# Ethics and Business

## An Introduction

KEVIN GIBSON

*Marquette University*

CAMBRIDGE
UNIVERSITY PRESS

CAMBRIDGE UNIVERSITY PRESS
Cambridge, New York, Melbourne, Madrid, Cape Town, Singapore, São Paulo

Cambridge University Press
The Edinburgh Building, Cambridge CB2 8RU, UK

Published in the United States of America by Cambridge University Press, New York

www.cambridge.org
Information on this title: www.cambridge.org/9780521682459

First published 2007

Printed in the United Kingdom at the University Press, Cambridge

A catalogue record for this publication is available from the British Library

Gibson, Kevin, 1955–
Ethics and business: an introduction / Kevin Gibson.
   p.   cm.
Includes bibliographical references and index.
ISBN-13: 978-0-521-86379-7 (hardback : alk. paper)
ISBN-10: 0-521-86379-1 (hardback : alk. paper)
ISBN-13: 978-0-521-68245-9 (paperback : alk. paper)
ISBN-10: 0-521-68245-2 (paperback : alk. paper)
1. Business ethics.  2. Social responsibility of business.  3. Corporate profits – Moral and
ethical aspects.  4. Business enterprises – Environmental aspects.  5. Globalization –
Moral and ethical aspects.  I. Title.
HF5387.G515   2007
174′.4 – dc22       2007012360

Library of Congress Cataloguing in Publication data

ISBN 978-0-521-86379-7 hardback
ISBN 978-0-521-68245-9 paperback

With love to Anna and Alex

# Contents

# Acknowledgments

I am grateful to many people for making this book possible. Foremost, I must thank Hilary Gaskin for her support and guidance throughout. Dale Jamieson has been a friend and mentor for over twenty years. Jennifer Gordon helped me realize what I wanted to say but had articulated poorly. James South, my department chair, has enthusiastically backed the project throughout, and I need to thank Dean Michael McKinney of the College of Arts and Sciences at Marquette University for the many things he has done on my behalf. I also need to express my appreciation to Dean David Shrock of the Marquette School of Business Administration, as well as to Dr. John Cotton, Dr. Jeanne Simmons, Sally Doyle, and Deb Reeder. I am indebted on a daily basis to Beth O'Sullivan and Lula Hopkins for keeping my work life on track. My wife, Elizabeth Lentini, has taken the dual role of cheerleader and patient critic, which is more than anyone could decently ask. My children as teenagers still light up my days and I feel very blessed that they are kind, caring, and curious individuals. My parents Ann and John Gibson have consistently encouraged me throughout my life. There are many others who contributed to the project, including my reviewers, who improved the book enormously, and friends and family, who helped in invaluable ways that they probably don't realize, but for which I am hugely indebted.

# Preface

*Ethics and Business: An Introduction* is an accessible, yet philosophically rigorous, book that gives readers the conceptual apparatus necessary to deal with the range of topics that they are likely to encounter. It is aimed at undergraduate students and students new to philosophical language. It reframes the way issues in business ethics are presented in order to give students a more unified, consistent, and conceptually elegant introduction to the field. There are numerous references to contemporary cases and 'real-life' examples, and each chapter comes with a case and discussion points at the end. The cases are designed as a springboard for further thinking, and hence are relatively short and open-ended.

Although it is explicitly philosophical, I believe this book will be appropriate for readers without any prior training in the discipline – for example, graduate or undergraduate business students. Philosophy should never be intimidating – and, in fact, most people engage in it naturally and unselfconsciously without realizing what they are doing. So while some of the discussions occasionally involve technical language, as they would in any discipline, the substance is easily within the grasp of students and business professionals.

There are two major features that set this book apart. First, the conceptual framework deliberately sets up a way of approaching issues built on basic moral principles. We cannot hope to cover every possible topic in the field, but if we can develop a clear way of approaching *any* topic then we will have accomplished a lot. The conceptual scheme is not exclusive or exhaustive, of course – for example, we could examine employee privacy from several perspectives. Setting up an analytical framework goes a long way to bridging the awkward gap between theory and practice, and provides introductory students with proper tools to get a good intellectual grasp of complex issues. Once we map it out, though, students are able to apply principles consistently across different topics and consequently construct arguments for a course of action from a reasoned argument rather than from awkwardly articulated intuitions.

Additionally, by situating business in the capitalist system we give a context for many of the forces that shape the way companies behave, and provide a backdrop to further analysis. My experience is that it is always worth laying out the fundamental framework within which the business world functions before moving ahead with discussions about individual or organizational morality. Clearly, in a profit-driven system there will usually be a paramount need for businesses to survive, grow, and make profits. At the same time, however, they are chartered by the public and thus instituted for the common good, and the pull to serve both investors and society is one of the foundational ethical tensions facing companies.

The second distinctive feature of the book is that it engages topics that are not often stressed in the literature, but are vital to any thorough examination of business ethics. They include:

- The impact of the growing "global economy" that may supersede or complicate issues of national sovereignty and business regulation;
- Feminist approaches to ethics in general and workplace concerns in particular;
- The relationship between business and environmental concerns, including discussions of economic sustainability and "triple bottom line" accounting.

In the words of one executive, the next billion computers are not going to be sold in the West. If a company is going to thrive in the global economy, they have to turn to thinking more broadly and in the longer term. Executives are coming to realize that they have a vested interest in developing and sustaining markets over time, that is, business ought not to be looking only at immediate returns, but at the communities that will become their consumers, and products lines that they can sustain for the foreseeable future. From this perspective, it is imperative that companies carefully re-examine what the overall business climate will be in a free international market and the nature of their interactions with all their stakeholders. Put bluntly, a simplistic notion of businesses operating by the ethics of a predatory jungle no longer applies, and companies will be forced to adopt a fresh approach to deal with changing conditions.

I have chosen to mention the law only where necessary, rather than use it as a basis for critical assessment of various topics. There is a temptation in life and business literature to use the law as a moral template, in the sense that following the law is morally sufficient, with the implication that if we have done nothing illegal we have done nothing wrong. While we have to admit that abiding by the law is a good start, it shortchanges the essential dialogue needed to establish appropriate standards and responses. The law cannot cover every case, and lawyers make a good living arguing about what precedent applies. Laws change or may not apply. It is usually easier and more productive to discuss the moral principles and policies involved in business dilemmas than to haggle over the merits of legislation, especially in the international arena. Furthermore, the law is a reactive instrument that often remedies harms that have already taken place, so if we wait around to have a case decided before we stop releasing a new chemical into the groundwater, the damage will have taken place before the case is decided. As we shall see, many cases fall into a legally gray area, where people are called on to use their discretionary judgment. Whatever the legality of giving notice about an impending factory closure, for example, doing so could be the morally decent thing to do. Finally, consider what a world would be like that relied on the law alone – everything would be regulated, and we would have armies of legislators, enforcers, judges and juries, and punishers. This vision alone should propel us into taking virtues of honesty, trust, fair dealing, and personal integrity seriously – in other words, it is well worth while to spend some time talking about the ethics as well as the legality of business.

In chapter 1 we look at the problem of ethical relativism, the notion that what is acceptable moral behavior is dependent on circumstances of time and place, or on each individual decision-maker. This is an important discussion for several reasons. First, if we are unable to defeat relativism in some way, then the whole ethical enterprise will falter, since it will have no leverage to criticize the behavior of others, and ethics will become a question of personal preference. Moreover, in the current global economy, the issue of varying standards across cultural boundaries has become immediate and pressing. For example, should businesses be allowed to use lower standards of worker rights (child labor, few safety measures) in overseas factories than in local factories, even though they may represent an improvement over previous standards?

This is not to say, of course, that there should be a single absolute standard for everything, a procrustean bed where the occupant is stretched or severed to fit. Rather, it demands we work out what values should be regarded as universal, and the conditions that let us treat others unequally, questions which naturally lead into an overview of ethical theory.

The chapter on feminism brings in an important perspective. Women make up almost half the workforce, and appear to carry disproportionate burdens. They still take on most household duties, and are over-represented in poorly paid employment. The chapter questions whether there is an essential difference in human nature between men and women, and asks whether the model we use for our work and private lives is still fitting for contemporary society or the more flexible workplace of the future.

The heart of the book examines business using the language of responsibility, rights, autonomy, and beneficence. By putting responsibility as a central focus we can group other concepts in a coherent way. When we ask, for example, whether a company is responsible for its actions, then the reader can draw fairly broad conclusions about the relationship between business and society that will apply to new and emergent cases. Responsibility is often elusive, and there may be cases such as the ferry disaster when the *Herald of Free Enterprise* capsized and 200 died. Although there was much blame to go around, no individual was held accountable. The survivors wanted the company to be charged with corporate manslaughter, but their case failed. At this point we critically examine what it means to be morally responsible (in contrast to legally liable) and the various conditions where we might properly morally censure a corporation and its employees.

Chapters 6 and 7 bring together some of the issues that have emerged thus far by introducing the terminology of rights and autonomy. Rights, which are often seen as a counterpoint to responsibilities, give us a way of establishing fixed points of business behavior – for instance, that there should be threshold levels of safety standards or that employers should be able to dismiss unproductive employees. Here we distinguish fundamental rights (sometimes referred to as "human rights") from rights that arise as a function of a legal system (what might be called "privileges"); and positive (claim) rights from negative ones (immunities). These distinctions will enable students to work through some of the arguments about, for example, sweatshops, so they can discuss the issues in a systematic way. Rights claims are often thought to override other considerations, so an employee's right to have access to a fire exit is more important than an employer's right to prevent pilfering by chaining the door shut. We will critically assess how these sorts of disputes can be played out. We will also look at recent claims that humans are not the only ones entitled to rights – perhaps animals and the environment should also be part of the discussion.

After rights and responsibilities, the third major concept I use is the notion of autonomy. Capitalism itself is founded on the idea that the consumer is sovereign, and individual free choice is a paramount good. Yet at the same time, we restrict sales and regulate goods in the market, often to protect people from themselves. Therefore if people choose to buy the drug Ephedra or other herbal supplements, perhaps they should accept the associated risks. In a similar vein, if a worker wants to use recreational drugs over the weekend, should that be any concern for an employer if there is no effect on his or her performance on the job?

The discussion in chapter 7 shows that the treatment of individuals as either workers or consumers is essentially two sides of the same coin. This is also an appropriate place to discuss advertising, which, if effective, sways us to buy things we otherwise might not have. The reason sales and marketing are ever morally questionable is because they risk offending personal autonomy. The chapter also covers the morality of discrimination. If an employer never hires obese people because he dislikes them intensely, his choice is an autonomous one, and if we restrict it, we are restricting his freedom, and we are led to issues of when something good for society matters more than individual choice.

Chapter 8 deals with beneficence. Roughly speaking, beneficence means that we have a duty to do good, The concept appears in a lot of contemporary literature under the banner of *corporate social responsibility*, and here we expand the analysis to discuss the general relationship between business and the community at large. The basic tenets of capitalism appear to promote doing only as much as the law requires on behalf of workers, consumers or the community at large. On the other hand, there are many cases where business has acted as an agent for moral good, and we will examine the strategic and intrinsic dimensions of corporate philanthropy. Some people have suggested that the greater power and influence of big corporations means they have correspondingly greater duties to act for the common good. This claim gets tested, though, when we consider whether they should interfere with sovereign states, even ones where the company could bring significant social benefits. Finally, our analysis goes to the issue of diversity, and whether firms have any duties to improve domestic societal wrongs, especially when past injustice is reflected in a homogeneous workforce.

The final chapter deals with the relationship between business and the planet. In broad terms, it is becoming increasingly apparent that unless we act properly to preserve and sustain the biosphere there will be a very bleak future for our descendants. The push for economic globalization can be thought of as the spread of free-market economics, which embodies certain assumptions about the desirability of consumption and wealth creation. This is especially pressing since one of the pressures in capitalism is constant growth, which effectively means the consumption of finite resources. We should also sound a note of urgency in that China is now the world's largest car manufacturer, and with India also becoming more reliant on petroleum there will be an exponential draw on our natural resources.

There is some movement toward including corporate impact on the environment as a factor in annual reports (so-called "triple bottom line accounting"), and also highlighting ecological stewardship in corporate mission statements (for example, Volvo). Still, globalization presumes that the market is an adequate mechanism for valuing the environment, which may not always be the case, especially if we are dealing with aesthetic, historical, cultural, or religious values.

As an epilogue, I return to the place of business in our lives and in our world. To make sense of our lives, I believe we need to find meaning in our work. Adding value means more than creating wealth – value is a moral term that speaks to the nature of human experience. Work, then, has a moral as well as economic aspect, and hence it is vital that we constantly remind ourselves that business is not an end in itself but a tool to enhance our lives. To do so, we need to develop institutions that support a virtuous trinity of consumers, employers, and workforce.

# 1 An overview of business ethics

## The Bhopal disaster

While most of the population slept during the night of December 3, 1984, a toxic cloud of over forty tons of methyl isocyanate (MIC) gas escaped from the Union Carbide plant in Bhopal, central India. Heavier than air, the gas blanketed the slums surrounding the facility and spread over the city of 800,000 people. At least 2,000 died immediately, although local estimates run into the tens of thousands.

Over twenty years later, there is still an arrest warrant out in India for Warren Anderson, the CEO of Union Carbide at the time, on a charge of culpable manslaughter. The plant, long defunct, has polluted the local aquifers with carcinogens and exposed open puddles of toxic waste. Local municipal workers tend to the area without any protective gear. Medical reports indicate that residents have compromised immune systems, growth retardation, miscarriage rates seven times the national average, and widespread incidence of cancer. Up to half a million people are said to be debilitated by chronic illness.[1]

---

[1] Drawn from: Randeep Ramesh, "Bhopal Still Suffering," *The Guardian* (UK) (November 29, 2004), available at www.guardian.co.uk/india/story/0,12559,1361575,00.html; Edward Broughton, "The Bhopal Disaster and Its Aftermath: A Review," *Environmental Health: A Global Access Science Source*, available at http://ehjournal.net/content/4/1/6, accessed January 20, 2006; "The Bhopal Disaster," Bhopal Municipal Corporation, available at http://bhopalmunicipal.com/disaster.htm, accessed January 25, 2006; Material available at www.dow.com, accessed January 25, 2006; Dinesh C. Sharma, "Bhopal: 20 Years On," *The Lancet*, 365 (2005), p. 111; Keerthi Reddy, "India: Dumping Ground of the Millennium?" *Vaishnava News* (January 31, 2001), available at http://www.vnn.org/editorials/ET0101/ET31-6533.html, accessed January 26, 2006; Gerd Leipold, "Trading in Poison," *The Telegraph* (Calcutta) (December 14, 2005).

A decade before the disaster, India had actively solicited investment by foreign companies and formed a joint venture with Union Carbide (UCC) to build a plant producing Sevrin, a common pesticide. However, by the early 1980s the Bhopal facility was operating at one-quarter of its capacity, due to poor harvests and reduction in the capital available to farmers. In 1982 a visiting UCC team declared the factory unsafe. By July 1984 the plant was up for sale, and UCC was planning to dismantle some components for shipment elsewhere. However, despite cutbacks and warnings, the plant continued to operate.

Union Carbide maintains that the spill was due to deliberate sabotage. Other independent investigations have pointed to poor maintenance and lax safety controls that led to water mixing with the volatile MIC. In 1991 the government of India negotiated a deal with UCC on behalf of the victims, which stipulated that legal jurisdiction was restricted to Indian courts. UCC paid $470 million in compensation and accepted moral responsibility. In return, all pending legal action against the company was dropped. When Anderson failed to answer the personal charges against him, the regional courts seized UCC's assets, including the now defunct and polluted plant. UCC (now part of Dow Chemical) insists that all the claims arising from the gas release were acquitted by the settlement and denies any enduring responsibility, maintaining that the regional government has now taken control of the situation.

In recent years, India's economy has steadily grown at about 8 percent a year, in part spurred by World Trade Organization rulings since 2000 encouraging foreign investment. Some commentators link the rapid growth and industrialization with poor environmental practices, dumping of pollutants, and risks to public health. These observers sense that business practices in developing countries may create conditions that would allow another disaster on the scale of Bhopal.

## The philosophical contribution

The Bhopal case typifies the complexity, mixed motives, and potential for benefit or harm characteristic of contemporary business activity. Merely reciting the facts or reviewing the legal decisions will fail to tell us what values have priority and how we might approach difficult issues. In the face of the intricacy of the various strands of thinking, it is critical that we can step back and work out a *normative* response, that is, what we *should* do. Philosophical inquiry is vital to any considered discussion since it can help us understand the nature of business and arrive at moral judgments.

Philosophy – literally, the love of wisdom – is hard to pin down as an academic activity. It embraces fundamental and abstract questions about human nature and our relationships, the existence of God, the meaning of language, and how we establish and implement our values. However, at the most basic level, philosophy has two primary functions:

• The examination of concepts
• The study of arguments.

At first glance, these may not seem to be highly significant activities, and yet they underlie all human behavior. We literally shape our lives by the way we organize our world – by the way we create the conceptual framework we use to make sense of things and by the values we embrace. For example, many people throughout the ages have laid down their lives for the sake of glory or liberty or have demanded rights of independence and sovereignty, and yet we rarely step back to examine exactly what these words signify. Thus it is worthwhile to spend time examining the meanings of these very basic concepts and how they apply to our lives.

This is especially true when we observe these concepts applied in business and the workplace. Most of the Western world operates under a capitalist economic system based on fundamental assumptions – assumptions that are often taken for granted, say, about the benefits of economic growth, or what constitutes a fair return on investment, or who should be responsible for harms that result from faulty products. The consequences of these assumptions are momentous for our quality of life. Furthermore, many of us will spend the majority of our adult lives in a work setting, usually employed by an institution or someone else, and we will inevitably be affected by baseline moral assumptions about justice and fairness, for example, in such issues as working conditions, terms of employment, privacy, assumption of risk, and concerns about health and safety.

In the Bhopal case, the Indian government had made value-laden decisions about the desirability of foreign investment, and Union Carbide was looking to realize a profit for its shareholders. The company's actions reveal certain assumptions about safety and the environment, at least in the Indian context, because UCC appears to have applied less stringent safety standards than at their American plants. Therefore it will be valuable at the outset to seriously examine the conceptual foundations underlying business and how they are put into practice.

The second major task of philosophers is to look at arguments. In the technical sense used by philosophers, arguments are a linked series of statements that force a conclusion. They can go wrong in a couple of important ways: either the statements themselves may be faulty, or the links may not connect as claimed. Analysis of this kind is critical because we often decide what to do based on a set of claims and what they purportedly conclude. So, for example, Dow Chemical claims that it has fulfilled its obligations to victims because the Indian government approved its legal settlement. A philosopher might examine whether paying a fine does, in fact, discharge one's duties of reparation.

In another common case, a business may lay off workers without notice because it believes that employees who know they will soon be out of a job will slack off and lower the morale of the firm. However, we might question the empirical claims involved and whether they will have the result management suspects. We are often misled by clever rhetoric or invalid arguments, and one of the philosopher's tasks is to sort out sound reasoning about any particular claim. In this case, the employer is making a causal claim about human behavior and comes to a conclusion primarily based on the effect on company efficiency. That is, a slacking worker will lower profitability, and profitability is the thing that matters most. But if we analyze the employer's argument closely we may see that it is not as obvious or compelling as it initially seems. For instance, we could empirically examine the premise that knowledge of the impending layoff will hurt productivity, or we might accept this premise yet still disagree with the employer's conclusion that it is right to keep employees in the dark. Perhaps there are moral reasons to treat people decently that are independent of the bottom line. If layoffs are imminent, perhaps it might be appropriate to give employees some time to adjust and make plans rather than escorting them to the door on a Friday afternoon. Thus we need to look carefully at both the assumptions at work in an argument and at the way these assumptions are linked to come to a conclusion.

One common way to critically assess an argument is to look for counterexamples that refute the claims being made. Thus, if it turns out that there are a number of cases where businesses have given notice of impending layoffs and found that the employees still worked diligently, that would speak against the assumptions implicit in the claim that the best way to deal with layoffs is not to give notice. We might contrast the Bhopal case with one where a company has undertaken to do whatever is necessary to remedy harms that its actions initiated, whether or not there have been intervening independent causes.

Another method of assessment is to abstract the principles at work and then see if they apply in other settings. For example, take the claim that a firm is responsible for any and all consequences arising from the use of its products. While this might be appropriate in, say, the case of damage resulting from exposure to toxic chemicals, the principle may not hold quite as well in cases such as obesity resulting from habitual consumption of fast food. Philosophers find it useful to examine the differences between cases and their underlying principles to determine the significant distinction – here it probably centers on the acceptance of risk by the individual consumer – and then see if the distinction has value in different contexts as well.

Philosophy differs from disciplines such as economics or sociology. In these disciplines, scholars study how people actually behave, and they produce *descriptive* reports. Thus an economist may examine the nature of economic growth in central India and balance the wealth created against the costs incurred. However, this is a neutral endeavor until policymakers make the further value-laden claim that, for example, growth *ought* to be permitted as long as the benefits outweigh the costs. Similarly, it may turn out that a quarter of all students in MBA programs admit cheating at some point in their academic career. Importantly, this tells us nothing about what the students *should* do. The very fact that many students cheat is instructive, yet we have to recognize the gap between a factual statement – one that can be verified – and the value claim that cheating is wrong. Economists and sociologists report behavior but do not suggest that because a lot of people act in a given way that it is therefore right. Thus, if we read a news report telling us that a third of all businesses in Australia routinely use illegal pirated software, we have purely descriptive information. The report does not automatically carry the ethical implication that pirating is wrong and should stop.[2] Disciplines such as economics are explicitly non-normative in that they make certain presumptions about human behavior – such as the

[2] Jim Macnamara, "It's Official – One Third of Business Software Stolen," Business Software Association of Australia news release (May 22, 2001).

desire to increase personal welfare – but do not take moral positions about them or their consequences. To bridge the "fact/value" divide, we need to adopt a prescriptive moral framework – one that explicitly tells us how we ought to behave.

Within philosophy there are numerous subdisciplines. Broadly speaking, ethics is the branch that discusses issues of morality. Morality deals with notions of good and bad, justice, fairness, right and wrong, and the way we develop and apply our values. Metaethics is concerned with the various theories that promote ideas of what constitutes the good. Another area, normative ethics, applies standards or norms and reaches conclusions about what we ought to do. Business ethics is the area within normative ethics that is concerned with the special moral issues and concerns that arise in business. These issues may be expansive, such as whether there should be any restraint on economic globalization, or specific, such as considering how a firm should deal with a dangerous plant, defective product, or an injured worker.

## Two meanings of business ethics

The term *business ethics* is ambiguous. It has at least two different meanings, with significantly different implications depending on its use. The first meaning of business ethics is in describing the rules of a game or practices in a limited domain. In sports or competitive games, players know which behavior is acceptable. It may be fair to bluff or lie to win in poker but wrong to mark the cards or use a confederate. This sense of the term is sometimes used to describe, say, the ethics of the gang, where shooting rivals is acceptable but ratting out someone to the police is not. When we use the term *ethics* like this to delineate a set of activities within a certain domain, it need not refer to behavior that is decent or moral.

This first use of the term *business ethics* appeals to people who have a strong sense of role morality, where individuals take on the behavior of the office that they hold rather than relying on their personal judgment. By this way of thinking, it would be appropriate for a professional to ask a client whether he should respond to a question as a friend or as an accountant, with the idea that different standards apply depending on the function that a person undertakes. When managers reporting to NASA were deliberating whether to ask for a postponement before what turned out to be a fateful launch of the space shuttle *Challenger*, the chair of the meeting literally said,

"Take off your engineering hat and put on your management hat."[3] The hats symbolize the various roles people take on in different situations.

Therefore, if the name of the game in business were just maximizing profit, this approach would allow a businessperson to act as if business were an amoral game where success is measured in financial terms alone. Part of the game, like not hiding cards up your sleeve, is that the threshold of acceptable behavior is complying with the law; beyond that, any artifice or brinksmanship that brings in more profit is not only appropriate but encouraged. Often those who hold this point of view will make claims to the effect that they have done nothing illegal, or they have paid the levied penalty, and therefore they have done nothing wrong.

The second understanding of business ethics makes no distinction among the different roles in our lives and in fact rejects the notion that we can divide our moral lives into discrete sections labeled "home," "family," "business," "romance," and so on, each with its distinct set of rules. Instead, this view proposes that we have a single set of standards that apply throughout our lives. The difference is that business presents us with new and different situations that require specialized assessment. Thus, relationships between producer and consumer may involve a set of considerations that do not apply to interactions between two people without the element of commercial interest, and questions of how to treat employees during a downsizing require special analysis. Nevertheless, the baseline of moral decency would be consistent throughout, and the same moral principles of justice, fairness, goodness, and what is right would hold in business as they do in our everyday dealings. By this light, the legal and ethical spheres may overlap, but we gauge correct action by personal morality rather than by reference to a legal code. Typical maxims of a manager who adopts this approach might be stated as questions such as "Would I be prepared to have my actions printed on the front page of the newspaper?" or "Would I think it acceptable if others treated me the way I treat them?"

## Instrumental or prudential approaches

We can also think about morality in terms of intrinsic and instrumental motivation. Those holding intrinsic views believe good should be done for

---

[3] Diane Vaughn, *The Challenger Launch Decision* (Chicago: University of Chicago Press, 1996).

its own sake, whereas instrumentalists would look for some form of payoff. Take the case of a company facing an opportunity to make a significant profit by lying in a negotiation. In broad terms, the company officials could decide to be honest because it is intrinsically wrong to lie, that is, they are faced with a choice about doing what they perceive as right or wrong, and irrespective of the consequences they decide not to exploit the advantage. On the other hand, instrumentalists would examine the situation to see what course of action is most economically beneficial. Again, the answer might be not to lie. Although lying would provide an immediate reward, there may be greater economic payoffs in the long run from acting honestly and benefiting from their enhanced reputation in the marketplace. On the web-based auction house eBay, research has found that sellers with excellent customer feedback are likely to sell their items for over 10 percent more than those with less positive responses.[4] The technical term used for following the moral path because of an anticipated reward is *prudence*.

The moral motivation involved here is that there has to be a reward (or, conversely, avoidance of distress). Essentially, instrumental approaches are self-interested, since they are concerned mainly with personal benefit. The benefits need not be immediate. For example, a company might invest in a poor community because it believes that doing so will mean that it will have an educated pool of workers in the future or because workers will be less inclined to change jobs if they enjoy the local amenities. Similarly, individuals may donate blood although they do not perceive any immediate personal benefit. Rather, they may see that this behavior enhances everyone's welfare, and they are better off in a community where there is an attitude of common concern. Actions that have a general benefit, although ultimately motivated by personal well-being, are described as *benign self-interest*. Take the case of a car repair firm: it may benefit in the short run by inflating the amount of work that needs to be done, but as with many firms it will retain its customers based on its credibility, and if that is lost the repair shop will have nothing to fall back on. Hence if customers start to question their bills, they are less likely to return, and the company will falter. Hence a prudential company might adopt the attitude that it makes economic sense in the long run to build a reputation for fair dealing and trust.

---

[4] Catherine Dupree, "Integrity Has Its Price," *Harvard Magazine* (July–August, 2003), http://www.harvardmag.com/on-line/070378.html, accessed June 11, 2006.

In another case, a firm sponsors a charity run to benefit sick children. The firm prominently displays its logo on the start and finish lines and prints its logo on the event T-shirt. The company is allocating resources to the charity, which may result in increased sales, but the effects need not be immediate or obvious. Moreover, there is some element of advertising in their sponsorship, and some critics might say that their actions are tainted merely because they involve some payoff (the same might be said if their donation were tax deductible). Others would admit that private firms in a capitalist society are often motivated by prudential concerns but focus instead on whether total welfare has been increased.

The rewards for prudential actions may not come soon or be measured easily, but that may not matter as long as the person involved believes in the reward system. Hence a faithful believer might resist temptation and do charitable works because of a promise of eternal salvation, even though there is no evidence that will occur; as a practical matter the evidence is secondary to the individual's belief. We might say business dealings are analogous, because despite the difficulty in proving that a business will benefit by doing good works, it may become self-verifying if everyone involved in commerce adopts the belief as a matter of course.

There is some anecdotal evidence that firms that act morally do better in the marketplace. As we have seen with reputation effects, the payoff might not be immediate, and so these things have to be looked at in the long term. Still, the evidence is not robust and tends to reflect the empirical difficulties firms have in finding out whether advertising is effective. For instance, it is hard to know if any single given action translates directly into individual purchasing decisions. We may choose to go to one department store over another because it offers scholarships to needy students, but the store may also have the quality and range of goods we prefer, among a constellation of other factors, and so it is hard to isolate corporate moral actions sufficiently to draw definitive conclusions.

A further confound is that companies that do a lot of good works and do well in the market – such as Johnson & Johnson, Merck, or Dayton-Hudson – tend to be well established, stable, and profitable anyway. This is not to deny that firms that act morally may do well in the marketplace, especially over time. However, it is not automatically true, and the empirical evidence is mixed, at best. The result is that we cannot firmly establish the claim that corporations benefit from ethical action. Nevertheless, acting well may still be a prudential strategy. Moreover, there may be very strong reasons to do the right thing intrinsically regardless of its instrumental effect on the bottom line.

## Rule-based approaches

An alternative view, often associated with the economist Milton Friedman, is that following the law fulfills the moral requirements of business. The rationale suggests that business is out to make a profit, and it should do whatever it can to maximize returns. This may mean causing pollution or bribing officials along the way. However, the moral yardstick involved is the appropriate law, and the firm will not do anything illegal. Suppose a manager is concerned about the declining population of songbirds near her business. By this view, she should work to maximize profits while at work and pollute up to the legal limit if that will enhance the bottom line, even if it jeopardizes the birds. The check and balance is that she can take her wages and do whatever she wants with them: if she chooses to support a wildlife organization that then mobilizes the political process to change the law, she is welcome to do so. At the point the law changes, so does the firm's obligation to the environment. But it is not her place to unilaterally make the decision to preserve more birds and lessen emissions if it will hurt the company, since her primary allegiance should be to the shareholders who own the firm and are looking to maximize their returns.

By this reasoning, the company may still voluntarily reduce pollution or do other good works that are over and above the law, but the acid test is profitability. If there is a benefit through improved public relations or avoiding a costly lawsuit, then the company will have an incentive to act beyond the legal minimum. However, absent any financial incentive, the company will rely on legal compliance as its ethical guide.

This view has some difficulties. Imagine a competitive world where everyone relied on the law as their gauge of appropriate behavior. In every transaction we would believe that the other party was predatory, and our only defense would be a close reading of settled law. It means that society would be deluged by lawmakers, regulators, and compliance officers, and a court system to adjudicate and punish. This shows us that although we may feel that sharp dealing is commonplace, in fact most of our business dealings are done against a backdrop of trust.

The watchword of rule-based systems is compliance. Minimally, compliance means making sure that the law is followed. Many companies have tried to institutionalize ethics by generating a code of conduct that lays out acceptable and sanctionable behavior. An illustration of this approach is accounting in America prior to the scandals of the late 1990s, where the profession was very much rule-governed, with a strict and comprehensive code of conduct. Yet the rules themselves restricted the scope of what accountants did, so that in auditing a company they had to make sure that the relevant accounting standards were met and the books were balanced, but they did not need to question business practices that appeared improper. In effect accountants were watchdogs, not bloodhounds. In the wake of the Enron and HealthSouth fiascos, accountants excused themselves on the basis that they had seen nothing illegal and therefore were not implicated in any wrongdoing, a claim that damaged the credibility of the profession and helped bring down Arthur Andersen, one of the largest accounting firms.[5]

## Principle-based approaches

One of the chief difficulties with a rule-based approach is that it does not deal well with new or difficult issues where it is unclear which standard should apply. Furthermore, in some cases rules will clash, and there needs to be a way to adjudicate between them. So, for example, a cooking spray that contains nothing but fat might be sold as "fat free" because the serving size does not reach the reportable threshold amount. That might be acceptable if the serving size were listed as more than a spray lasting one third of a second, which seems unrealistic and manipulative. In a similar vein, a soup manufacturer might claim that it has reduced the amount of sodium in its product, whereas all it has done is to reduce the recommended serving size from twelve ounces to eight. A firm might demand that its employees submit to drug testing and then use the samples to test for susceptibility to genetic diseases, or a sales agent may want to treat her client to a lavish dinner that goes against company policy but not the law. Using the law or rules alone gives little guidance on vague issues, and in some cases prompts ingenious people to research the law for the purpose of discovering its loopholes.

---

[5] See, generally, *Barbara Ley Toffler Final Accounting: Ambition, Greed, and the Fall of Arthur Andersen* (New York: Broadway Books, 2003).

An alternative is to move to a more principle-based approach, where moral considerations are thought of in more general and abstract terms. The benefit is that when a novel issue arises people will have a point of reference from which to work. For example, if an overarching principle is to "do no harm," then it can be applied to a wide range of more concrete issues. The associated problem, of course, is that applying principles in any given situation will require a degree of interpretation, which in turn will rely on the moral discernment of the individual involved. In practical terms, a principle-based approach is likely to require more training and time for moral consideration than simply following the rules.

## Ethical relativism

Some American educational institutions have an "honor code" along the following lines: "I will not lie, cheat, or steal, and I will not tolerate those who do." While most students feel comfortable with the first clause, they tend to be less compliant with the second, because they believe that individuals should be responsible for their own actions, but there is no moral imperative to interfere with the conduct of others if it does not affect them directly. Very often they may disapprove of poor behavior by other people, but will not do anything about it because they feel each of us should be in command of our own actions. However, there may be problems with that attitude as well. Consider an exam where it turns out that most of the students have brought in calculators with some of the answers already programmed in. Sticking to the honor code in that kind of situation may leave the honest students feeling they are foolish to put themselves at a disadvantage when they aspire to a higher moral standard than the prevailing norm. Many of these same dynamics are echoed in business dealings, especially across different cultures.

Our experience shows us that people have varying moral judgments, and it is tempting to believe that all moral beliefs and principles are relative, in the sense that someone's judgment seems to apply to that individual in that situation at that time. This implies that it will be difficult to criticize anyone else's actions, and consequently we would have no grounds to intervene and tell them they are mistaken. It would also mean that there is no absolute standard of morality that is universally accepted, since everything will be context-dependent. In the case of sweatshop labor, for example, a relativist would say that the use of child labor has to be seen in the context of the prevailing standards of the local culture and that we are in no position to judge the actions of others.

We could think about the difference by imagining two camps with no passage between them. The first is what might be termed *absolutists*, or *objectivists*, who believe that there are moral truths that hold throughout space and time. They might claim, for example, that torture or incest are wrong, and that they always have been and always will be whatever the situation. For them, the fact that certain societies have allowed these practices does not show that standards vary by context but instead shows that humans make mistakes and can become enlightened over time.

The other camp might be termed *relativists*, or *coherentists*. Their view is that we cannot make moral judgments apart from understanding the context involved, and they would allow that the acceptability of acts depends on the individual facts and the prevailing norms. This is not to say that they believe that anything goes, however. The coherentist label means that they feel the object of moral theory is to make sure that our values are internally consistent and do not contradict each other. Thus they also believe that we can be mistaken, and moral progress is possible. Slavery, for instance, goes against the belief in individual liberty and therefore is condemnable by a coherentist on the grounds that the two beliefs need to be aligned.

One version of relativism says that we only generate norms within a cultural context, and so the meaning of the word *good* within a society is that it is in accord with an accepted practice. Hence there is no objective sense of right and wrong, but only what the society has sanctioned over time. This would explain some radical differences in the way that different cultures deal with some issues. For example, it is inappropriate for women to take an active role in business affairs in some countries in the Middle East, or abortion is legal and accessible in some countries but not others.[6] It also means that the notion of good may change over time. Thus the subjugation of women was once widely accepted, but societies have changed, and what was once thought of as proper is now condemned.

However, just because we find differences between societies does not mean that they cannot be criticized. A more sophisticated relativist position

---

[6] This view is taken from Ruth Benedict, "Relativism and Patterns of Culture," in R. Brandt, ed., *Value and Obligation* (New York: Harcourt Brace, 1961).

would suggest that it is possible to assess different cultures once we truly understand what is going on. Thus it could be that one society takes heroic medical measures for its elderly members, whereas another believes in minimal intervention. What initially look like opposite approaches may, in fact, be manifestations of the same human concern. So, each society may respect its elderly and wish the best for them, but the way this is manifested turns out to be quite different.

The counterclaim by absolutists is that without an anchor, there is no way to validly criticize practices. In effect, there have to be some overarching principles – such as respect – that allow us to compare different practices.

It may be that the camps are not as different as they originally seem to be, so that we can draw on insights from both. Initially, though, it is important to realize that the mere existence of moral disagreement does not mean that there is no moral truth or that it could never be found. Take the analogy of religion: clearly there are many different religions, but we do not take from that fact alone that a spiritual quest is meaningless and futile.[7] The plurality of religious beliefs actually underwrites the validity of the religious dimension of human life. Similarly, the fact that there are disputes over morality may reinforce the fact that moral values are a constant and important feature of human life.

A better model is perhaps a sphere with a crust that represents variations and a core that is constant. Consider the anthropological fact that contracts form the basis of human society. Even in a basic society there will be some exchanges. Unless we keep our word about them, society cannot operate. Thus if we want some anchor point, we could say that society requires a concept of contracts to function. Again, that is not to say that people would never break contracts. The point is that the very idea of a contract requires an agreement in principle that people keep their promises, and someone who does not would be punished in some way in order to preserve the practice. This is a very minimal level of agreement, but it shows that there will be some universal agreements. The list could be expanded: all human societies have systems for looking after their young and forming families. From this start we could develop a core of common values that all humans share. The question then becomes whether the core is small with a wide band of disagreement, or whether the surface of differences only represents a thin crust. As we saw in the case of respect for the elderly, many societies

---

[7] I am grateful to Tom Beauchamp for this analogy.

may have similarities in principle that are manifested in different ways. Thus societies may have a notion of a fair profit that is contrasted to usury or exorbitant gains, but the actual percentages involved may vary considerably in practice.

The upshot is that there are valid ways to deal with relativism in business. While there may be startling differences in standards of moral acceptability across cultures, that does not mean that they are all equally legitimate. It will be important to find out the operating beliefs that lie behind particular actions and start the discussion at the level of the underlying principles involved. Hence, although there are no countries that endorse the practice of bribery, there may be different understandings of what constitutes a bribe. The second step is to decipher whether there are threshold values that should never be compromised: just as genocide is never acceptable, we might say that it is universally wrong to expose workers to deadly hazards unawares, or to deprive native people of traditional lands without compensation merely because the land has desirable mineral deposits. As we shall see in a later chapter, the language of rights may be a useful way to frame the debate. Furthermore, we can examine the moral posture of a company within a culture for inconsistencies that may be resolved. We also need to be sensitive to the prevailing norms of the country and determine whether there are legitimate differences that merit accommodation or whether we should impose our domestic standards.

## Egoism

The other major challenge to developing an ethics of business is posed by *ethical egoism*. An *egoist* would say that one should put one's own interests and concerns above those of others, regardless of external ethical standards. This is critical in discussing business behavior because many practitioners tend to have an initial intuitive reaction that business operation is predatory and competitive, and therefore a special kind of self-interested morality has to apply: the law of the jungle, where only the strong and ruthless survive. Although we may not be able to defeat egoists, it is still possible to show that even if we grant their premises there may nevertheless be good reasons for moderating behavior in the business realm.

There is a long tradition of egoism that believes we are all out to do whatever is best for ourselves, and ethical action is no more than a social construction upheld by the legal system. Over 2,000 years ago the Greek philosopher Plato (427–347 BCE) used the character Glaucon to illustrate the point in his work *The Republic*. Glaucon tells the story of a shepherd who discovers a magical ring that can make him invisible. The question posed is that if we were released from the constraints of the law, would we still behave decently? Glaucon concludes that our conscience would be overcome by the temptation to do whatever we want if there were no personal consequences.[8]

## Machiavelli and Hobbes

Current advocates of egoism often appeal to the works of two major historical figures: Niccolò Machiavelli (1469–1527) and Thomas Hobbes (1588–1679). Machiavelli is best known for his work *The Prince*, which was published after his death. He considers the nature of a principality and advocates that a bold leader should acquire and use power to his personal advantage by whatever means possible. He felt that whatever private morality someone had, if the individual was a leader he had to be prepared to act to promote his own interests above all others. In the public sphere, right and wrong did not matter as much as praise or blame. The prince had to act expediently for himself in every case and do whatever was necessary at the time. This meant, as he put it, that although it was desirable to be both loved and feared by one's subjects, if it came down to one it was safer to be feared.[9] He says:

> Hence it is necessary for a prince wishing to hold his own to know how to do wrong, and to make use of it or not according to necessity . . . He need not make himself uneasy at incurring a reproach for those vices without which the state can only be saved with difficulty, for if everything is considered carefully, it will be found that something which looks like virtue, if followed, would be his ruin; whilst something else, which looks like vice, yet followed brings him security and prosperity.[10]

There is some debate about Machiavelli's sincerity in what he wrote. However, his work has been influential in advancing an attitude that leaders

---

[8] Plato, *The Republic*, trans. Benjamin Jowett (New York: Random House, 1947), Book II, 358d–361d.

[9] Niccolò Machiavelli, *The Prince* [1512], trans. W. K. Marriott (New York: Alfred A. Knopf, 1992), chapter 17.

[10] Machiavelli, *The Prince*, pp. 70–71.

need to be self-promoting without concern about the welfare of others, and to adapt their morality to changing circumstances.

Yet the prince has to maintain complete control, since he will be under constant threat from ambitious rivals, and few people or businesses will ever have that much power. It is more realistic to think of people and businesses as having public visibility and being vulnerable. It is worth learning from the English philosopher Thomas Hobbes, who also starts from the assumption of constant competition and moral relativism:

> For moral philosophy is nothing else but the science of what is good and evil in the conversation and society of mankind. Good and evil are names that signify our appetites and aversions . . . Hereby it is manifest that during the time men live without a common power to keep them all in awe, they are in that condition which is called war; and such a war as is of every man against every man . . . where every man is enemy to every man, the same consequent to the time wherein men live without other security than what their own strength and their own invention shall furnish them withal. In such condition there is no place for industry, because the fruit thereof is uncertain: and consequently no culture of the earth . . . no arts; no letters; no society; and which is worst of all, continual fear, and danger of violent death; and the life of man, solitary, poor, nasty, brutish, and short.[11]

His view is that we are necessarily self-interested but at the same time at risk from the actions of others, and once we realize that, we need to create a society that has sufficient power to dominate us all, like a super police force. However, for our purposes, the insight that matters most is his recognition that it is not always in our interest to compete or dominate: the features of a life worth living come from cooperative endeavors. In many ways we might describe his posture as strategic rather than moral, since it is the way rational people would behave. We can be indifferent to the situation of others and only care about their welfare insofar as it affects us personally, but then grasp that humans necessarily live in communities and exchange goods and services, and so the individual may be best served by mutual cooperation.

---

[11] Thomas Hobbes, *Leviathan* [1651], ed. J. C. A. Gaskin (Oxford: Oxford University Press, 1998), p. 84.

## Game theory

We can model Hobbes' view of strategic morality using game theory. *Game theory* is the term mathematicians and social scientists apply to competitive scenarios where individual parties are seeking to maximize their own outcomes. The name is somewhat misleading, since some of the subjects they have studied include nuclear strategy and economics. The theories are useful in many disciplines because they can provide quantitative data about rational choices under varying conditions. For simplicity's sake, many of the dynamics are represented by two sides that have to make decisions that will result in a payoff. The most straightforward case is a zero-sum game, where a win for one side ($+1$) represents a loss ($-1$) for the other. Hobbes assumed that self-interest in an unregulated competitive environment would necessarily lead to destructive behavior, and we can see that is certainly one possible outcome. On the other hand, there may be other options, especially if we see that many, if not most, encounters are not zero-sum – there is a greater payoff if we work together. So, for instance, a person might be more adversarial in a one-time encounter because playing "hard ball" may be very effective. However, if we have to deal with the same people over and over, we tend to be more cooperative. Thus if two gas stations are on opposite sides of an intersection, neither is served well by consistently cutting prices to beat the other. While they do not have to directly collude, each could independently reason that the maximum profit is achieved by each posting the same price. In repeated computer simulations, the evidence suggests that defection by one side (say, undercutting the rival station) would be met with defection, and it is very hard to restore cooperation in the future.[12] Thus a fully rational player would strategize that it is worthwhile to cooperate voluntarily and perhaps forsake the allure of immediate profits, because the long-term benefit matters more than the short-term gains.

The actions of corporations acting internationally provide a helpful indication about the limits of egoism. A firm that operates away from its home base is usually free to operate by the rules that apply in the host country. If the overseas laws are lax, then the natural temptation will be to exploit the potential economic efficiencies. Extrapolating, we can imagine that there

[12] See B. Bottom, K. Gibson, S. Walker, and J. K. Murnighan, "When Talk Is Not Cheap: Substantive Penance and Expressions of Intent in the Reestablishment of Cooperation," *Organization Science*, 13.5 (September–October, 2002), pp. 497–513.

are regimes where, for example, child labor and exposure to asbestos are legal, and trying to organize a trade union is a criminal offense. Should the company take advantage of the more relaxed laws to improve its bottom line or stick to the standards that it operates with at home?

The descriptive evidence is that some companies do make the most of weaker laws in developing countries, especially in the unskilled or low-skilled industries such as apparel and assembly work. Thus there are reports of workers suffering physical abuse, of people being forced to work long hours without breaks or overtime, and of employees being made to spend their earnings at a company store at inflated prices, effectively making them indentured servants.[13] Corrupt regimes may permit or encourage these practices because of the promise of hard currency and side payments to those in power.

## Nike

The striking feature of business behavior is not so much the existence of exploitative conditions, though, but the fact that such features are not universal. One reason for these constraints is that there is always some level of transparency involved, and so our actions, even overseas, will leave a trail. There may be long-term self-interested reasons to maintain certain standards. The Nike case is instructive here. When reports surfaced in the 1990s of worker abuse in third world sweatshops, Nike responded by saying that the factories were run by their subcontractors, and so it had little control over them. Thus a dress that retailed for $100 in the United States netted $15 to the contractor but less than a dollar to the seamstress, or a pair of sneakers made in Vietnam cost the manufacturer less than 1 percent of its final retail price.[14] However, after a string of bad publicity, including being highlighted in the comic strip "Doonesbury," the stock price and earnings slumped over 25 percent in 1998. Nike chairman Phil Knight publicly admitted there had been problems and announced a series of measures to address them including international monitoring and a higher minimum wage for

---

[13] See, for example, Elizabeth Martinez, "Sweatshops Firsthand," *The Nation* (November 19, 2001); http://www.sweatshopwatch.org/, accessed October 3, 2005; http://www.global-exchange.org/campaigns/sweatshops/, accessed October 3, 2005.

[14] Jeff Ballinger, "Nike Does It to Vietnam," *Multinational Monitor* (March, 1997).

overseas workers, greater transparency, better air quality in the factories, a minimum age for employees, and education programs. While it would be wrong to make direct causal connections, Nike is no longer considered an archetype of global exploitation, and its earnings have consistently risen in recent years (up 12 percent in the 2005 financial year, to $13.7 billion). We can conclude by saying that even if morality in business turns out to be self-interested and firms act strategically, the evidence indicates they will be motivated to maintain certain standards and build a solid reputation rather than descending into Hobbes' war of all against all.

## Morality and strategy

Thus there may be prudential reasons that cause companies to resist complete exploitation, just as individuals may see that over the long term, their own benefit lies in cooperation. Nevertheless, there are difficulties in taking a strategic approach to morality: it depends crucially on the calculations involved – the actions of the company are still profit-driven, and so if the numbers were to show that they could make more money by acting badly, there would be no independent reason not to change their behavior.

The moral problems of expedient changes in moral attitude are further highlighted by the presence of public relations specialists. Company sales, as we have seen, may depend on the way that a company is perceived. The Nike case is often used as an example of a successful public relations campaign, one that changed the public perception of what was going on. Taking this logic to its conclusion, the lesson for a corporation would be that hypocrisy pays. That is, the truth of the matter is immaterial, since the important variable is the public image. So if we had a company that could cleverly mask its operations or consistently confuse the public through some well-promoted charitable work, then if these campaigns cost less than, say, raising the minimum wage of overseas workers, that would be the most appropriate course of action. The owners of a business could say that they are a self-interested operation with the sole goal of maximizing returns, and this would certainly be a legitimate posture to adopt in a competitive free market.[15] Further, they could gear all of their operations based on a game-theoretic strategy. In this

---

[15] Milton Friedman, "The Social Responsibility of Business Is to Increase Its Profits," *New York Times Magazine* (September 13, 1970).

sense, morality would become subordinate to strategy and a matter of expedience. If they could maximize profits by using cheap labor overseas they would do that, and if it turned out that customers would pay a higher price for organic goods or union-made apparel, they would follow market demand. Notice that they follow the moral tide, so that they will do whatever it takes to make the most profit. They are constrained from out-and-out competitive behavior only because they realize there may be a future payoff.

There is something jarring about the notion that a company should alter its moral stance depending on its cost-effectiveness like a chameleon changing its color to suit its surroundings, and yet this is the correlate of an egoist working out what is in his best interest and plotting his behavior accordingly. Still, we should again return to the positive aspect of business behavior and look for a common element that underlies these discussions. Many companies do have a baseline of acceptable behavior that is independent of external monitoring. Further, the fact that many consumers choose to not buy brands associated with sweatshop conditions illustrates that there will be a point where individuals are willing to pay more to preserve higher principles. Thus even in a corrupt regime where there are virtually no laws restricting the terms of employment, many foreign companies are unwilling to compromise what they perceive as basic human rights. In the same vein, consumers are often willing to accept that there are relative standards that mean workers overseas do not have the same complement of benefits as workers at home. However, there is a point where consumers feel that their economic welfare matters less than guaranteeing the humane treatment of the people who produce their goods.

## Responses to egoism

The magic ring story suggests that, left to our own devices and without any accountability, no one could resist the temptation to do whatever it took to increase personal power and wealth. However, that may not be entirely true. The likelihood is that some people and companies would, in fact, restrain themselves without concern for the consequences because they recognize that it is wrong to deprive others of life, liberty, or property, based on the idea that humans are entitled to individual rights.

There is also another line of response against egoism, based on the character of the person involved. Glaucon, along with Machiavelli, Hobbes, and many others, believed that human nature was essentially self-aggrandizing, power-hungry, and hedonistic. Gyges (Glaucon's shepherd) covets the king's wife and his realm and gets what he wants. Now it could be that there is more to human nature, and indeed many people would not use the ring at all or would do so to improve the general welfare rather than just their own. We are rarely called to publicly declare what our values are and what we are going to do to bring them about. Businesses, on the other hand, very often do make public statements of their core values, and often these incorporate a lot more than the desire to return yield to investors. They have statements about public responsibility and their corporate practices: in effect, a summary of the corporate character. So, for example, Nike changed its corporate mission statement in the late 1990s from one that declared an ambition to be the best sports company in the world to the more recent version:

> To bring inspiration and innovation to every athlete* in the world (the asterisk comes from Bill Bowerman, one of our founders, who said that if you have a body, you are an athlete).

The mission is more focused on serving the customer than enhancing the company. Of course, we should acknowledge that there may be some rhetoric in these statements, but nevertheless, they do not have to make them at all, let alone broadcast them and follow up by directing resources to substantiate what they espouse. If we look at some of the top international companies, we find that the vast majority make announcements of this kind on their web sites and in their company literature.

The effect of having a mission statement along these lines is that it shows the company may not have a purely egoistic nature after all. A publicly held corporation will be interested in making a profit, to be sure. However, the evolution of mission statements that are more outwardly directed to other stakeholders seems to indicate that a company will also hold a set of values that may sometimes conflict with increasing investor returns, at least in the short run.

One question we will explore further in this book is whether a company does the right thing in terms of acting ethically, and expects that profits will follow, or does it seek profit as its paramount goal and see ethical action as the most advantageous strategy to achieve it? Although there are undoubtedly companies that act as if their sole goal is constantly increasing profits, there are many others that believe that their prime mission is one of service, and improving human welfare and earnings are seen as a secondary benefit. It is important to make sure that we do not treat business as some kind of monolithic structure, too. Individual corporations vary widely both in their goals and in their perceptions of the appropriate means to achieve them.

## Summary

The Bhopal disaster underscores the difficulty in fully analyzing ethical issues in business and the number of factors we have to consider: The facts of individual cases can be highly significant. In Bhopal circumstances set the stage and a series of problems came together to make the gas leak as widespread and deadly as it was. There are many stakeholders with widely varying interests in the case, and many of them are incompatible. Some commentators will emphasize the perceived difference between legal and moral responsibility, the acceptability of risk, and the nature of compensation. There are diverse cultural expectations that have complicated the issues, as well as tensions between rich developed nations and poor developing ones. We also have to think about the long-term effects of business activity: although the incident happened over twenty years ago, its damage to human health and the polluted environment will affect the region for years to come.

This preliminary survey has told us some of the things that philosophers can do and their limitations. Philosophy is unlikely to be able to transform hard questions into simple ones, and in fact will probably show how complex and nuanced moral questions are. Nor will it provide a simple algorithm for telling us exactly what to do in any given situation. However, it does offer the promise of developing a reasoned analysis of business practice, and a framework for making decisions on a normative basis.

In the rest of the text we will look in more detail at several of the key concepts that frame ethical debates in business. First we will look at the ethical theories that underlie business ethics so that we have a basis for evaluating the issues that arise. Then we look at the nature of capitalism and some of its implications for corporate and individual actions. Next we examine what is meant by the key concepts of responsibility, rights, autonomy and beneficence. We will also look at some of the challenges posed by feminist perspectives. This will better equip us to systematically study the morality of business and its impact on our lives.

## General issues for discussion

1. Are there any absolute rules that should never be broken, whatever the circumstances? Defend your view.
2. Does morality change when you are in different roles, such as a business executive?
3. Are those hurt in industrial accidents owed compensation? Who should pay it?
4. Does moral motivation matter? If a company does good works, should we be indifferent to the fact that they may lead to increased profits?
5. How much do you think reputation matters in business? Would you pay a premium for an item if it came from a retailer with a reputation for being honest?
6. If you were giving employees ethical training, would you stress knowing the law and the company rules, or try to explain the principles behind the rules?

## Case – pornography

Pornography is big business in America. Conservative estimates have Americans spending over $10 billion a year on so-called adult entertainment, comparable to the amount spent going out to movies or professional sporting events. Thirty years ago the industry was relatively small, until the time the home video cassette recorder became popular. Then demand increased exponentially, because, in the words of one industry spokesman, "We went from 1,000 adult movie theaters in less than 10 years to 80 million adult movie theaters, and that is what basically happened with the VCR." The trend has continued with the spread of the World Wide Web and almost 100 million households with computers. According to some estimates, 20 percent of American households with a VCR or cable service will pay to watch pornography, and 10 percent will pay to watch frequently.

One of America's largest cable operators, Comcast, made over $50 million from shows featuring erotica in 2002. Most of the other cable companies made huge profits, but tended to roll the income into other areas, so the sector is not highlighted in their financial reports. Most of the big hotel chains now offer in-room, on-demand video rentals, and according to some sources, over 50 percent of guests rent at least one sexually explicit feature. One provider, LodgeNet, based in South Dakota, makes almost $200 million a year selling videos to hotels. A spokeswoman for the company remarked, "We feel good about what we do. We're good corporate citizens. We contribute to local charities."

Larry Peterman owned a video store in American Fork, Utah. Over 4,000 residents had signed a petition demanding the store be closed, and in the mid-1990s local prosecutors charged him with fifteen counts of pornography for renting such movies as "Jugsy" and "Young Buns II." The basis of the prosecution was that the videos violated community standards.

The defending attorney, himself a devout Mormon, investigated the spending practices of the community by obtaining records from local hotels and cable companies. Larry Peterman answered the petition by showing that he had almost 4,000 store members who had rented at least one sexually explicit movie in the previous year, while the evidence showed that far more had been watched through cable or satellite rentals. It turned out that the consumers were renting "adult" material at almost double the national average: 20,000 movies had been rented through cable in the previous two years, the local Sun Coast store was deriving 20 percent of its revenue from the 2 percent of its stock that was designated for adults only, and the Provo Marriot next to the courthouse had sold almost 3,500 pay-per-view adult movies in a single year.

One hotel chain, Omni, decided to get out of the market, and according to industry sources will lose almost $2 million a year. However the chain is now endorsed by religious groups and reportedly got over 50,000 letters supporting the decision.

The largest providers of adult material are not known as providers of smut. DirectTV, a satellite provider with over $200 million annual adult rentals, is owned by General Motors. AT&T also has a major stake in the industry, although it does not publicize its involvement. In the words of one executive, "How can we? It's the crazy aunt in the attic. Everyone knows she's there, but you can't say anything about it." The owner of a company called Hot Network commented, "The biggest problem I have is the image of the adult business. People think it is run by the mob, or a bunch of guys with gold chains. I grew up in Paris, Illinois. I have a master's of business administration degree." Another trade spokesman noted that although the rise of broadband capability would undoubtedly attract large companies to industry, the main factor was the huge profit margins: "This just happens to be a business where you can't lose money."[16]

## Some questions from the case

1. Are there moral standards that apply to everyone, or are they all relative?
2. Is there any legal product or service that a firm should not provide?
3. How do you react to the claim that a firm is morally neutral, and only fulfilling consumer demand?
4. Why do you think the parent companies often disguise their involvement in the industry if the product is legal and popular?
5. If you were a shareholder of Omni, would you agree with the decision to get out of a highly profitable sector of the market?
6. What would you say about the claim that selling pornography is acceptable because everyone else in the market is doing so?

---

[16] Material in this section is drawn from "Porn in the U.S.A.," *60 Minutes*, CBS News (September 5, 2004), accessible at http://www.cbsnews.com/stories/2003/11/21/60minutes/ printable58504.shtml, accessed January 17, 2006; "How Utah Video Store Pornography Prosecution Led to Criticism of Marriott Corp.," *Mormon News* (October 27, 2000); Terry Neal, "GOP Corporate Donors Cash In on Smut," *Washington Post* (December 21, 2004); Timothy Egan, "Wall Street Meets Pornography," *New York Times* (October 23, 2000), available at http://www.nytimes.com/2000/10/23/technology/23PORN.html, accessed January 20, 2006.

# 2    Insights from ethical theory

## Gleaning at the grocery

Owen Bedborough was working his way through college with a part-time job in a grocery store, part of a highly profitable national chain. He did not expect to encounter any moral dilemmas, but as the weeks went on he became more and more troubled. Some of the staff would purchase food for their breaks, but the checker would not scan all the items. When he mentioned it to one of his coworkers, he was told that it was one of the unofficial perks of working for barely more than minimum wage. She also pointed out that it was quite routine for staff to use their company discount for friends and family, and that he would hurt a lot of people if he reported it any further. He also noticed that customers near the fruit would sometimes sample grapes directly from the display, and some would go as far as to eat a small bunch before returning the stalk to the shelf. He relayed his concern to the shift manager; he was instructed to ignore it unless the person looked homeless, and then to call security. When he worked at the checkout, he would sometimes be given government food stamps for cola drinks and prepackaged candy. He wanted to tell the customers they would be much better off using them for healthy food, but said nothing. However, the main moral dilemma he faced involved the store policy of disposing of meat that had reached its sell-buy date. Part of his duties involved sorting the meat on display, and then throwing out-of-date packages into a dumpster behind the store which he then had to lock to prevent scavenging. Prepackaged meat is usually good for several days if kept cool and then thoroughly cooked, and when he questioned his supervisor about the policy, he was told that the company was simply protecting itself. By getting rid of the meat this way before it spoiled the store avoided potential lawsuits through anyone getting sick from its products, even if they had recovered them after they had been thrown away. Owen routinely told his roommates when he would likely be throwing food into the dumpster and for several months, if no one were around, they would meet him behind the store and take it home instead. One day the manager was watching the security camera, observed what was going on, and fired Owen immediately.

## The value of theory

Owen faced a number of ethical issues in his job. Like him, our intuitions are often spontaneous and inconsistent, and it is not obvious what we should do or how much we should get involved. The analytical framework of ethical theory can help us sort out our thinking and develop a more coherent and justifiable basis for our behavior. In this section we will look at some classical ways of considering moral questions, and see how they can apply to some business situations.

At the outset, we can see that ethical issues rest on foundational beliefs about justice: Owen might defend his actions on the basis that good food was going to waste, that he was only acting like every other employee, or that no one was being hurt by his actions. These rationalizations, like other ethical intuitions, beg an explanation of the principles behind them, and once we bring them into the light we can start to develop arguments about what we should do. Reflection at this abstract level can also help us work out how we should react – whether we approve of an act, tolerate it, or should intervene to change what is going on. Owen's case also demonstrates that merely saying that we should follow the law is often an insufficient guide, since the law may be ambiguous, not apply to a particular set of circumstances, or not be enforced, and, as the proverb says, a law that is not enforced is no law at all.

## Justice

Justice has been a subject of philosophical inquiry since the time of Plato. In very rough terms, a theory of justice seeks to establish what is right and fair at a somewhat abstract level, and then suggest appropriate remedial action. Thus in civil issues (contrasted, say, to criminal ones) the central questions will involve the distribution of rights and goods within society. Two main theories will concern us in dealing with business: *libertarianism* and *egalitarianism*.

A libertarian view suggests that the paramount virtue is personal choice in a context of maximum liberty. That is, everyone should be free to decide their own fate, and we are only responsible for others as far as we choose to be. It is often linked with a strong belief in personal property rights, so that we can give and receive freely, but have no entitlement to make demands on others. Hence we choose to train as poets or plumbers, but cannot complain if the market rewards one more than another, and have no right to subsidence at the expense of others. Advocates, such as Robert Nozick (1938–2002), would say that we should not preconceive outcomes, as long as the system itself is fair.[1] Thus, it would be fine if Bill Gates, one of the world's richest men, won the lottery, since he would have bought his ticket like everyone else. The fact that it strikes us as unfair that a rich man gets richer is incidental, and no cause to penalize him for the benefit of others who were not as lucky. Similarly, they would say that if we make capitalism as fair as possible by removing as many barriers as we can – such as taxation and regulation – then a free market will serve us best by allowing as many individuals as possible to maximize their own choices. So if people choose to attend monster truck rallies rather than go to the opera, that is a reasonable outcome, and certainly no reason to subsidize the arts. Inequalities are thought of as differential rewards that reflect applied talent that ought to be encouraged, rather than an incentive to redistribute personal holdings.

In contrast, an egalitarian view starts from the premise that we all share in one another's fate, and we should not be unduly rewarded for attributes that are, after all, a function of genetic luck. Consequently it would actively promote redistribution of rights and property to give everyone equal opportunities. Egalitarianism's most famous recent articulation has been through the work of John Rawls (1921–2002).[2] He devised a highly abstract set of thought experiments through which we might have insights in developing social policy.

Broadly speaking, Rawls asks us to imagine that we are behind what he terms a "veil of ignorance" where we know the basic facts of human psychology and economics, but we do not know who we are as individuals, and then asks us to propose general guidelines for a just society. His aim to get us away from advocating things that would extend our own privileges.

---

[1] Robert Nozick, *Anarchy, State and Utopia* (New York: Basic Books, 1977).
[2] John Rawls, *A Theory of Justice* (Cambridge, MA: Harvard University Press, 1972).

So we are aware that there are 6 billion people in the world and slightly more adult women than men, for example. He believes that we would be rational, but risk-averse, and under these anonymous conditions we would design a society that provides the maximum opportunities for everyone: because we do not know whether we were men or women, had physical or mental challenges, or the nature of our family background, he thinks it would be reasonable to create policies that give everyone a fair chance.

It is very important that we do not make the mistake of saying that Rawls wants wholesale equality; rather, he believes that it is perfectly acceptable if differences arise, as long as they make everyone, including the least advantaged, better off. We can imagine that society would benefit if there were a selection system that led to those with the right aptitudes and interests becoming doctors or software designers, for example, since it is rational to use disproportionate resources and training to reward those people for their potential to improve society taken as a whole. Rawls would endorse social and economic differences emerging through on merit and by processes that were open and fair to everyone. In his terms, justice is a matter of fairness, and given his background condition of ensuring the quality of life for everyone in society, equality of opportunity rather than equal shares becomes the paramount consideration for framing social policy. The effect of applying Rawls to business ethics is that we have to take impartiality seriously, and accept that some redistribution may be appropriate, based on the fact that many of the privileges that we enjoy may be a function of luck rather than merit.

A concept of justice will give us the background conditions for developing morally acceptable structures in society and business. However, we are still faced with the question of what constitutes right action, and to help us examine that issue we will now turn to look at three different classical ethical approaches.

## Utilitarianism

A well-known phrase is that "All is well that ends well," a motto associated with utilitarianism, one of a family of theories that take the paramount gauge of morality to be the consequences of an action. Utility is a measure of welfare, which is often interpreted as human welfare. The significant element of an act is the amount of good or evil it produces. Hence a company that donates money to preserve a tract of natural prairie would be judged on whether the donation increased human enjoyment, rather than whether the company board of directors had ulterior motives or whether the land had some intrinsic value. In very rough terms, utilitarianism correlates to cost/benefit analyses in business settings.

The term *utilitarianism* was coined by Jeremy Bentham (1748–1832), and the theory was later refined by John Stuart Mill (1806–1873). Mill's insight was that utility offers a single criterion where we can compare and assess moral action. He formulated the greatest happiness principle, often expressed in the maxim that we should act to bring about the maximum good for the maximum number, or as he puts it:

> Actions are right in proportion as they tend to promote happiness, wrong as they tend to produce the reverse of happiness. By happiness is intended pleasure, and the absence of pain; by unhappiness, pain and the privation of pleasure.[3]

Although his claim is often accepted at face value, we should note that it involves two highly significant elements. First, it demands impartiality – as Bentham said, each should count for one and no one for more than one. In practical terms, this means that we cannot give our friends and families moral preference, and a worker in an apparel factory in an undeveloped country will have the same standing and entitlements that we do. Second, the theory demands that we have an obligation to all concerned in a moral decision. Thus, we cannot benefit a few well-off consumers if it means that a larger group will suffer. Mill also believed that we have a natural sympathy to one another and that we are capable of distancing ourselves sufficiently to make impartial moral decisions.

The sort of happiness that Bentham and Mill talk about should be broadly construed. Mill thought of it more as an intrinsic good, something good in and of itself. Thus a student who gets so wrapped up in a subject to the point of exhaustion might qualify as being happy, because the activity brings her personal fulfillment.

Recent theorists have tended to abandon the language of maximizing happiness, pleasure, or the good and instead have concentrated on taking

---

[3] John Stuart Mill *Utilitarianism* [1863], ed. Samuel Gorovitz, chapter 2 (Indianapolis: Bobbs-Merrill, 1971), p. 18.

personal preferences as a way of assessing right action. By this view, maxi-mizing utility means assessing what individuals would prefer from a range of available options and then doing that which, on aggregate, will give most what they want. Herbert Simon has described this approach as "satisficing."[4] It goes some way to overcoming the difficulties involved in trying to measure and compare individual conceptions of happiness.

There is a traditional distinction made in utilitarian theory between act and rule utilitarianism. An act utilitarian would be more likely to make snapshot decisions, based on the circumstances of the moment, whereas a rule utilitarian would be more concerned with general application of the principle. Thus in a case of a company wishing to demolish a historic building to expand its factory, an act utilitarian would refer to the balance of welfare in this particular case, whereas the rule utilitarian would appeal to the background laws and policies that are themselves justified by improving welfare. Perhaps the easiest way of understanding the difference is by noting that an act utilitarian does not have to weigh every individual decision but can live by moral precepts. The distinction is that he or she would be much more likely to allow moral exceptions; it might be acceptable, for instance, to lie on occasion, if justified by the circumstances.

## Some issues in utilitarianism

A persistent concern voiced by critics is that utilitarianism may pose a threat to minority groups. That is, if we acknowledge that the significant measure is utility in the aggregate, then it means that individual dissenters may suffer. If we could all have cheap oil for the foreseeable future by displacing a native tribe from their homeland in the Amazon, then it seems that the welfare of the majority should prevail.

There are two lines of response to this challenge. The first is based on the theory itself and suggests that we have utility in institutions such as the family and being able to enjoy secure lives. Recall that under the theory we have to recognize that others will have similar interests, and they should be weighted equally with ours. The net result is that in displacing the tribe we not only have to think about their immediate distress but also the general

---

[4] Herbert Simon, *Report of the Research Briefing Panel on Decision Making and Problem Solving* (Washington, DC: National Academy Press, 1986).

lowering of welfare if everyone were subject to being expelled from their homes without recourse. Mill suggests that there is utility through having a just society, and infringements on that must be included in any utilitarian calculus.

Another response uses the terminology of rights and suggests that we may be entitled to self-determination, privacy, physical security, and a number of other fundamental rights – not because of their place in overall utility but because all humans are automatically entitled to them. Both sets of reasoning would preserve the sanctity of minorities and show that the theory is subtler than merely summing up the immediate benefits and distress caused by an action. Utilitarianism necessarily looks at the long-term effects for the greatest range of people that could possibly be affected.

Another issue in utilitarianism is the calculus applied. Although there has been a lot of work done on methods of calculating welfare, nevertheless making those kinds of calculations about the future are necessarily speculative. For example, if we harvest Alaskan snow crabs at the present rate, they are likely to be unavailable to future generations, and their diminishing numbers may have an effect on the ecosystem. Similarly, carbon dioxide emissions caused by current industrial practice may be leading to global warming. However, we cannot know at the moment that people in the future will have similar preferences to ours, or that our predictions about the future state of the world will come to pass. Therefore there are a number of questions we should pose in making a utilitarian calculation, including:

a. Who counts in the calculation?[5]
   • Does everyone in the world count equally?
   • Who counts for more, and why?
   • Do future generations figure into the calculation?
b. How do we deal with differing tastes?
   • What if a consequence means a lot to some and very little to others?
   • What about people who are never satisfied?
c. How do we account for the various probabilities?
   • Are all the outcomes equally likely?

[5] See, for instance, Mill, *Utilitarianism*, where he says, "I must again repeat, what the assailants of utilitarianism seldom have the justice to acknowledge, that the happiness which forms the utilitarian standard of what is right in conduct, is not the agent's own happiness, but that of all concerned" (p. 268).

- Can we balance a probable good consequence against an unlikely disastrous one?
- How far can we predict a causal chain?

## Supererogation

A further concern in utilitarianism is supererogation, or going beyond what is expected. In ordinary life, we do not have to do things that are above and beyond normal expectations. For example, if you can swim and see a child in distress in a lake, it is nice if you try to help the child and could be considered heroic. However, there is normally no moral requirement that you risk your life to save another. First aid training, for example, stresses that the first thing a rescuer needs to do is make sure that he or she does not become another victim.

American law reflects this same attitude. There is no legal duty to recognize an obligation based on common decency. In the words of William Prosser, an expert on tort law:

> A physician is under no duty to answer the call of one who is dying and might be saved, nor is anyone required to play the part of Florence Nightingale and bind up the wounds of a stranger who is bleeding to death, or to prevent a neighbor's child from hammering on a dangerous explosive . . . or cry a warning to one who is walking into the jaws of a dangerous machine. The remedy in such cases is left to the "higher law" and the "voice of conscience" which, in a wicked world, would seem to be singularly ineffective either to prevent harm or to compensate the victim.[6]

In short, we are not our brother's keeper in the eyes of the law. In contrast, some countries, including Germany, France, and Japan, have Good Samaritan laws that require bystanders to help unless it puts them in harm's way.[7]

Doing the heroic act is what philosophers call "supererogatory" (from the Latin "above" and "ask for"). In the context of the workplace, an employee's primary duty is to the employer. Thus Owen ought to work diligently when

---

[6] W. L. Prosser and W. Keeton, *Prosser and Keeton on Torts*, 5th ed. (St. Paul, MN: West Publishing Co., 1984), 375–376.

[7] Photographers at the scene of Princess Diana's fatal crash in Paris were investigated because they were taking pictures instead of helping the injured.

stocking shelves, but it is not as clear whether he has a moral duty to go beyond his assigned tasks or report petty theft. Supererogation may be a problem for the utilitarian because if we take the demand to maximize welfare seriously, then there will be no distinction between the decent and the heroic: we will inevitably face a constant demand to do as much as we can.

The issue is illustrated by the actions of the pharmaceutical firm Merck. In doing research for veterinary products, researchers discovered that its drug Mectizan could cure river blindness, a parasitic disease carried by flies in sub-Saharan Africa. Merck was then faced with the dilemma that it had a sure cure for a crippling disease, but those afflicted were in no position to pay for it. Merck committed to supply sufficient doses to all who need it free of charge for as long as it takes to eradicate the disease. The life cycle of the parasite means that it could easily take over fifteen years at a cost of $1.50 per person affected every year. By May 2003, Merck had donated 250 million doses. The test of a superogatory act may be how we answer the question of whether Merck's actions were merely decent, all things considered, or, alternatively, heroic. We might respond that the company did more than it had to and would not be held accountable for failing to act. At the same time, moral approaches do not assess actions by what is conventionally accepted but rather look to what we should do. Taken this way, the notion of supererogation falls away, in that we can fairly readily see what we ought to do, and the problem is more a question of overcoming human frailty and self-interest.

## Partiality

An additional consideration of utilitarianism is the partiality issue. In some television commercials, donors to charities overseas are promised that in return for their money they will receive a picture of the beneficiary and periodic letters. Why does the charity bother to do this? Simply, because it works. These charities know that by personalizing a starving child in a far-away land, more people will respond with generosity. In fact, we do not do well when presented with the faceless or distant. We all know how difficult the world is, but it is not until we are shown stark pictures and personal descriptions of deplorable situations that we realize the urgency and humanity of those who are suffering. Partly, this is a defense mechanism. If we empathized with all suffering in the world, we would be overwhelmed and rendered incapable of doing anything. Psychological evidence suggests that we mainly reserve our pity for those with whom we can associate.

Since the eighteenth century utilitarianism has made the initial assumption that we are all of equal value, and we should care as much about individuals who are distant and unknown to us as we do about our close family. However, it appears we *do* care more about the ones we love, and we shield ourselves from nameless statistics. When these nameless statistics become real, often through the power of television, we lower our barriers and see them as human beings in need.

In terms of the business world, then, this dehumanization of those with whom we do not have contact means that it is much easier to pass on suffering to people we don't know and don't care about, including future generations. We do treat people differently, and we favor those known and near to us.

A final issue to consider with regard to utilitarianism is the "sour grapes" lesson. In Aesop's fables, a fox covets some juicy grapes hanging from a vine. He tries, in vain, to take them. He departs, declaring that the grapes were probably sour anyway. Jon Elster describes this phenomenon as "adaptive preference formation." He says:

> Why should individuals want satisfaction to be the criterion of justice . . .
> if people tend to adjust their aspirations to their possibilities? For the
> utilitarian, there would be no welfare loss if the fox were excluded from
> consumption of the grapes, since he thought them sour anyway.[8]

One of the implications of the "sour grapes" phenomenon is that we cannot rely solely on personal satisfaction of the individuals, since they may have been led to expect an unjustly poor outcome and feel indebted for it. Thus workers who expect to be fired if they are injured on the job may be grateful if they are allowed to take a half-day off without pay instead, or victims in Bhopal may be grateful for any compensation at all, however small it is.

[8] Jon Elster, "Sour Grapes: Utilitarianism and the Genesis of Wants," in B. Williams and A. Sen, eds., *Utilitarianism and Beyond* (Cambridge: Cambridge University Press, 1982), p. 219 (corrected).

## Utility is not always fair

So far, we have assumed that it is possible to have a solution that creates the greatest good for the greatest number. However, many of the decisions we make have moral overtones by virtue of the fact that the resources under discussion are limited and have to be assigned on some criterion of fairness. We should note that mere acceptance of an outcome is not the same as a fair distribution.

Imagine the following case: a multinational company makes an offer to a company in a developing country that will only provide a marginal return for the supplier. The multinational has what is termed the "threat advantage" since it has options unavailable to the supplier, whereas this may be the only offer the supplier gets. This outcome will give great utility to the multinational, and some – more than none – to the supplier. Overall, there is an increase in utility, but it is skewed by an unequal distribution. Some commentators have criticized utilitarianism on the grounds that although it recommends increasing utility, it generally has little to say about the allocation of the utility itself. To counter this tendency in free markets, a movement has arisen called "fair trade" or "trade justice" that advocates minimal levels of returns to producers irrespective of the bargaining leverage that the consumers may have. Thus, for example, some importers of coffee will agree to a guaranteed price with farmers even though the prevailing world market price drops lower. This may go against the self-interest of the consumers in purely economic terms, but it means that they are assured that the producers will not be gouged by loss leading or predatory practices by large firms.

## Duty-based theories

In stark contrast to theories that deal with outcomes, deontological approaches believe that it is a mistake to judge actions by their results. A deontologist would say that we need to act out of a principle of obligation that does not rely on any particular consequence. For example, a customer may have received too much change at a store. She could reason that the world would be a better place if people gave back the extra money or that it would make her feel guilty if she did not. However, a deontologist considers that we have duties (Greek: *deon*) and obligations to do the right thing, no matter what the consequences. That is, she should return the money just because it is morally correct regardless of the outcome. Similarly, a deontologist would reason that it is improper to lie to potential customers, even though the lie might facilitate sales and never be discovered, merely on the grounds that lying is wrong.

## Some issues in Kantian capitalism

The foremost philosopher associated with deontology is Immanuel Kant (1724–1804). Kant believed that ethics is based on reason and freedom. Broadly speaking, people have the mental capacity to make moral decisions – and so we hold individuals accountable for their actions in ways that children or animals are not. Further, we have the freedom to choose our actions – in other words, we are autonomous agents. This gives rise to a system where we ought to respect one another's humanity, meaning that we should not treat people as we would treat a machine. Imagine a tollbooth collector, for example. Although the function he has could be done mechanically, we should recognize that he is a person with dignity and worthy of respect.

Kant's system is rational in the sense that it does not rely on outside evidence. He believed that we could work out the commands of ethics in just the same way that we could reason through a logic problem. So, for example, if we know that line A is longer than B, and B is longer than C, it follows that A will be longer than C. To many people, this is both obvious and compelling, with the sense that if the first two claims are true, then the last necessarily has to be true. This means that moral rules are not subject to evidence, but that they are proven like mathematical formulae, and have the same irrefutable force.

Deontology takes motives to be of paramount importance in assessing morality. Kant understood that we often act out of self-interest or because we are following directions. On the other hand, he felt that the highest good comes about when we perform an act for the sake of goodness itself, rather than looking to any particular outcome. Merck's act in donating drugs to impoverished Africans, for example, may have been done out of a desire for good publicity or to gain political leverage. However, the public announcements from Merck do not appear to justify their acts on these grounds; instead, their behavior seems to be based on the moral belief that there was no alternative in the face of terrible human suffering. Similarly, Johnson & Johnson, the makers of the analgesic Tylenol, reacted to a fatal tampering of their product by recalling the entire line off the shelves nationwide at a huge cost. Someone had spiked seven bottles with cyanide, but very quickly it emerged that the contamination had occurred at the store rather than in the factory. Whatever had happened was beyond the firm's control. James E. Burke, chairman at the time of the crisis, said that he was advised that the company could deny any link to the killings or just issue a local recall. However, he ordered a nationwide recall and has recounted that he felt he had no other choice, since it was the only possible moral course of action – that is, it was as compelling as a conclusion in a logical proof.

George W. Merck once claimed in an influential speech that "We try never to forget medicine is for the people. It is not for the profits. The profits follow, and if we have remembered that, they have never failed to appear."[9] The view he was espousing suggests that there is a correlation between doing the right thing and profitability. However, it is significant that the company does not do what it perceives as morally correct in order to generate profits. In that sense, the company does not have an instrumental morality. Profits are seen as a function of being moral. Similarly, we can see how one can have a for-profit company that has a deontological mission. It may be organized to provide a service or product but still operate in the belief that profits are a by-product of a business functioning for overall welfare.

## Kantian principles

Following Kant, we can propose three elements that determine moral worth. The first is that motive is all-important. The second principle asserts that the motive itself has to be of the right type that seeks goodness for goodness's sake: an action's moral value is due to the maxim from which it is performed, and not to its success in realizing some desired end or purpose. Thus if a company discloses to its workers that there is a health hazard associated with the chemicals used to produce compact disks because of a legal requirement or with the aim of reducing sick leave, then according to Kant it would not be fully moral since it did not act from moral obligation

[9] George W. Merck, 1950 address, Medical College of Virginia, cited in www.merck.com/about, accessed September 14, 2005.

alone. The third says: "Duty is the necessity of an action performed from respect for the law."[10] The point he is driving at is that actions cannot be subjective, but ones that everyone would assent to if they considered them rationally. Moreover, when he refers to the law, he means the moral law. He believes that we could rationally determine a set of moral prescriptions (for example, "Do not lie," "Do not steal," and so on) that are clear to everyone. These would then take on the force of a law – they are commands that would have to be complied with even if we found it inconvenient or against our immediate self-interest. He used the term *categorical imperative*, since the laws would not allow exceptions and hence apply *categorically*, and *imperative* because we do have the liberty to choose to do otherwise.

For Kant, maxims can be tested by whether they are consistent, which means that they have to apply universally without contradiction. So, for instance, he considers whether it would be permissible for someone to borrow money by making a promise to repay that he cannot keep. He reasons that to be consistent he would have to allow everyone to do the same, which would lead to universal distrust. He thus has to reject a course of action that might be immediately attractive but cannot withstand his test. Another important implication of his approach is that we have to treat people as we would wish to be treated or, as he puts it, "One must act to treat every person as an end and never as a means only." This does not mean that we cannot employ others in pursuit of our goals, but rather that we ought to respect people as people, not just as "human capital." Thus it would be acceptable to contract individuals to add value in a business, but we also have to realize that they are not there exclusively as a means to our ends – they are likely to be harmed if sacked without notice, put in unhealthy working conditions, or not paid a living wage. In Kantian terms, we have to treat all people – employees, suppliers, agents, customers, and everyone else – as "ends-in-themselves."

## Kantian capitalism and stakeholders

Kantianism is manifested in the recent emergence of so-called stakeholder theory. Traditional theories of the firm contend that its paramount function is to maximize returns to shareholders, either through dividends

---

[10] Immanuel Kant, *Foundations of the Metaphysics of Morals*, trans. Lewis White Beck (Indianapolis: Bobbs-Merrill, 1959), p. 16.

or increased share value. The executives of a firm are essentially hired agents who should do everything they legally can to increase profits. This sort of motivation means that the key decision in any case will always come back to whether or not it will be efficient by lowering costs or raising returns. Consequently, the individuals are functionaries of the firm and are assessed by their ability to add value. If a company has what is sometimes euphemistically called "surplus overhead" – that is, more workers than it needs – then this approach would advocate swiftly getting rid of them.

An alternative view has arisen in the last twenty years, spearheaded by R. Edward Freeman, who coined the term "Kantian capitalism."[11] Freeman believes that we need to reconceive the nature of the corporation as a responsible member of a community with the associated duties and privileges: it would be a partner rather than a scavenger. Freeman uses the term *stakeholder* to flesh out his analysis. Essentially, any party that might be affected for better or worse by corporate actions will have an interest or stake in its future. This would include customers, suppliers, and the community, for example. Some relationships would be more official or contractual, such as a customer at a restaurant, whereas others would be more remote groups – perhaps the coffee growers in a different country.

Freeman suggests that the firm should not be run for the paramount sake of one group in particular – that is, the investors – but that management needs to consider the interests of all stakeholder groups when making its decisions. Thus the owners or shareholders in a fast-food restaurant have duties beyond operating the site profitably. He would claim that they should care about the community in which it is located – perhaps, for example, by opening up a play area, making sure the employees are treated humanely, and checking that they are not degrading the local environment. The deontological factor is that profit by itself is not the overriding function of the business: a firm should operate in this way because it is a minimally decent way to deal with others and the community.

The reason we should care about others is that we respect them as ends-in-themselves, not just as instruments of our personal ambitions. Freeman has taken the Kantian notion of respect to mean that the job of management is to consider all of the stakeholder interests with equal weight, a task he

---

[11] See, for example, R. E. Freeman, "A Stakeholder Theory of the Modern Corporation," in T. Beauchamp and N. Bowie, eds., *Ethical Theory and Business* (Englewood Cliffs, NJ: Prentice-Hall, 1994), pp. 66–76.

says requires the wisdom of King Solomon from the Bible. That is, he gives no primacy to shareholders but feels the company has a fiduciary duty to all its stakeholders. In making a decision about whether to relocate a factory, for example, executives would need to think not only about the increase in efficiency and consequent greater returns but also about the effects of a shutdown on its current workers and the local community.

Norman Bowie has also championed Kantian capitalism. For him, it means that the relationships within the firm must change: we need to give individuals more autonomy and meaningful work. It would also extend to providing a salary that ensures independence and an environment that is safe and healthy. He would encourage worker participation and fairness in the workplace.[12]

It is important to note the kind of justification that Freeman and Bowie appeal to. It is not that the firm will be worse off if they fail to enact these more humane measures, but that behaving any other way would entail a self-contradiction. Bowie gives the example of a company renegotiating a settled contract. Using the test of Kant's categorical imperative, if everyone behaved similarly, then the concept of a contract would lose its meaning, and it would be hard to engage in commerce. Similarly, a disgruntled employee might feel justified in stealing groceries from her employer. However, stealing as a generalized practice would ultimately undermine the notion of private property. Importantly, we should recognize that Kant is not trying to justify commerce or private property as such, but saying that if you have adopted these operating concepts then you cannot engage in practices that would undermine them.

Kantian approaches to capitalism are foundational in that they look to the very basic ideas that make the system operate at all. One of their main points is that there has to be a moral underpinning to any market economy since it would collapse without a set of shared understandings about appropriate behavior. Following Kant, these approaches have expanded the initial claim to non-contradiction within the system to a moral demand to respect individual stakeholders.

Kant believed that moral issues could be resolved by reference to a single overarching principle. However, we can imagine cases where obligations

---

[12] Norman Bowie, "A Kantian Approach to Business Ethics," in Robert Frederick, ed., *A Companion to Business Ethics* (Oxford: Blackwell, 1999), pp. 3–16.

might conflict. Plausibly there are times when it would be acceptable to lie, perhaps if a life were at stake. We may have duties to supply drugs at no charge to sick people overseas, but what if the very survival of the firm is in question? One problem with Kantian capitalism is that it does not seem to readily supply a standard by which conflicting obligations can be judged.

One suggested solution has been proposed by the English philosopher W. D. Ross (1877–1971). Ross thought we had a number of *prima facie* (at first glance) obligations based on our everyday moral reflection.[13] They include reciprocity, reparation, gratitude, justice, beneficence, and self-improvement. Although justice is an all-embracing demand, the others are targeted toward specific groups or individuals. For instance, we have baseline duties to everyone but special duties to those who have helped us in the past or those we have harmed. Thus if a company has been assisted by a tax break from the local community, it will have generalized duties to produce returns to its shareholders and produce safe goods, but in case of a conflict it should put community interests ahead of others, all other things being equal.

So far we have looked at the shareholder approach that suggests that the central concern of business is maximizing returns to company owners, and a stakeholder view where profitability is secondary to moral action. We might also chart an intermediate position, where companies take account of stakeholder interests but realize that this approach is also more profitable. It may be, as in the Merck case, that the moral mission is correlated with profitability. On the other hand, we could imagine a board of directors consciously adopting a public stakeholder stance because it functions to enhance the corporate reputation and builds a future client base. Discerning the difference between the two positions might be difficult, since outwardly they would look the same. One test might be to see how the company reacts if it falls on hard times – if it maintains its duties to stakeholders even if the evidence shows doing so is a losing proposition. However, Freeman makes the point that for a private firm to be a vehicle for enhancing overall welfare, it needs to stay in business – that is, make a profit. Therefore giving some primacy to the needs of the owners could easily be justified.

The language of stakeholder benefits is prevalent in current business, and it appears to reflect a sincere commitment on the part of companies to act as good corporate citizens. Although some of the language may be used

---

[13] W. D. Ross, *The Right and the Good* (Oxford: Clarendon Press, 1930), p. 21.

rhetorically or to enhance the firm's reputation in order to become more competitive, there is significant evidence that many very successful companies do, in fact, adopt a deontological stance on the basis that taking care of others or enhancing community welfare requires no further justification than it is simply the right thing to do.

## Virtue theory

A third perspective relies on developing character as opposed to discovering the right action in any particular case. Consider that if we were to ask someone how he would like to be remembered, it is likely that the response would be something along the lines of "as someone who was kind, generous, caring, compassionate, friendly, and humorous." The point is that he typically would not point to particular acts or achievements but instead looks to general character traits. The exercise gives us an insight into virtue ethics, which challenges the relevance of putting so much stress on the particular outcomes, as does utilitarianism, and reverence for rational decision procedures, as does deontology. Virtue theory is more concerned with character and what it means to have a life well lived. It echoes our common belief that we judge people by more than just their effectiveness in increasing welfare or by how well they fulfill obligations.

The key figure in virtue theory is the philosopher Aristotle (384–322 BCE). Aristotle's system is *teleological*: in other words, purposeful or end-directed. He believed that we should aim to achieve *eudaimonia*, perhaps best translated as "human flourishing." It is specifically human because he sees the ability to reason and express ourselves in action as distinguishing us from all other living things. We learn best from role models in society and making the most of our talents. Instead of working out an algorithm of correct action, we can model ourselves on heroic people we aspire to be like, asking what they would do in this situation. Moral goodness is achieved by encouraging and shaping our virtues. He says:

> Virtue, then, is of two sorts, virtue of thought and virtue of character. Virtue of thought arises and grows mostly from teaching, and hence needs experience and time. Virtue of character results from habit [ethos]; hence its name "ethical," slightly varied from "ethos."[14]

[14] Aristotle, *Nicomachean Ethics*, trans. T. Irwin (Indianapolis: Hackett Publishing Company, 1987).

The virtues do not exist in isolation, though. They have to be expressed in a particular context, and our moral character involves moderating our virtues between excess and deficiency, much like a rudder steering a ship. We need to balance the feelings of fear, boldness, desire, anger, pity, pleasure, and pain between too much and too little. Hence, it is fine to be trusting, but we have to strike the balance between not trusting enough and being gullible. We have to have feelings, in Aristotle's words, at the right times on the right occasions toward the right people for the right motives in the right way and to the right extent, and our ability to judge correctly characterizes goodness. Thus anybody can fly into a rage, but a virtuous manager has to be able to direct her anger appropriately so that the right person gets the right message at the right time to get things done properly. Too little anger will make people think nothing is wrong, but too much may leave employees feeling resentful. Moreover, it is part of the manager's job to praise or reward those who are directly responsible.

Virtues may not be taught by mere classroom instruction. Aristotle believed that humans have both reason and desire, and there are two types of corresponding virtues: intellectual virtues and practical virtues – those of us with character apply the virtues appropriately in real situations. Intellectual virtues by themselves can make someone clever or wily but not necessarily good. So a hacker who develops a computer virus is undoubtedly very bright, but his intellect is probably misdirected. Aristotle believed that we have to combine cleverness with the ability to know when and where to apply it, which comes from experience and from listening to respected members of the community. It does not preclude competition, so just like athletics, everyone is encouraged to develop personal excellence, and doing so does not entail disrespect to others.

Moral training is also a question of developing the right habits (Aristotle's "ethos" mentioned above). We could make an analogy with car seat belts, which were once optional, and then made mandatory by law. As people started wearing them, they became habituated, and most people now have an automatic reaction to buckle up in a car. Similarly, virtue training will first enforce the disposition to find the mean between excess and deficiency, but then it will become more normal and habitual until it eventually becomes an internal characteristic. However, it would be wrong to portray virtue theory as automatically demanding a uniform response. Explicitly, every person will have to judge his or her best action in specific situations.

A central element for an Aristotelian is to conceive of actions as part of a continuing personal history, that is, one with a future and a past. Just as learning to play an instrument takes time and practice, we can only judge an individual on overall character. The perspective of time will allow us to gauge a person by building a profile of actions in a range of circumstances and seeing the continuing motivational dynamic (*energeia*) behind actions. Furthermore, virtue theory necessarily looks at the context of an act, something that Kant wants to ignore.

Another feature is that virtue theory recognizes that our actions take place within communities and have to be judged in those terms. Thus on an individual level it makes sense that the qualities of a good marine and a good librarian are different, although we can judge each by how well they fulfill their respective functions. Firms operate within the societies that charter them, and so we should not judge them in isolation. Moreover, as members of a community firms will have clearly articulated rights and responsibilities that go beyond the vague directive to do the right thing.[15]

Public corporate statements and popular management literature often use virtue language. JPMorgan Chase provides an example of a brief statement of core values along these lines:

> Behaviors and principles that describe what we stand for – integrity and respect – and what we deliver – excellence and innovation.
> - Integrity – Striving at all times to do what's right and adhere to the highest ethical standards.
> - Respect – Valuing the perspectives and expertise of all to surface the best ideas and insights.
> - Excellence – Achieving high-quality results by continuous improvement and superb execution.
> - Innovation – Going beyond the commonplace to break new ground.[16]

The list could be expanded, of course. The contemporary philosopher Robert Solomon has published a list of over forty business virtues, ranging from

[15] Daryl Koehn, "A Role for Virtue Ethics in the Analysis of Business Practice," *Business Ethics Quarterly*, 5.3 (July, 1995), pp. 553–539.

[16] JPMorgan Chase, 2003 Community Partnership Report, http://www.jpmorganchase.com/cm/cs?pagename=Chase/Href&urlname=jpmc/community, accessed June 30, 2006.

ambition to zeal.[17] However, being true to the spirit of Aristotle's philosophy, these cannot be promoted in isolation but have to be used judiciously to the right effect. Additionally, the environment of the firm has to be conducive to individuals developing their virtues so they can flourish and have the happiest and most rewarding lives possible, which leads to the question of the moral status of the corporation itself.

## The virtuous corporation

While it makes perfect sense to ask if people are virtuous, is the claim that "Enron acted badly" meaningful, or can we say a company itself is good? One way of thinking about this is to consider that many firms have a distinct *culture*. There may be a set of unwritten corporate policies and shared understandings that are not written in the code of conduct, and those who are in tune with them and act accordingly will thrive whereas those who do not will flounder. Thus there may be a Citibank way of dressing or an acceptable way of going through channels at FedEx that reflects the nature of the company. These understandings are not linked to individual executives or employees but represent the way the company operates.

The effect of a corporate culture is that it may lead to behaviors where no one individual may be held accountable. In the case of the space shuttle *Columbia*, for instance, an engineer had suspected that there was significant damage to the wing and tried to get satellite pictures taken to determine if he was right. However, the bureaucratic nature of NASA held up his request because the engineer did not use the correct channels to report his concern. As it turns out he was correct, and the investigatory board faulted the authoritarian and rigid culture at NASA. Yet, at the same time, no individual was held accountable.

So it could be that every individual in an organization can sincerely say that they were not to blame for an incident, yet they were part of a collective whole that was nevertheless responsible. Consequently the firm cannot be reduced to just its members, but takes on a moral agency of its own. Thus we can argue that it is not just people who can be morally assessed by virtue ethics, but corporations as well.

[17] Robert Solomon, *A Better Way to Think About Business: How Personal Integrity Leads to Corporate Success* (New York: Oxford University Press, 1999).

Virtue theory is attractive in many ways, but nevertheless it has some weaknesses that make it prone to criticism. As we have seen, the theory is context-based and therefore will tend to reflect prevalent norms and attitudes. Accordingly in a society that believes the good life is one of constant acquisition and consumption and where successful business leaders are venerated as celebrities, it would be natural for young people to model their lives after such figures. Aristotle assumes that we have sufficient critical acumen to distinguish among people who are truly worthy and those who are not, but this may be a difficult task for most of us: in contemporary times it seems difficult to name more than a handful of people who consistently stand out as natural role models or heroes.

The lack of an outside principle of right and wrong can also lead to what is termed the "good Nazi" problem. In this case, someone is loyal, brave, courageous, and has many other noble qualities, but unfortunately is working for a corrupt and evil system. In essence, ideally we need some independent external criterion to establish that the contextual norms are not immoral, otherwise the prevailing norms may be immune to criticism.

Virtue theory also begs questions about the moral status of firms and how we should consider the relationship between business and society. Whereas it is fairly straightforward to describe the qualities of a good citizen in a specific society, it is more complicated to frame what we think an ideal corporation would be like, especially given its primary obligations to survive, grow, and make profits in a worldwide marketplace. After all, Aristotle's original notion of flourishing was an exclusively human activity, based on our abilities to reason and contemplate.

## Summary

Stepping back, we can claim that ultimately corporations exist to serve human demand. As we shall see in the next chapter, capitalism has its own logic that sometimes needs to be monitored and corrected. Like a fire, capitalism makes a good servant to human flourishing, but a poor master, since left unchecked it may lead to excessive, unreasonable, or harmful acts. Adam Smith came to a similar conclusion in 1776:

> The violence and injustice of the rulers of mankind is an ancient evil, for
> which, I am afraid, the nature of human affairs can scarce admit of a
> remedy. But the mean rapacity, the monopolizing spirit of merchants and

manufacturers, who neither are, nor ought to be, the rulers of mankind, though it cannot perhaps be corrected may very easily be prevented from disturbing the tranquillity of anybody but themselves.[18]

Ethical theory provides us with an analytical framework that starts us on the path to making decisions about what we should do in any particular case. At this point let us return to Owen, faced with his various moral quandaries and conflicting intuitions. Ethical theory will allow him to organize his intuitions and begin to make reasoned arguments. The dilemmas that Owen confronted at work will still involve hard thinking, but by incorporating the language of outcomes, duties, and virtues he may be able to better sort out what he should do and make a persuasive case to others. These approaches, as we have seen, are often nuanced and will not provide a direct recipe for right action in every case. Still, the move from unreflective action to a justified one is a considerable advance, so that if we are ever called on to explain our plans and acts we can do so in a principled and coherent fashion, rather than relying on personal feelings alone.

At the same time, in examining business ethics it is vital to acknowledge that moral decisions do not occur in isolation, but always take place within a wider context, and hence we need to understand the pressures and institutions capitalism fosters that encourage some behaviors and censure others. Therefore we will now turn to look at the moral implications of capitalism and then bring in more conceptual tools to facilitate discussion about what constitute appropriate ethical responses to difficult situations.

## General issues for discussion

1. What makes a decision an ethical one?
2. Do you think business, as contrasted to the people in a business, can be virtuous?
3. How much should we take potential consequences into account when making an ethical choice? How much work should we put into making sure our assessment of outcomes is correct?
4. When can we stop doing good? Is there a difference between decent and heroic behavior?

---

[18] Adam Smith, *The Wealth of Nations* [1776], ed. Edwin Cannan (London: Methuen, 1904), Book V, chapter 3, para. 38.

5. Which form of ethical theory do you think applies best to the realm of business activity?
6. Should a firm do good because it will lead to profits? If not, what other reasons are there?

## Case – terminator seeds

In 1998 the US Department of Agriculture and Delta and Pine Land Company, the world's largest cottonseed producer, received a patent for "Control of Plant Gene Expression." The process is sometimes referred to as the Genetic Use Restriction Technologies (GURT). There are two major forms. The first creates seeds or plants that are sterile, so that a farmer could not harvest the next generation of seeds for future use. The second requires specialized treatment by a chemical that effectively acts as a genetic switch that turns on the enhanced qualities of the crop. The nickname "Terminator" has entered common use in describing these technologies, after the movies starring Arnold Schwarzenegger as an unstoppable robot.[19]

Agriculture companies see this as a way of protecting their intellectual property. They spend millions of dollars in research, and want to assure that they have an income stream from their products, since without any controls new varieties could be widely reproduced and disseminated from just a few original plants. The technology also has the promise of greater control on the farm – for example, a farmer could trigger harvesting at an optimal time, or ensure that windblown seeds do not interfere with crop rotation. The American government has supported GURT on the basis that it will stimulate private development of crop breeding of new and more useful varieties that "could be crucial to meeting future world food needs, conserving soil and water, conserving genetic resources, reducing negative environmental effects of farming, and spurring farm and other economic growth."[20]

Critics suggest that the technology will affect a centuries-old way of life, and hold farmers hostage to big firms, in that they would be the only suppliers of viable seeds and could charge whatever price they choose. It has become a highly sensitive issue in developing nations, especially India,

[19] Patrick Mooney, executive director of the Canadian Rural Advancement Foundation International (RAFI), an opponent of the technology, coined the term.
[20] "Why USDA's Technology Protection System (aka "Terminator") Benefits Agriculture," United States Department of Agriculture, Agricultural Research Service, available at http://www.ars.usda.gov/is/br/tps/, accessed March 9, 2006.

where most farmers capture the seed from crops for future use, while at the same time Monsanto and other companies are trying to increase their influence in the agricultural market. The Indian Agricultural Minister suggested that using terminator seeds threatened biodiversity and could lead to the gradual extinction of traditional varieties, and banned them from being imported.[21] Monsanto's position is that the technology would be safe if and when it is marketed, and it has the potential to increase protection from pests and drought resistance.[22]

A worldwide moratorium was enacted in 2000 after the United Nations Convention on Biological Diversity recommended against field testing or commercializing seed sterilization technologies. This has been successively challenged. Australia, Canada, New Zealand, and the UK have all supported GURT, and have backed language that suggests the applications be assessed on a case-by-case basis. This would bring international regulation in line with existing rules governing the already widespread use of genetically modified organisms.[23] (In the United States, over half the soybeans and a third of cotton and corn planted in a year are genetically engineered to resist pests or herbicides, and about 70 percent of processed foods contain genetically modified organisms.)

Currently the US government, Delta, Syngenta, DuPont, Monsanto, BASF, and several American universities all hold "terminator" patents. Delta and the US government are actively promoting commercial uses of terminator seeds. The other big companies have made public statements saying that they currently have no plans to introduce GURT.

## Some questions from the case

1. In general, should a company be compensated for the use of its intellectual property?

[21] "Indian Government: Shri Sompal's Statement Regarding Threat of American Terminator Seed to Agriculture," *M2 Presswire* (December 2, 1998).

[22] Bill Lambrecht, "Critics Vilify New Seed Technology that Monsanto May Soon Control: 'Terminator' Would Prevent Saving of Seeds by Making Them Sterile," *St. Louis Post-Dispatch* (November 1, 1998).

[23] Charlene Sweeney, "Britain Gives the Green Light to GM Terminator Technology," *Sunday Herald* (Scotland) (March 5, 2006); John Vidal, "Canada Backs Terminator Seeds," *The Guardian* (UK) (February 9, 2005); "Terminator Five Years Later" ETC group, Issue 79 (May/June, 2003), http://www.etcgroup.org/search2.asp?srch=terminator+five+years+later, accessed March 9, 2006.

2. How should we go about comparing the purported benefits and risks of so-called terminator seeds?

3. Is it unjust for governments to interfere with the free operation of the market?

4. What qualities would a "virtuous" chemical company have? Would they differ from the qualities of any other company?

5. Do you think it would ever be acceptable for impoverished farmers to steal the seed from rich suppliers? For a poor country to have its scientists synthesize and reproduce proprietary formulas?

6. Genetic modification could make barren areas fertile and result in an end to world hunger. Why should we restrain that potential?

# 3 The capitalist system and its ethical implications

## The Body Shop

Anita Roddick was struggling to support herself and her two young children when she opened a shop to sell homemade cosmetics in 1976. The ingredients were natural and exotic, and customers were invited to refill their bottles. Soon the business had become popular, and she wanted to open a second store. Her local bank manager told her to wait a year, but instead she made a deal with a local used car salesman, Ian McGlinn, who bought a half share in the company for £4,000 (approximately $7,000), and he has not taken an active role in the business since.

The products attracted customers through promotions that touted ecologically friendly practices, natural ingredients, animal welfare, and fair trade with indigenous peoples. Roddick teamed with the organization Greenpeace in a "save the whales" campaign to substitute jojoba oil for whale spermaceti in cosmetics. She has promoted causes ranging from banning animal testing to fostering the use of ingredients grown by small farms in the third world. She has supported a wide range of social causes and has allowed her workers to dedicate one day a month to outside activism.

The business grew rapidly, and franchises opened around the world. At its height, there were some 2,000 stores in 48 countries. Roddick publicly floated the company in 1985, and by 1992 shares were trading at 360 pence, more than triple their initial price. Roddick and her husband ranked among the richest people in Britain. McGlinn's initial investment turned into a net worth of over 150 million pounds.

However, other manufacturers began to promote similar products, including the French company L'Oréal, which emphasizes its commitment to sustainable development. Estée Lauder and many others have banned animal testing. The expansion into America failed to take into account powerful competitors such as Bath & Body Works. Moreover, press reports disclosed that many Body Shop products were synthetic in origin, that the company had been less philanthropic than its claims suggested, and that its fair trade practices were exaggerated. Roddick countered the bad publicity by commissioning an independent report that faulted the company in areas such as wages, working conditions, product quality, and management accountability but also stated that "The Body Shop demonstrates greater social responsibility and better social performance than most companies of its size."

By the late 1990s, the share price had tumbled, largely due to the overly ambitious expansion program and difficulties with franchisees. Under shareholder pressure, Roddick stepped down as chief executive. At the time she described the company as a "dysfunctional coffin" that had lost its soul since going public. She also claimed that all beauty products besides moisturizers were "complete pap" and declared, "No one really needs anything we sell."

Roddick moved on to publishing inspirational books, promoting her favorite causes, and giving talks on ethical business practice. In March 2006, The Body Shop agreed to a takeover by L'Oréal, netting Roddick and her husband almost $230 million. As she remarked: "This is without doubt the best 30th anniversary gift The Body Shop could have received."[1]

We cannot discuss business ethics without some understanding of the capitalist context that dominates world markets. No transaction in our society happens in isolation, but within a certain context and as part of a much wider system. Therefore, before we look at more individual topics, it is worthwhile to examine capitalism in broad theoretical terms. The story

---

[1] Sources include: Craig Cox, "Social Auditing," *Utne Reader* (August 25, 1998); Will Self, "I Want a Relationship with the Cosmos," *The Independent on Sunday* (UK) (March 11, 2001); Susie Mesure, "Body Shop Potions Work for Now but Christmas Could Still Be Dismal," *The Independent* (UK) (October 14, 2005); Susie Mesure, "Body Shop warning delivers body blow to investors," *The Independent* (UK) (January 12, 2006); Richard Creasy, "The Body Builder: The Recluse Who Loaned Anita Roddick 4000 Pounds and Sat Back as it Turned Into 115 Million," *The Mirror* (UK) (May 14, 1998); Jon Entine, "Body Flop," *Toronto Globe, Report on Business Magazine* (May 31, 2002); Matthew Beard, "Anita Roddick Says Body Shop Has Become a 'Dysfunctional Coffin'," *The Independent* (UK) (August 25, 2001); Emma Clark, "The End of Anita's Heyday," BBC News Online (February 12, 2002), available at http://news.bbc.co.uk/2/hi/business/1816041.stm, accessed February 10, 2006; "Body Shop Agrees L'Oreal Takeover," BBC News Online, http://news.bbc.co.uk/2/hi/business/4815776.stm, accessed March 17, 2006.

of The Body Shop is instructive in showing us a number of key features in capitalism and the behavior that they promote.

## Features of capitalism

Capitalism is an economic system with profound influence over our everyday lives. Many of us spend significant parts of our lives working for a corporation or other economic entity; we constantly shop for goods and services, both out of necessity and recreationally. Our landscape is filled with commercial stimuli, dictating many of our entertainment options, especially on television. Corporate sponsorship pervades research, sports, and cultural activities. Indeed, many of the relationships we have with others have an economic basis.

Undoubtedly capitalism has resulted in a high standard of living and an abundance of high quality goods and services at an affordable price. At the same time, though, we should consider some of capitalism's other effects, including constant consumption of finite resources, relentless marketing, an imbalance between rich and poor, and the rise of corporate power. Additionally, as capitalism becomes more global it will challenge some of the restraints placed on it by sovereign nations.

It is important to see that businesses do not operate independently but against the backdrop of a system based on certain assumptions: people operate out of self-interest; consumers are discerning enough to demand things that will increase their well-being; competition is good; the market will reward those who are industrious and innovative; economic growth should be encouraged; and, perhaps most important, the invisible hand functions to promote our mutual best interest, although it is irrational and guided by individuals operating uncooperatively.

In this chapter we will critically assess these assumptions and the dynamics they stimulate as well as some of the ways in which the market system fails. We will see that in practice governments have considerably modified the capitalist model, and that the rise of globalization poses a challenge to government restraint. Finally, we will briefly reflect on the logic of capitalism and its potential effect on human fulfillment.

Imagine a society where everyone is self-sufficient – they all make their own clothes and cultivate their own food. Two dynamics are likely to develop as the society grows. First, jobs are often accomplished more efficiently if the tasks are broken down into discrete elements, each performed by a particular person who may well become a specialist in that area. Second, exchange is mutually beneficial. Thus if someone has a talent for making clothes and sewing whereas another excels at tending animals, they may all be better off when they partition jobs and then exchange the resources that result.

A huge shift in the economic system came about with the industrial revolution. The use of powered machinery allowed a quantum leap in productivity, but the investment required was largely beyond any one investor. The most efficient means of raising large sums of money has been to pool the burden, so that many people share in the enterprise. This is typically known as share ownership, and the financial vehicle for the project is a corporation. Shareholders may be paid a dividend out of profits or may trade their stock as it changes value. The central feature of a for-profit corporation, though, is its ability to shield individual members from personal liability. Debts incurred by the corporation belong to the corporation and not the individual owners. Furthermore, corporations are perpetual, in that they survive the coming and going of particular individuals, and thus projects and assets can be maintained over time.

Thus when The Body Shop went public, its ownership was divided among share buyers, and then the shares were later traded. The firm continued after the majority of shareholders felt their financial welfare would improve if Roddick stepped down as chief executive officer. We might imagine the scenario as owners showing up at an annual meeting and raising concerns about the strategy of the company, but this is getting to be more unusual. In the last twenty years or so, big institutions like mutual funds or insurance companies are now the holders of many shares. Shares will often be traded based on computer models of expected performance. This means that someone who has a private pension may invest in a mutual fund, which then spreads its assets as productively as it can across a wide portfolio of investments. In this case, the individual is not a direct shareholder of the company, since his money is pooled and redistributed. Therefore even when people invest in a "socially responsible" fund that seeks out investments that conform to certain ethical standards, the degree of anyone's personal support of particular companies will be hard to track.

A key element in capitalism is that company shareholders do not increase their wealth by investing their labor, but instead they use money to make money – hence, they became capitalists. Ian McGlinn did no work to earn his millions, but he did put substantial resources at risk to promote a new business – Anita Roddick's Body Shop. In contrast, think of a cook, earning a wage in a restaurant kitchen. He adds value by cooking the food with expertise, which is then sold to customers. However, his pay probably is less than the amount of the value added to the food. Certainly the restaurant owner has to pay for other workers, suppliers, and overhead, but she also wants to realize a profit for taking the risk of investing in the enterprise.

Corporations are typically run by corporate officers who are agents of the owners, that is, the shareholders. These executives have a fiduciary duty to run the firm so that it produces a return to the shareholders, and face significant pressures to survive, grow, and become ever more efficient. They have to do this in the face of competition and government regulation. It is not surprising therefore that the ethical dimension of business decisions may sometimes be an afterthought. At the same time, companies exist to serve people, and are chartered by society to benefit all, and so we have a legitimate interest in regulating and auditing business activity by promoting elements that will improve the quality of our lives.

Firms have become a significant social and economic powerhouse within society. They have the ability to shape public and legislative opinion and throw their weight behind political causes. The top 200 corporations have combined sales representing 27 percent of the world's economic activity. And if we look at the gross domestic product of a country and corporate sales, and then of the hundred largest economies in the world, over half are corporations. Almost half their activity is split among four areas: banking and insurance, telecommunications, retail/wholesale, and cars and auto parts. As a point of comparison, General Motors has a bigger economy than Denmark, IBM is bigger than Singapore, and DaimlerChrysler is bigger than Poland.[2]

In an ideal capitalist system there is a free market where the means of production are privately owned, and there is no central control of investment, production, distribution, or prices of commodities. People buy from a wide variety of potential vendors when they judge that their welfare will be increased, but they may also refuse to buy. Prices are established by the dynamics of supply and demand. The market allows the manufacturer who

---

[2] From Sarah Anderson, John Cavanaugh, and Thea Lee, *A Field Guide to the Global Economy, 2000* (Washington, DC: Institute for Policy Studies, 2000).

produces best quality and most affordable goods to prosper, and the system punishes firms that fail to deliver what the market wants. There are demands within the market, sometimes for things that people do not yet realize that they want. The Body Shop was able to tap into a demand for cosmetics associated with an ecological sensitivity, and Anita Roddick was richly rewarded for supplying a demand that no other retailer had pinpointed.

Capitalism relies on the generation and reinvestment of profit. Profit is a return over and above the cost of producing and marketing a good or service. A traditional view of business is that its main function is to return profit to the owners of a corporation. Profit acts as an incentive and reward for those who successfully predict where the market will go. A company may invest substantial amounts in research and development hoping to capture a new market, and in this way capitalism rewards risk-taking and innovation. A maxim in investing is that "risk equals yield." In a capitalistic system, someone who sees the potential in ecological cosmetics, internet auctions, or nationwide overnight delivery service can become very wealthy, although there is the correlative risk of championing an internet grocery or beta-max video recorders and losing everything.

A simple assertion by free market advocates is that merit will be rewarded. If individuals command a product or service that the market will support, then they will get what they deserve: a brain surgeon ought to be highly paid because of the intelligence and industry it takes to acquire those skills, and someone like Bill Gates, the founder of Microsoft, merits his fortune because he had the vision and ability to fulfill a market demand. This claim rests on the assumption that the market is a proper gauge of human success, and meeting needs will reap a reward. Critics might claim that this is approach unfairly benefits someone who has been lucky enough in the genetic lottery to have come into the world literally gifted with the right intelligence and aptitudes.

Property rights are another pillar of capitalism. Largely derived from the work of the philosopher John Locke (1632–1704), we have developed certain assumptions about ownership. In rough terms, we may hold legal title to property, and then we can give it away, exchange it, or dispose of it as we see fit. However, there may be conditions that would cause society to restrict your freedoms. If you owned a culturally significant piece of art, you might be prevented from destroying it or shipping it overseas, or similarly if the government needed your land for a new airport you might be compelled to sell it.

Locke asserted that we come to own something by mixing our labor with it. Imagine the case of a woman who goes fishing at sea. She has a boat and nets, and if she catches fish, we consider that she is entitled to them: she may take them to market and pocket the profits. The resource that she exploits is held in common, but by virtue of her hard work and expertise, she now owns the fish. However, nowadays most workers do not work for themselves or harvest a common resource. They generally do not have an ownership interest in the business or the product. Thus if you have a job in a factory, you are typically paid an hourly wage, and your function is to add value to the goods or services by your labor. The owner of the business hires workers based on an exchange of labor for compensation, and in the competitive realm of capitalism, the employer seeks to get as much work for as little as possible, and conversely the workers try to get as much compensation for their labor as they can.

Embedded in the notion of private property is the idea that we are distinct individuals, each capable of making independent decisions and with separate interests from everyone else. Again this sounds obvious, but it may not be as clear-cut as it appears at first. In a very real sense, humans are social creatures, and we identify ourselves in relation to others. This means that we necessarily live in societies where we have relationships with others involving partiality and obligation. So while it may initially seem that we all exist independently, a more accurate picture would show us living as parents, children, caregivers, and dependents, among other roles.

Allied with the idea that we are unique individuals is the sense that we are ultimately trying to maximize our own welfare. One view that we have encountered earlier in this book also suggests that even apparently altruistic acts are motivated from self-interest, so that giving to charity or volunteering really amounts to acting so that we feel good about ourselves. *Greed* is not a pejorative term from this perspective, since it is natural for everyone to look out for themselves and should be expected.

## The invisible hand

Systematic self-interest turns out to be a fundamentally beneficial attribute in a free market. Consider a supermarket. One that offers a wide range of products will attract more customers than one with more limited offerings. The store does not offer the array just to be nice to customers but because it recognizes that its greater appeal will maximize its subsequent profits. The same logic will hold true of other goods and services: almost paradoxically, looking out for ourselves will necessarily result in an increase in overall welfare. Adam Smith first described this phenomenon in his 1776 work *The Wealth of Nations*, where he wrote:

> It is not from the benevolence of the butcher, the brewer, or the baker that we expect our dinner, but from their regard to their own interest. We address ourselves, not to their humanity but to their self-love, and never talk to them of our own necessities but their advantages . . . Every individual . . . neither intends to promote the public interest nor knows how much he is promoting it . . . by directing industry in such a manner as its produce may be of the greatest value, he intends only his own gain, and he is, in this, as in many other cases, led by an invisible hand to promote an end which was no part of his intention. By pursuing his own interest he frequently promotes that of the society more effectively than when he really intends to promote it.[3]

The free market is uncoordinated in that there is no central authority that dictates the number of cars to be produced or what color they should be. Individuals send signals to producers through their aggregated economic choices, and the market responds. Thus if there is a surge in demand for low carbohydrate foods or cars with low fuel consumption, then manufacturers will alter their production to accommodate the market.

Ideally, competition works to make firms produce goods more efficiently – that is, creating more output for a given input – which drives down costs, a benefit that is then passed on to consumers in the form of lower prices. The boost in efficiency can come in a number of ways: increased use of technology, to be sure, but the pressures also encourage companies to minimize labor costs, both directly and in terms of overhead and benefits, and from production processes that comply with the law but go no further. In theory, at least, lower prices increase demand that spurs employment and gives workers more purchasing power, enabling the economy to grow overall and improve the general standard of living.

---

[3] Smith, *Wealth of Nations* [1776], ed. Edwin Cannan (London: Methuen, 1904), Book IV, chapter 2, para. 2.

Another objective in the ideal market is constant growth, and it is often assumed that a growing economy is a healthy one. Still, growth inevitably means greater consumption, which will have ethical implications. In simple terms, products are the result of raw materials being fashioned in some way. A plastic toy in a fast-food meal is typically a petroleum by-product, and the materials in the toy will last for hundreds of years without degrading and rarely go through recycling. The net effect is that we have transformed a finite natural resource into a disposable good. The low costs of production will also act as an incentive to replace rather than to repair products: for example, it is much easier to buy a new compact disc player than have a broken one fixed. An emphasis on expanding sales also leads to the development of goods that have "built-in obsolescence," meaning that they are designed with a limited life span that forces consumers to purchase new goods. Consider that we could use rechargeable batteries, pens that are refillable, or long-life light bulbs, but we choose not to. Many older computers work perfectly well for the limited range of ordinary uses – e-mail, word processing, and spreadsheets. Yet it is in the interest of manufacturers and software developers to create products that require constant upgrading.

While increasing consumption is good for the market, it does mean that we are continually adding to landfills and depleting our resources. The amount of waste that the average American generates has almost doubled in the last forty years, and in the mid-1990s every household in the developed world produced two metric tons of trash every year.[4] The resources of the earth are enormous, to be sure, but they are nevertheless finite. Future generations may face shortages and pollution based on our economic activities and the lifestyle we promote.

Another way to reflect about the potential effects of constant growth is to look at energy use by people in the developed world. In 2001, Americans and Canadians used an average of the equivalent of 8,000 kilograms of oil energy per person, Europeans and Australians used about 4,500 kg., whereas people in the developing world used an average of 828 kg.[5] Thus if everyone

---

[4] "Briefing: Throw-Away Culture," BBC News Online (June 26, 2002), http://news.bbc.co.uk/hi/english/static/in_depth/world/2002/ disposable_planet/waste/, accessed August 31, 2005.

[5] Organization for Economic Cooperation and Development, International Energy Agency (IEA), *Energy Balances of OECD Countries (2003 Edition)* and *Energy Balances of Non-OECD Countries (2003 Edition)*; electronic database available online at http://data.iea.org/ieastore/default.asp (Paris: OECD, 2004); http://earthtrends.wri.org/searchable_db/index.cfm?theme=6&variable_ID=351&action=select_countries, accessed January 10, 2006.

in the world enjoyed the energy-lavish lifestyle of those in the west, there would be a massive drain on the world's non-renewable energy resources.[6] Imagine, for example, the environmental effect of China having the car ownership rates of America. In 2002 America had a population of 296 million and 220 million vehicles on the road, whereas China had a population of 1,310 million and 14 million cars and trucks.[7]

## Market morality

If business is responsive to consumer choices, then it implies that business is a mere conduit for buyers' demands and suggests what we might term *market morality*. The idea is that there may be a great deal of talk about environmental concerns, but unless purchasers actually buy recycled goods or dolphin-friendly tuna their expressions can be discounted as essentially meaningless or superficial, since what matters is where they spend their money. If it turned out, for example, that consumers refused to buy Body Shop products once they discovered that they contained synthetic materials, then their values, represented by their purchasing choices, would impel the retailer to change its practices. On the other hand, if there was a great deal of media coverage and public censure, but consumers still shopped at the store, then we can assume that people did not care that much after all.

However, the basic signal that a producer gets from the market is fairly crude: either people buy goods or they do not, and so consumer reaction to moral issues can easily be conflated with other factors. A more accurate picture would recognize that there are a constellation of reasons why consumers make a particular purchasing decisions. They may be concerned with animal welfare but also want an effective soap that smells good and is the right price. They may enjoy the service provided by the retailer or feel that any other retailer would be similarly suspect.

The point is that consumers and shareholders have a very unsophisticated mechanism by which to signal their moral beliefs and preferences to corporations. If sales of the product go down or the shares lose value, the company will take notice. A regular shareholder may sell shares, say, because

[6] BP/Amoco, *Statistical Review of Energy* (London: June, 1999).

[7] http://www.mnsu.edu/emuseum/information/population/, accessed January 10, 2006; http://www.oecd.org/dsti/sti/transpor/road/index.htm, accessed January 10, 2006.

the company has dealt with a corrupt regime overseas, but the signal that the company gets is blunt and undifferentiated – the company has no way to know what the shareholder's reasons are for selling. The company only knows that its stock has been sold.

A further implication of thinking that the market system is primarily driven by consumer demand is that it will have no independent moral duties other than obeying the law and serving its clients. If customers are willing to buy cosmetics tested on animals, luxury soap that is no more effective than something a quarter of the price, speed trap detectors, or chewing tobacco, then an effective business will fulfill those demands without internally sanctioning its own behavior or questioning the consumer values.

Furthermore, the assumption that consumers are considered sovereign in the marketplace also implies that producers and marketers ought not to be held responsible for trying to influence them. For example, women are often told through advertising that they should aspire to an ideal body type and that the effects of aging should be disguised and remedied. This message, echoed by media that lionize the young and beautiful, may create a desire for goods that are unnecessary and vastly overpriced – for example, Americans spent over $44 billion dollars on cosmetics and anti-aging products and services in 2004.[8] Nevertheless, there is a considerable body of evidence suggesting that in fact our decisions are significantly manipulated or directed in certain ways. This is an important moral finding, because it means that any ethical analysis in business should look beyond consumer buying patterns, and also consider the way the firms shape our desires to fulfill their objectives rather than our own. It is especially true in the case of luxury goods. Consider that there is practically no advertising of staples, fruits, and vegetables, whereas cosmetics, soda, and fast food are regularly promoted and tied to attractive images.

## Market failures

When ideal conditions are relaxed certain problems called market failures arise. Here we will look at consolidation and negative externalities. These

---

[8] Vanessa Gisquet, "Best Age-Defying Foods," *Forbes Magazine* (February 2, 2005), available at http://www.forbes.com/health/2005/02/02/cx_vg_0202feat_ls.html, accessed February 10, 2006.

are morally significant because they can lead to injustice and exploitation that may require correction by an external force, such as government legislation.

## Consolidation

There is a tendency for firms in a competitive environment to form oligopolies (small groups of companies that control a market) or monopolies (single firm control). Once they have acquired a significant market share, they will use their wealth and power to maintain dominance. An example might be an airline that is the only one to fly between two cities. If a new airline starts up, the established firm may sell tickets at a loss for as long as it takes to force the newcomer out of business.

There may also be prohibitive costs to starting up a company, or the advertising and distribution systems may be controlled by a parent entity. Take the market in soft drinks in the United States as an example. It is dominated by three very large firms: Coca-Cola (43 percent), PepsiCo (32 percent), and Cadbury-Schwepps (15 percent).[9] It would be unrealistic to think that a new company could easily enter the market or, if it did, that it would not meet stiff competition from the market leaders. Another example of such dominance shows up in manufacturing firms in the United States where the top 1 percent hold over 80 percent of the assets, and four major appliance makers have 98 percent of the market, and although there are over 1,200 firms engaged in beef processing, the top four have captured 85 percent of the market.[10] Think of the brand leaders that come to mind when considering items such as ketchup, copying machines, or computer operating systems. Several brands have come to dominate the market so completely that their names – Kleenex or Xerox – have become eponymous with the product. Additionally, some industries, such as commercial airplane manufacturers, have such high initial costs and huge overhead that it is not surprising that older firms have consolidated and now have a virtual monopoly.

---

[9] Parija Bhatnagar, "Coke, Pepsi Losing the Fizz," CNN/Money (March 8, 2005), available at http://money.cnn.com/2005/03/07/news/fortune500/cokepepsi_sales/, accessed July 7, 2006.

[10] R. C. O. Matthews, ed., *Economy and Democracy* (London: Palgrave Macmillan, 1985), p. 239; Richard Du Boff, *Accumulation and Power: An Economic History of the United States* (Armonk, NY: M. E. Sharp, 1989), p. 171.

Once a company has cornered a market, it can maintain artificially high prices and restrict innovation. Moreover, the moral concerns about consolidation include worries about the possibility of a few large firms developing disproportionate power and influence, which can be employed to the benefit of shareholders at the expense of the common good. For example, some pharmaceutical companies have a monopoly on certain drugs: the evidence appears to point to the fact that they use their position to maximize profits and restrict the market.[11] In stakeholder terms, this directly favors one particular group – the shareholders – while hurting others unduly.

## Externalities

Another reason that capitalism is impure is the presence of negative externalities, that is, costs of production that are not borne by consumers. Although these costs may be spread among many more people and therefore become imperceptible or slight, they are often incurred without the permission of those who will be forced to pay. People living near a coal-fired power plant, for example, may get soot on their laundry when it is hung out to dry. Strictly speaking, the problem would not have arisen but for the power production, and the extra cost of cleaning ought to be incorporated into the cost of producing the power rather than borne by the residents themselves, with the effect that the higher – but more realistic – price would lead to lower consumption and less pollution.

In another case, imagine that a car has a leaky oil pan that would cost $600 to repair. The owner may have to put in a pint a week, with an annual cost, say, of $120.[12] At first glance it seems that the owner should just keep topping off the oil rather than fixing the problem. On the other hand, the hidden cost is the environmental burden placed on the general community and future generations by the leaking oil contaminating the groundwater, which could easily cost millions to clean up. When we incorporate the new cost, the balance swings dramatically back to getting the car fixed.

Negative externalities are widespread and tend to skew discussions about ethics in business. Take apparel made in a third world country, for instance.

---

[11] Bruce Japsen, "NIH Rules Abbott Can Keep its Monopoly on AIDS Drug," *Chicago Tribune* (August 4, 2004).

[12] This example is derived from Mark Sagoff, "At the Shrine of Our Lady of Fatima," in *The Economy of the Earth* (Cambridge: Cambridge University Press, 1988), pp. 24–49.

Very often consumers are indifferent to where clothes come from and how they arrived at the local store. So, for example, a shirt may well be made in one of the world's poorer countries, perhaps under harsh labor conditions. It would be unusual for the workers to have health benefits, unemployment insurance, or pensions. The retailer finds it more economical to have the article assembled there and pay for shipping instead of having it made closer to the final sales point. In sweatshop debates people often say that labor is more expensive in the first world, which is clearly true. However, some of the costs of labor in the developed nations include items paid by the employer such as unemployment insurance or maintenance of health and safety standards. It is not as if these costs disappear completely overseas, though. Externalities do not show up in the price of the garment, but the burden is nevertheless real and falls elsewhere, in this case, on the workers and their dependents. If those costs were considered equally in calculating labor costs, then we would find there is actually much less difference across the world than is often claimed.

## Commons

A further complication to the market system is that there are a number of resources described as "commons." Imagine a village where anyone can graze their sheep and cows in a common area. This will work well as long as everyone who uses it does so responsibly. However, what if one person starts exploiting the area? In all likelihood, others will similarly abuse the property to promote their own welfare. The answer to this dynamic in agrarian history has been to privatize the resource – that is, to turn the commons into a series of privately owned plots. However, there are resources such as the sea, water, and land that could plausibly be privatized but might be better treated as a communal resource immune from the market.

In dealing with commons issues, there will often be tension between what is in our immediate personal interest and the long-term good taken as a whole. This is compounded by the psychological fact that sometimes despite knowing what we ought to do we are inevitably influenced by the behavior of others. In the case of the oil leak, there seems to be very little merit in *me* having a tight seal on my gasket when everywhere I go I find that there are black patches in parking lots, and my personal heroism in having my engine repaired will do little to change the overall situation.

Therefore, individuals may ignore the results of the full calculation until everyone else comes to the same realization of the true costs involved.

## Regulation of the market

Governments often intervene in the workings of capitalism, either to correct market failures or because of concerns about aggregate welfare. The government may intervene directly or indirectly, through regulation, taxation, and government spending, and consequently the way that capitalism is manifested in contemporary society represents a considerable modification of the ideal model. Some advocates of the free market, such as Ayn Rand or Robert Nozick, believed that the government's role should be as minimal as possible – perhaps just to maintain national defense and enforce contracts.[13] They would say that any attempt by government to adjust the distribution of wealth (described by Nozick as patterning, since it follows a pattern of "from each according to . . . to each according to . . . ," where a centralized administration fills in the blanks) is bound to fail on the grounds that the only just reason for someone to give away their resources is through their personal choice rather than being forced to.

Unrestrained capitalism has a history of business cycles, since firms often take time to react to market signals: during boom times there are not enough resources to fill demand, and during a downturn there are underutilized resources. These effects may be mitigated somewhat by the intervention of government. It may set forth economic priorities that give clear indications of favored sectors of the economy, or it may invest directly, say, in government-subsidized housing, road construction, or military spending. While this is not planning in the sense of direct mandates about the number of shoes or cars that may be produced in a given year, nevertheless the significant amount of government spending in the gross domestic product may stabilize a national economy. As a point of contrast to Nozick's position of minimal interference, we can point to the fact that currently US state and federal governments account for between a quarter and a third of the nation's gross domestic product.[14] Among other things, this means

---

[13] See, for example, Ayn Rand, *Capitalism: The Unknown Ideal* (New York: Dutton Signet, 1966) or Robert Nozick, *Anarchy, State, and Utopia* (New York: Basic Books, 1977).

[14] http://www.gpoaccess.gov/usbudget/fy00/descriptions.html, accessed August 28, 2005.

the government is a huge player in the marketplace and can sustain or ruin companies by how it awards contracts.

Moreover, governments can help correct falsely low prices caused by producer costs that are externalized. A curious thing to many people is that the difference between the lower cost and the higher one that includes the externalities (known as the "shadow price") does not have to be used to compensate those harmed: it could be imposed in the form of a tax that then goes to other uses. For the purpose of the market, all that is required is that the price of goods and services to the consumer accurately reflects their true costs, all things considered.

Just as the government protects certain political rights such as freedom of speech or assembly, it has been involved in maintaining personal rights in the workplace. These include minimum wage laws, unemployment insurance, Social Security systems, restraint on the number of hours that can be worked, limits on child labor, immunity from many forms of discrimination, and entitlements to privacy and safety. In a perfect market, these would likely be part of the terms of employment that could be negotiated – for example, someone might demand higher wages if there were no restrictions on the number of hours that the employer might demand without overtime payments. Historically, though, legislators have often imposed minimum standards, especially where they feel there is unequal bargaining power.

Government action, then, can moderate the tendency in capitalism toward market failures and social injustice. Recently, however, many countries have encouraged the globalization of business. The ethical concern is that as capitalism expands around the world, there will be few mechanisms to rein in its potential harms in the way that national governments do at present.

## Globalization and its implications

International business describes business done between different countries, and the practice is as old as human trading. In contrast, globalization refers to the integration of national economies to form a single market. Globalization takes the liberal market approach worldwide, promoting an unchecked flow of capital and goods, and the paramount motivation of profit maximization.

International markets have historically been protectionist, in that nations try to preserve and promote domestic industry by altering the market through tariffs and taxes. So if Britain had a computer chip industry that was threatened by cheap imports from China, the government could impose a tax that artificially increased the price of the imports and consequently made the domestic product more competitive.[15] This has the political benefit of maintaining employment and safeguarding an industry. However, at present very few economies are self-sustaining, and the fundamental idea behind globalization is that unconstrained capitalism without any national barriers will make business more efficient by opening up markets and boosting fair competition, and this will inevitably lead to greater prosperity worldwide.

Globalization has arisen in the last two decades, fuelled by the formation of the World Trade Organization (WTO) in 1995. By 2005 it had 149 member states that accounted for more than 95 percent of the world's trade. It administers WTO agreements on trade and provides assistance to member nations and developing countries.[16] Nominally it helps exporters and importers conduct business, although it has taken on an increasing role as an unelected international trade manager and arbiter of disputes. As with capitalism in general, there is a presumption that consumption is a good thing and growth should be encouraged, and trade should be on a "laissez-faire" (let it happen) basis. In general, WTO supporters believe regulation and intervention should be kept to a minimum and limited to the governance of contracts and breaking down trade barriers.

The logic is that if jobs are lost, say, in Calgary, Canada, because a manufacturing firm can find cheaper labor in Mexico, this is actually a net advantage. The Mexican economy benefits through the new development, and consumers do well because of the lower costs of goods. If Mexico has an expanding economy, then the workers will have more money to spend and demand higher wages, leading to an increase in aggregate welfare. The company does well because of the increased efficiency. The apparent losers are the workers in Canada. However, they are part of a cycle of a developing economy where there will be a greater demand for higher-skilled and service

---

[15] This is nothing new, of course. Much of Adam Smith's *Wealth of Nations* [1776] discusses the imposition of tariffs on imported corn.

[16] http://www.wto.org/english/thewto_e/thewto_e.htm, accessed January 9, 2006.

workers rather than low- and semi-skilled ones, and once they have adapted to the transition they will prosper, as well. The problem, from this perspective, is that countries may try to protect industries that are no longer efficient. It requires unilateral free trade for the system to work.

The problems with capitalism will be echoed in the globalization debate, especially in terms of externalities and pollution. Free trade implies a level playing field where companies can compete on the basis of their efficiency. However, if a country has a developed infrastructure that imposes costs on businesses, we should expect that firms will relocate wherever costs are lower. Many developed countries dictate minimum wage rates, safety regulations, and environmental protection. In a global free market, these could all be seen as unfair and costly restrictions on trade. Given the incentive for business to relocate to lower its overhead, governments may be tempted to loosen these controls in order to remain competitive in the world market. A similar argument could also be made about welfare programs in general, since they effectively impose taxes on business. Any country that remains committed to maintaining a certain standard of living and security for its citizens through regulation and taxation will face challenges from countries where social programs are not such a priority.

The motivation for business to become ever more efficient also means that low-skilled work inevitably takes the form of a "race to the bottom" where producers are willing to relocate anywhere they find lower overhead. Some developing countries may be desperately poor and in such need of hard currency that they will tolerate practices that might be considered unconscionable in the developed world.

One response is that this dynamic has existed since the time of the industrial revolution. If we trace the low-skilled apparel industry from the appalling slum conditions of Manchester, England, we can see that it followed developing economies – from England, to the Northeast of America before at the turn of the twentieth century, then to the South of the United States, before transferring to Japan and China at the time of the Second World War, and then later to the developing economies of Southeast Asia. Some commentators have associated the moves with increasing labor activism and emergent skill levels in the local labor force.[17] The argument

---

[17] See, for example, Pietra Rivoli, "Labor Standards in the Global Economy: Issues for Investors," *Journal of Business Ethics*, 43.3 (March, 2003), pp. 223–232.

goes that unskilled or low-skilled jobs are the necessary first rung on the ladder of economic development, and in their historical context they will bring an overall increase in welfare.

One tenet of globalization is mobile capital, where money is easily transferred across national borders and can be invested wherever there is most potential yield, so that jobs can be moved to available labor. However, there is currently no correlative freedom for labor to move to the jobs. Borders are open for trade, but often closed for aspirant immigrants. Depending on the skill level involved, this has meant that firms are more likely to relocate or outsource than go through the difficulties associated with work permits. Thus an American telephone company may find it easier to route service calls to India rather than sponsor relocation of the workers. Moreover, rigorous border controls have often resulted in a significant undocumented labor force in many of the developing nations who are ripe for exploitation by unscrupulous employers.

At present, industrial pollution is generally governed by national standards. As controlling waste is an expense, a firm is faced with the decision to spend money conforming to local regulation or moving to an area with fewer controls. So although there is domestic accountability for individuals and companies that pollute, industry might hunt for a host country with fewer concerns. There is a historical element to this discussion as well. The industrial revolution in Europe and America caused massive pollution at the same time as it spurred dramatic economic development. Other countries, for example, China or India, may claim that pollution is the price of industrial development, and it is bigoted of the Western countries to deny it to them – it is as if they are pushing away the ladder to development once they have climbed it, thus preventing others from following suit. One difficulty with issues involving pollution is that it knows no borders, and it is typically easier to prevent than clean up. Still, if consumers are more concerned about lower prices than environmental health, then practical global regulation may be unrealistic. Moreover, if market forces govern pollution, then typically poorer nations will be more willing to compromise their standards or accept pollutants. Some of these nations may be under the control of a despot who is more interested in personal aggrandizement than the general welfare, and if companies are dealing with these heads of state, then they may reach deals that have a deleterious effect on third parties, often the native peoples.

Globalization has also been criticized on the grounds that it transfers power to undemocratic and unelected bodies such as the World Trade Organization (WTO). The member states agree on joining that they will abide by the rulings of the WTO. As in the classic prisoner's dilemma, one of the chief difficulties in opening trade is that if one country imposes tariffs, then others will follow suit until everyone has trade barriers. Therefore, in order for the WTO to have any leverage, members must initially agree to set aside their partisan programs and abide by the WTO's decisions. For example, in July 2005 the WTO upheld a case brought by Brazil against the United States. The United States had been giving subsidies to its cotton farmers, allowing them to sell at artificially low prices. The WTO ruled that Brazilian, African, and Asian farmers could not get good prices because of the availability of cheap American cotton, and ordered America to cut back on its subsidies. In another ruling, President George W. Bush lifted tariffs on foreign steel in 2003 when the WTO's highest court found that they infringed on global trade. The Americans had imposed the tariffs for a three-year period, hoping to give their domestic industry time to recover from a slump, but the action led to an appeal to the WTO by rival manufacturing countries. If America had not lifted its tariffs, then the WTO would have allowed affected countries to impose retaliatory tariffs on American imports. The ruling not only hurt America's steel industry but also hundreds of thousands of retirees who depended on profit-sharing plans.[18] These judgments angered many Americans who felt that their national interest was compromised because their domestic policy was being dictated to by an undemocratic transnational authority. An additional worry to many is that WTO hearings are typically closed to both the public and the media, which adds to feelings that it is autocratic.

There have been two lines of response to the claims of usurped authority. One is that although some particular sectors may be hurt in the short run, the widespread benefits of free trade in promoting jobs and trade will serve as a counterbalance. The second is that joining the WTO has always been voluntary, and the terms of membership are open and transparent. Thus

[18] See, for example, "Steel Tariffs Ended," PBS Online NewsHour (December 4, 2003), available at http://www.pbs.org/newshour/bb/international/july-dec03/steel_12-4a.html, accessed July 7, 2006; Trade Law Centre for Southern Africa, Africa Growth and Opportunity Agency, Business Report, "WTO Rules in Favor of Brazil, Against the USA" (July 3, 2005), available at http://tralac.org/scripts/content.php?id=3469, accessed July 7, 2006.

the time to raise the sovereignty issue has now passed for present members – if it was a real issue it should have been fought over in national political discussions before the country applied for membership. Moreover, supporters note that the rules of the organization are written by member states and its leadership is selected by members through open competition.

Another line of criticism is that although the WTO is nominally neutral, it will inevitably reflect the power of the member countries since it is run by the rich, and the smaller and poorer countries will fare badly. The argument is that developing countries are unable to compete fairly with richer trade partners, and may need time and internal protections to mature their commercial enterprises before they can take on international competitors. For example, it is difficult and expensive to develop a domestic automotive manufacturing capability, and it might be appropriate to allow that to come about before allowing open and free competition from multinational companies.

In short, traditionally national governments have taken it upon themselves to moderate the effects of unrestrained capitalism. Some believe that this leads to its own problems, and the best means to achieve human happiness is to let the system operate unchecked. However, with the rise of global capitalism, the power of individual nations will be severely limited. It would not be surprising, for example, to see a company shop around for a base that least limits its ability to pollute. In the absence of enforceable international regulations, the ultimate responsibility for ethical standards may well rest with consumers, who will have to make decisions about what they are willing to tolerate for cheaper goods and greater convenience.

## Summary

Finally, let us return briefly to The Body Shop. In many ways, Anita Roddick's rags-to-riches story shows capitalism at its best, since she seized an opportunity to do well by supplying ecologically friendly cosmetics and was well rewarded for it. Her company made money for its shareholders, expanding internationally by providing goods to willing consumers at competitive prices and at the same time employing thousands.

However, another side of the story can be told by means of a radical critique of capitalism. Typically, the wages that the company paid were low, sometimes below the European Union threshold of decency standard (similar to American minimum wage).[19] In the words of a former manager, "It's a sweat shop. It's a cruel organization, a mean-spirited company. Benefits are average, at best. Pay is 75% of what other cosmetic companies offer and here we work 60–80 hours a week. Workers are fired on Anita's whims and get no severance. They have no daycare facilities."[20] Using language that originates from Karl Marx, we might say that workers who are paid only a fraction of the value they add to goods and services come to realize that they are the means to someone else's enrichment, and become alienated from their labor: they have no real investment in the endeavor, and work becomes a commodity, something that can be bought and sold, without any personal meaning. Often they work to survive but cannot hope to better themselves.

This perspective on capitalism raises two important concerns that are particularly pressing and immediate when we consider its global spread. First, it forces us to confront the nature of work itself. Many people are in fact alienated from what they do for a huge proportion of their lives and cannot wait for the end of the workday. They have little interest in doing more than they are paid for, do not care about the product or its application, and resent time away from their "real" lives. While there have been some movements to engage workers in profit sharing, or more horizontal management systems, these are rarely adopted wholeheartedly, and owners often revert to traditional work arrangements if they feel vulnerable or threatened. The challenge, then, is how we can adapt the capitalist model to make work more meaningful and fulfilling.

The second concern is that greater efficiency in business does not necessarily translate into better work lives for employees. For instance, computer workstations have revolutionized office and retail operations. Consider that twenty years ago, banking was largely a matter of personal interactions and transferring paper materials. Nowadays it is very much a matter of electronic transactions often completed in seconds. Similarly, robotic machinery now completes assembly-line tasks more quickly and more accurately than human factory workers did just a few years ago. Yet the dramatic increase in productivity has not led to a shorter work week or to a more relaxed work environment – indeed, it has had the opposite effect: people are working

[19] http://www.mcspotlight.org/beyond/companies/bs_ref.html, accessed June 14, 2006.
[20] Jon Entine, "A Social and Environmental Audit of The Body Shop: Anita Roddick and the Question of Character," available at http://www.jonentine.com/body_shop, accessed June 14, 2006.

longer hours, and some technologies such as laptop computers and cellular telephones allow us to continue working from home or while traveling. Fewer workers are required, but their output needs to match ever-greater demands, with the consequence of enriching the owners while at the same time raising unemployment.

Thus while capitalism undoubtedly provides us with a high standard of living and material goods, we should also reflect on the fact that it also encourages us to work ever longer and harder, leading to a paradox where it affords us a quality of life that we may have little time to enjoy, and where the constant urgency of work demands may jeopardize our opportunity to benefit from lives of meaning and fulfillment.

## General issues for discussion

1. Should there be any restraint on capitalism?
2. Are businesses amoral, in the sense that they only reflect the values of their consumers?
3. What do you see as the main ethical issues arising from globalization?
4. Do you consider sweatshops and massive industrial pollution to be a stage in the development of a capitalist economy?
5. How free are consumer choices? How free do you believe workers are to determine their own terms and conditions of employment?

## Case – fool's gold

Bre-X was a small Canadian mineral exploration company founded in 1988 by David Walsh. In 1991, its stock was trading at 4 cents (Canadian) a share. Two years later Walsh met with a charismatic geologist called John Felderhof. By now, Walsh was down to his last $10,000. Felderhof persuaded him to use it to buy the mineral rights of a remote area of Indonesia known as Busang where local villagers had been observed panning for gold.

One form of exploration is core drilling, where samples are brought to the surface in a hollow tube and then examined for mineral content. Felderhof brought in a Filipino geologist, Michael de Guzman, to evaluate the site. Shortly after Bre-X started operations in the area, reports came back from the local assay office that the ore was rich and would be easily extractable. Felderhof explained that a volcano had collapsed back on itself, and the resulting heat and pressure had created one of the world's richest pockets of gold. The initial estimate for the site was 71 million ounces, worth $25 billion, and production costs were predicted to be half the world average. Felderhof said off the record that he was comfortable with a figure of 200 million ounces. By 1994 Bre-X stock was at $1.45 a share.

Financial analysts eagerly promoted the stock. Egizio Bianchini of Nesbitt Burns, Inc., a subsidiary of the Bank of Montreal, visited the site in November 1995 and enthusiastically claimed, "I know for a fact there's more gold. I've seen it . . . Bre-X has made one of the great gold discoveries of our generation." First Marathon Securities sent an analyst to the site, and after his return they reported, "among gold exploration companies, Bre-X remains our favourite." In 1996 analyst Michael Fowler wrote "The bottom line is that our previous 52.74 million ounce resource estimate for the deposit will be easily surpassed, and plus 60 million ounces are likely."

At its height in 1997, the market value of Bre-X had reached $4 billion (US), representing a 100,000 percent growth in three years. De Guzman sold shares that netted him millions of dollars, and Walsh cashed in shares and options worth $35 million and then moved to the Bahamas. Felderhof made his home in the Cayman Islands after realizing almost $30 million. At the time, the major national paper in Canada commented, "If David Walsh and John Felderhof were already not so rich as to be practically above suspicion more complaints might be heard about their offhand approach to corporate disclosure and insider trading."

The government of Indonesia wanted to be involved in the operation, and suggested that Bre-X partner with Barrick, a firm tied to the daughter of President Suharto. Board members of Barrick included the former US president George H. Bush and former Canadian prime minister Brian Mulroney. Bre-X favored a partnership with a firm associated with one of Suharto's sons. The Canadian press characterized the Bre-X founders as business heroes, describing their "fate to make one of the great gold strikes of modern times under the nose of one of the world's most famously corrupt governments, and to be none too quick to realize what they were up against." Eventually, in February 1997 an intermediary, Mohomad "Bob" Hasan, brokered a deal where the American firm Freeport-McMoRan would run the mining operation and Bre-X would have a 45 percent share. Walsh issued a press release announcing the agreement and reiterating the $25 billion figure. As part of its due diligence, Freeport drilled its own samples to verify the lode.

In mid-March, de Guzman took a helicopter ride to meet with Freeport representatives at the mine. He jumped or was pushed out 800 feet above the jungle. Rumors began to circulate that his original samples had been tampered with and salted with gold flecks. Analysts challenged the reports, and still recommended their clients to buy Bre-X stock. On March 24, Gordon Capital in Toronto issued a release that said "Quality of Busang asset not in question . . . Buy this undervalued asset. We maintain our belief that the Busang gold deposit will become a world class gold mine." On the 26th Bre-X was trading at $15.50. Later that day, Freeport issued a report saying there were no significant amounts of gold in the samples they tested. The report was questioned as a ploy to drive down prices in a takeover bid, or based on faulty testing. The market reacted and by the end of the day, Bre-X stock was at $2.50. The Ontario Municipal Employees Retirement fund lost $45 million, the Quebec Public Sector Pension fund lost $70 million, and the Ontario Teachers Pension Plan lost $100 million.

Walsh held onto his stock and hinted that the report was fueled by a political agenda. He died in 1998 at the age of 52 of a brain aneurysm. Felderhof was charged with fraud in absentia, but the Cayman Islands has no extradition treaty with Canada.[21]

## Some questions from the case

1. Should the stock market be regulated by the government?
2. What is the value of a share in a company? How is it determined?
3. How are investment analysts paid? How credible should their reports be?
4. What is the role of the press in reporting on business affairs?
5. Should there be any safeguards for investors in a capitalist system?
6. What damage did the fall of Bre-X cause, if any?

[21] Sources include: "Bre-X Minerals Ltd," *PR Newswire* (February 26, 1997); "Bre-X Minerals Ltd," *PR Newswire* (May 4, 1997); Jennifer Wells and John Schofield, "Bre-X Bubble Bursts," *The Canadian Encyclopedia*, at http://www.thecanadianencyclopedia.com/PrinterFriendly.cfm?Params+M1ARTM0011316, accessed February 22, 2006; Doug Smith, "Bre-X: The Saga Continues," *Canadian Dimension* (September 1, 1997); "There's One Born Every Minute," *Canada and the World Backgrounder* (May 1, 2003); Anthony Spaeth, "The Golden Shaft," *Time Magazine* (May 19, 1997); Richard Behar, "Jungle Fever," *Fortune* (June 9, 1997).

# 4     Feminism

## Morgan Stanley

Allison Schieffelin worked for Morgan Stanley in New York from the time she graduated from Northwestern University's Kellogg School of Management with her MBA. Twelve years later she was earning over a million dollars a year. In 2000 she was fired and escorted from the office days after what her employer described as "an abusive confrontation" with her boss. She filed suit and four years later settled for $12 million.

The basis of her case was that Morgan Stanley had systematically practiced sexual discrimination and retaliated when she complained. Her case had been taken up by the US government's Equal Employment Opportunities Commission (EEOC) on behalf of 300 women who had worked at Morgan Stanley. If the case had gone forward, many of these women had been expected to testify against the company. One of the incidents Schieffelin recounted in her lawsuit was when two clients were invited by male colleagues to attend a weekend in Las Vegas approved by their manager. When Schieffelin asked why she wasn't included, she was told it was "because the men would be uncomfortable participating in sexually oriented entertainment with a woman colleague present, especially one who knew their wives."[1]

In 1996 Schieffelin had complained to the EEOC because apparently less qualified men were being promoted ahead of her, and subsequently her duties were reduced and she was passed over for promotion. She complained that she was being treated unfairly: she claimed similar behavior was praised as "aggressive" in her male colleagues while she was described as "snippy." In 1997 her boss suggested that she was too focused on her work, and she

[1] Complaint available at http://www.newsday.com/media/acrobat/2004-07/13313354.pdf, accessed April 21, 2006.

should direct her energy into "the important things in life" like "having a family" and a "full personal life."

Another incident Schieffelin recounted in her lawsuit concerned one of her directors. After attending sexual harassment training, this director felt constrained by the admonition to not tell sexual jokes and told his colleagues to use a private internal telephone line as "the rude wire." Schieffelin was repeatedly excluded from all-male golf outings with clients paid for by the company, and often meetings were set up in strip clubs or topless bars. When the company arranged for dinners for women to express their concerns, they were told that sexual harassment was "a cultural thing . . . that could not be changed overnight" and "the way forward was to improve things for the next generation of women and Morgan Stanley."

## Women at work

Labor shortages during the world wars stimulated women's entrance into the workplace. During the Second World War, over 6 million women took up work outside the home, many of them married and over 35. The rise of labor-saving devices, baby formula, and food storage technology contributed to their ability to take paid work outside the home. Women became more educated, and a booming economy provided greater employment opportunities. The spread of the women's movement in the 1960s led to a shift in attitude against the "feminine mystique" of women being fulfilled as mothers and homemakers. Women tended to get married later and had fewer children. The inflation of the 1970s prompted many families to have both parents work to maintain their standard of living.[2] Currently, half the households in America rely on both partners working.[3]

In the United States and Europe, women now represent a fraction under half of the workforce. Businesses that ignore concerns of women lose out not only by missing the potential of valuable human resources such as Allison Schieffelin, but also because they develop a reputation for intolerance and injustice.

---

[2] Marie Richmond-Abbott, "Women Wage Earners," in Janet Kourany, James Sterba, and Rosemary Tong, eds., *Feminist Philosophies* (Englewood Cliffs, NJ: Prentice-Hall, 1992), pp. 135–149, at p. 137 n. 2.

[3] Lawrence Mishel, Jared Bernstein, and Sylvia Allegretto, *The State of Working America 2004/2005* (Ithaca, NY: Cornell University Press, 2005).

Two-thirds of women with children work, with participation highest among the 35 to 44 age group (77 percent), and half of the women with children under the age of 3 work outside the home.[4] The more educated women are, the more likely they are to seek a job: 84 percent of female college graduates are in the workforce, contrasted to only 50 percent of women with less than four years in high school.[5] However, the work world seems hostile to women. When median earnings are calculated, women earn about 75 percent of men's wages, although such comparisons are complex because women tend to be employed in a narrow cluster of job categories. They undertake two-thirds of all part-time work, are overrepresented in low-paying jobs, and on aggregate get fewer benefits and are more likely to be laid off.

Some of these jobs have disproportionately high entrance requirements and low salaries – for example, elementary school teaching or nursing. Women have entered the professions, especially law and medicine, yet the vast majority of women are occupied in less than twenty job categories, notably clerical and service occupations. Even in medicine, women tend to specialize in certain areas including pediatrics, public health, and rehabilitation, while they are underrepresented in surgery. In law, women are more likely to be involved in family law or trust and estates than litigation. Research shows that married working women still shoulder the vast majority of household chores and childrearing duties.[6]

At this point we should pause to consider whether the workplace is a gender-neutral environment, and be mindful of the fact that most philosophical work done in the area has been written by men about a labor force presumed to be male. Women's experience in the workplace requires that we turn to insights from philosophers who can inform their ethical analysis with a feminist perspective.

---

[4] "Facts on Working Women," US Department of Labor, Women's Bureau, No. 93–2 (June 1993); M. Thewlis, L. Miller, and F. Neathey, "Advancing Women in the Workplace," European Equal Opportunities Commission, available at http://www.eoc.org.uk/EOCeng/EOCcs/Research/statanalysis.pdf, accessed April 25, 2006.

[5] "Women in the Labor Force in 2004," US Department of Labor, Women's Bureau, www.dol.gov/wb, accessed April 20, 2006.

[6] H. Presser, "Employment Schedules among Dual-Earner Spouses and the Division of Household Labor by Gender," *American Sociological Review*, 59 (1994), pp. 348–364.

## Feminism in business ethics

Broadly speaking, feminist philosophers are united in their belief that women should be treated as full and equal human beings, but beyond that feminism is an extensive field with a wide range of perspectives.[7] Here we will concentrate on two strands of feminist thinking: essentialism and equality. To illustrate these two feminist approaches, we'll use an analogy.

Consider the Olympic Games and what comes to mind are images of athletes running, jumping, and throwing. Now think of the world record holders in these events. Inevitably, they will be men, that is, the fastest runner in the world is a man. We segregate the events so that women compete against women, though undoubtedly there are many women who can run faster than most men. Nevertheless, it is unlikely that the fastest woman in the world will outrun the fastest man. This seems natural, given the differing physical abilities of men and women. However, we seldom question the nature of the games themselves – how the contests emerged and what they measure – since we take running fast and jumping high to be natural ways of gauging our physical achievements. Still, if one were to take a random group of college students and train them for a marathon, the odds are that the winner would be a man, but more women would finish the race since women in general exhibit greater endurance. Similarly, if we had events that rewarded balance, flexibility, and coordination – such as the gymnastics balance beam – women would probably outperform the men.

The question this brings up is whether the games are in some sense natural contests, or whether they emerged from skills necessary to men in ancient battle, where running, throwing a javelin, or lifting heavy weights were prized qualities that were promoted through peacetime contests and childhood games. It could be that they are so ingrained in our society that we think that there is only one proper way to exhibit athletic prowess and that is through the type of games that have come down through history. So if it were possible to design them again from scratch, we might find more categories like the floor exercises, where athletes design a routine of dance-like moves and acrobatic skills that would not automatically favor one gender over another.

[7] See Alison Jaggar, "Feminist Ethics," in H. LaFollette, ed., *The Blackwell Guide to Ethical Theory* (New York: Blackwell, 2000), pp. 348–374.

The example of the Olympics illustrates that there are at least two ways we can address issues of gender in business. The first occurs when we deal with discrimination in the workplace, striving to help women perform up to their potential and receive appropriate recognition. Thus we try to remove barriers to education, provide equal opportunity in hiring and promotion, make sure that men and women doing the same job get paid equally, and so forth. The second way is more radical: it suggests that we need to change the very structure of the workplace, since just like athletic games, it has evolved around a set of male-oriented assumptions about the nature of work and the place of women. The template of what is considered normal is fashioned on men's experience and values. Women are systematically disadvantaged, and however well they adapt and "play the game," the way society and business are structured works against them. Some women may mimic men, according to this view, and a few may be more successful than many men, but in general women are hampered as long as we maintain our prevailing attitudes about women as primarily nurturers and homemakers, and therefore we need to rethink our assumptions about the role of women, work, and business.[8]

## Women's nature

Women's human nature has been characterized as distinct, and the differences may be summed up in a number of conceptual dichotomies: mind/body, reason/emotion, permanent/changing, culture/nature. These are value-laden terms, and historically they have been associated with masculinity and femininity, with the more praiseworthy terms being male. For example, reason has always been highly prized in philosophy, and emotional or intuitive responses have been regarded as contaminating influences. The stereotype of women as being more emotional fixed their nature as being less rational. This led to two results: first, women were thought to have a natural domestic role and thus were taken less seriously as philosophers; and second, insights that were not rationally based were systematically dismissed.

[8] Iris Marion Young, *Justice and the Politics of Difference* (Princeton: Princeton University Press, 1990); Deborah Rhode, "Occupational Inequality," *Duke Law Journal* (December, 1988), pp. 1207–1241.

The debate over whether men and women have essential differences con-tinues in contemporary times where there is some suggestion that men and women are "hard-wired" to have differing ethical responses and personal values. Others accept that these differences exist but ascribe them to social-ization. A third view is that the apparent differences are, in fact, illusory. Still when male managers were asked to characterize both male and female managers, women were perceived as less self-confident, less emotionally sta-ble, less analytical, less consistent, and having poorer leadership qualities than men.[9] However, these perceptions of deficiencies may well refer to a set of characteristics such as compassion or sensitivity that other commen-tators might see as strengths and that should be legitimated and honored rather than corrected.

The dispute over the alleged difference in human nature between men and women has a long history. The philosopher Jean-Jacques Rousseau said in *Emile* (1762) that women have different aptitudes and talents from men and therefore ought to be educated differently. Mary Wollstonecraft responded in her *Vindication of the Rights of Woman* (1792) that although men are obviously stronger, there are no discernible differences in character traits or ability to reason between the sexes that are not the product of social conditioning and domination:

> I earnestly wish to point out in what true dignity and human happiness
> consists. I wish to persuade women to endeavour to acquire strength,
> both of mind and body, and to convince them that the soft phrases,
> susceptibility of heart, delicacy of sentiment, and refinement of taste, are
> almost synonymous with epithets of weakness, and that those beings who
> are only the objects of pity, and that kind of love which has been termed
> its sister, will soon become objects of contempt.[10]

## The female voice

The controversy over whether genders have special qualities can be illus-trated through the recent empirical work of Lawrence Kohlberg and Carol

[9] M. E. Heilman, C. J. Block, R. F. Martell, and M. C. Simon, "Has Anything Changed? Current Characterizations of Men, Women, and Managers," *Journal of Applied Psychology*, 74.6 (1989), pp. 935–942.

[10] Mary Wollstonecraft, *A Vindication of the Rights of Women* (New York: Penguin, 2004), p. 82.

Gilligan. Kohlberg devised a set of hypothetical cases and used subjects' responses to these cases to create a scale of moral development. One case involved a woman who desperately needed a drug that she couldn't afford, and the question posed was whether her husband would be justified in stealing the drug from a pharmacist who was charging an exorbitant amount and who refused to donate the drug or reduce his price. Roughly speaking, Kohlberg rated people who reacted out of fear of punishment lower than those who followed societal convention, and subjects who were motivated by universal moral principles rated highest of all.[11] Typically, women rated lower on Kohlberg's scale than men, a finding that Gilligan later explored. She concluded that his experiments were biased toward a disposition she called the "male voice." We should note, though, that she does not suggest that all and only men have the "male voice," or that women could not show it; rather, it reflects a set of responses commonly associated with men.

Gilligan found that men were more concerned with rules and rights, whereas women tended to look to responsibilities and relationships, especially ones of care. Her experiments suggested that women fear isolation and abandonment and that women develop connections with others, whereas men fear intimacy and think of themselves as separate from others. Alison Jaggar characterizes the woman's voice as valuing "care, attentiveness, trust, and love for others" over and above impersonal qualities of equality, rights, respect, and justice.[12] These insights have led to what we might term an *essentialist view*: that there is something essential to women's nature and experience particularly demonstrated within close relationships and in the practice of nurturing that is valuable and ought to be brought to bear in ethical discourse.

## Ethics of care

Many feminists have adopted an *ethics of care* that suggests that we should start from a view of human nature that we are interdependent, bound in relationships such as family and friends, and partial. This goes against the

---

[11] Lawrence Kohlberg and Richard Kramer, "Continuities and Discontinuities in Childhood and Adult Moral Development," *Human Development*, 12 (1969), pp. 93–120.

[12] Jaggar, "Feminist Ethics," p. 359.

traditional (male) view that many classical philosophers espouse wherein individuals are considered independent, unconstrained, and equal. Some feminists advocate this model of personal relationships and cooperation as a basis for society at large.[13] Thus in a case where a worker has to take time off to care for the needs of an aging parent, a manager would not look to universal and impartial principles of justice removed from the particular context of the issue at hand, but rather approach the situation with empathy and an open mind, considering the special factors involved. Care in this sense should not be confused with soft-heartedness, though. Its proponents say that it sometimes leads to tough decisions, but the decisions derive from rationality tinged with humane concern.[14]

One difficulty with such a personal ethics is that the experience of care is individual, and the approach can easily lapse into relativism, where there is no apparent independent criterion of right and wrong. Moreover, dealing with each issue as independent and contextually bound means that there are few norms that cut across different cases, making it difficult to institute broad policy or to address wide-scale problems.

The other main standpoint, following Wollstonecraft, challenges the essentialist view, believing that claims about special qualities are more a product of social conditioning, class, and culture than about the experience of being female.[15] All the same, these feminists believe that classical ethical theory exhibits biases that need to be redressed and that we should strive for an inclusive ethical consciousness, sometimes called *gender egalitarianism*; thus rather than accept the dichotomies of, say, reason and emotion and then contest which is more appropriate to ethics, this view suggests that we draw ethical insights from both without necessarily assigning gender characteristics to either. Perhaps there are no separate and autonomous female values that are not the product of social conditioning. Nevertheless, society may have systematically devalued women's experience, and by taking seriously the perspectives and experiences of women we may challenge our social and moral priorities.

---

[13] Virginia Held, *Feminist Morality: Transforming Culture, Society and Politics* (Chicago: University of Chicago Press, 1993).

[14] Nel Noddings, *Caring: A Feminine Approach to Ethics and Moral Education* (Berkeley: University of California Press, 1984).

[15] Joan Tronto, *Moral Boundaries: A Political Argument for an Ethics of Care* (New York: Routledge, 1993).

## Issues of equality in the workplace

The call for equality between the sexes is still problematic, since equality may not be equivalent to sameness. Women experience menstruation, pregnancy, childbirth, lactation, and menopause, and any account of equality in business has to deal with the realities of our existence. This inevitably means that we cannot treat equality between the sexes as being gender-blind, especially if we take male experience as the model of normality.

It might be useful at this point to recall Rawls' veil of ignorance: if we believe in a fundamental equality between the sexes and then set societal structures and policy while ignorant of what gender we would be, we might design a world that gave equal opportunity to women and men without penalizing women, say, for bearing children. For example, we might consider pregnancy and maternity leave to be a normal human occurrence instead of treating it – as many businesses currently do – as an illness or career deficit. This line of thinking would promote gender equity rather than take on the difficulties of identical treatment that the term *equality* connotes.

The Global Compact initiative of the United Nations, designed to promote good corporate citizenship, has over 500 signatories including many major multinational companies. One of its clauses is a paramount commitment to non-discrimination in business practice.[16] If we treat gender equity seriously, a company that signs onto the compact is committed to removing sexist bias throughout the company as a priority, which implies a major shift in many business practices. To examine what that might mean, we will now turn to some particular issues that confront working women. Dual burdens make it difficult for women to do the same work as men. Women have often been reluctant to take jobs that involve frequent travel or long hours because it conflicts with a perception that they should be the primary homemaker and childrearer. This may lead employers to create a career path that has fewer demands and more flexible hours, sometimes disparagingly called the "mommy track." The term came about after the *Harvard Business Review* ran an article that began, "The cost of employing women in management is greater than the cost of employing men." Its argument was that if companies did not invest in women-friendly initiatives such as day care and flexible

[16] http://www.unglobalcompact.org/AboutTheGC/TheTenPrinciples/humanRights.html, accessed April 24, 2006. I am grateful to Maureen Kilgour for pointing this out to me.

hours, they would lose valuable employees. However, businesses took the finding to justify putting women on less competitive career paths while maintaining current practices.[17]

Perceptions about potential may become self-verifying, too. In 1968, 15 percent of all managers were women. Given a career path, that means that forty years later, all things being equal, there ought to be roughly that proportion of women in top management today. This is known as the *pipeline effect*, which suggests that increasing the number of women in higher levels of management is contingent on the number of junior entrants years earlier. However, women make up only 3 percent of top management positions today. This statistic supports the notion of a so-called glass ceiling where women get promoted only to a certain level and find it very difficult to get beyond that plateau.

One theory is that men will become more comfortable with women in power positions when there are sufficient numbers of women in such positions to demonstrate that they are fully capable. In spite of this, one study indicates that while this occurred with small numbers, once the proportion of women reached 15 percent there was a backlash effect, probably stimulated by the men feeling less secure and more threatened.[18] Moreover, women who do get promoted to senior levels are at greater risk of being given difficult or precarious jobs, sometimes described as a "glass cliff." As the researchers described the phenomenon,

> There seems to be an unwritten law that says "think female, think crisis"
> . . . if a company is doing well, then the "jobs for the boys" rules still apply,
> but if it is in trouble, no man wants to give the job to their friends, it seems,
> so for many the answer is to get in a woman.

They also found that women perceived they had fewer opportunities than men and were more willing to accept difficult assignments.[19]

---

[17] Felice N. Schwartz, "Management Women and the New Facts of Life," *Harvard Business Review*, 67.1 (January 1, 1989), pp. 65–67.

[18] A. Harlan and C. L. Weiss, "Sex Differences in Factors Affecting Managerial Career Advancement," in P. A. Wallace, ed., *Women in the Workplace* (Boston: Auburn Publishing Service, 1982), pp. 59–100.

[19] Michelle K. Ryan and S. Alexander Haslam, "The Glass Cliff: Evidence that Women are Over-Represented in Precarious Leadership Positions," *British Journal of Management*, 16.2 (June, 2005), pp. 81–90, available at http://www.management-issues.com/2006/8/24/research/not-so-much-a-glass-ceiling-as-a-glass-cliff.asp, accessed December 28, 2006.

Much overt discrimination and sexual harassment has been prohibited by legislation. For example, in the United States, harassment is defined as:

> Unwelcome sexual advances, requests for sexual favors, and other verbal or physical conduct of a sexual nature constitute sexual harassment when this conduct explicitly or implicitly affects an individual's employment, unreasonably interferes with an individual's work performance, or creates an intimidating, hostile, or offensive work environment.[20]

However, even if harassment is made illegal, many women may justifiably feel reluctant to follow up on an accusation and believe that they will be branded as a complainer or not a team player if they object to workplace behavior.

Discrimination may be institutionalized or more covert, so the effect is largely the same. Men may be given more important projects, for example, or the floor sales staff in a department store may be divided so that women sell clothing whereas the men sell appliances, and thus the commission sales favor the men.[21] As Schieffelin noted in her complaint about Morgan Stanley, similar behaviors were positively described as aggressive or competitive in her male colleagues and given negative connotations in her case. Discrimination can also occur in such seemingly trivial forms as using a formal title for a man while calling a woman by her first name, describing her using language with sexist connotations such as "perky," and talking about the world of work in military or sports metaphors.

Unconscious bias is also reflected in the schism in awareness of executive men and working women about the state of emancipation in the workplace: a 1997 Family and Work Institute study found 50 percent of all male CEOs believe that conditions for women have greatly improved, while only 25 percent of women agree; 40 percent of women say that changes in their companies have been minimal or nonexistent, which goes against the perception of 94 percent of CEOs.[22]

The difficulty in ensuring equal treatment in business is illustrated in a legal case brought before the United States Supreme Court.[23] Johnson Controls owned a plant making batteries and warned women working in the

---

[20] http://www.eeoc.gov/types/sexual_harassment.html, accessed April 21, 2006.

[21] Richmond-Abbott, "Women Wage Earners," p. 136.

[22] http://www.familiesandwork.org/announce/workforce.html, accessed April 21, 2006.

[23] http://biotech.law.lsu.edu/cases/EEOC/johnson_controls.htm, accessed April 24, 2006.

area that some of the chemicals they were exposed to were potential feto-toxins (dangerous to fetuses); Johnson Controls asked the women to sign a form showing they were aware of the risks should they become pregnant. However, when eight pregnant women on the line tested at critical levels for lead exposure, the company followed federal guidelines and barred them from working in the area. The women's union sued on the basis of sexual discrimination, citing additional evidence that a man who wanted to become a father was not allowed to transfer out without penalty, and one woman had undergone sterilization to keep her job. The court ruled for the women, on the narrow legal grounds that the law was silent about risks to fetuses and that the workers were given sufficient warnings.

Still, the issue remains that pregnant women – and potentially pregnant women – may deserve special consideration. One question is whether the women ought to have been treated differently, since there are documented risks to men as well. At least in this case both men and women did have other employment options, and the risks were known and public, which allowed them a degree of autonomy. Some commentators suggest that the issue of pregnancy is dramatic, but the essence of the case is that we should provide a safe working environment for everyone, regardless of gender.[24]

## Private lives and public work

The contemporary philosopher Jean Grimshaw has suggested that we cannot look at issues of gender in the workplace without challenging the split that the market economy makes between our private lives and our public work.[25] The prevailing assumption is that we have our personal lives, and then we go off to work as a distinct activity. She notes that this view operates best when the public domain is supported by a subordinate private sphere – which is largely the realm of women. Thus a career couple organize their lives around work demands, but the woman largely maintains the household, and she often adjusts her ambitions around the male's; women who fail

[24] Joan Callahan, "Let's Get the Lead Out: Or Why Johnson Controls Is Not an Unequivocal Victory for Women," *Journal of Social Philosophy*, 25 (1994), pp. 65–75.

[25] Jean Grimshaw, "The Idea of a Female Ethic," from P. Singer, ed., *A Companion to Ethics* (Oxford: Blackwell, 1991).

to compromise may shoulder a disproportionate burden to maintain equal status. She feels that as long as we continue to compartmentalize our lives into public and private, women will inevitably be dealing with a double task that is inherently unfair. Grimshaw advocates a change in perspective, where we assess our life burdens as a whole without distinct borders. Hence our personal lives may involve concessions because of work demands, but conversely, there may be times we have to compromise work, for instance, if we have to cater to the needs of an ailing parent. The breakdown of public and private barriers may also be a double-edged sword, though, in that it is very useful to be able to work from home, but the same technologies that liberate us from having to go into a office or factory may mean that we are also much more likely to bring work home. Her approach will not lessen the various demands we face – the fact that work can be done more flexibly does not imply there will be less of it, of course, and domestic chores still have to be tackled. Nevertheless, she suggests the melding of work and private life may be a first step in achieving gender parity.

There is some evidence that at least among professional workers some traditional gender stereotypes are breaking down, and the public/private distinction is less rigid than it used to be. A study of 800 two-career couples found no meaningful difference in the way men and women responded to work-life balance questions. More than 75 percent said they would look for family leave policies in a new employer; 60 percent said they would seek formalized flexible work programs and the opportunity to work at home or to telecommute. More than 50 percent said they would seek supported childcare.[26] These findings suggest that employers seeking the best applicants ought to consider building better options for work–life balance and providing opportunities for employees that are neutral with regard to gender roles.

## Disproportionate burdens

One final consideration is whether the benefits and burdens of business have a disproportionate effect on women. One area where this appears to

---

[26] Catalyst Inc., New York, press release, "Catalyst Study Finds Dual-Career Couples Want Freedom and Control" (January 20, 1998), available at http://www.catalystwomen.org/pressroom/press_releases/dual_career_couples.htm, accessed April 21, 2006.

be the case is when we look at the effects of globalization. According to the United Nations, women have entered the workforce in significant numbers in states that have embraced liberal economic policies.[27] Specifically, women are employed in large numbers – over 80 percent – in Export Processing Zones (EPZs) and Special Economic Zones (SEZs). These are trade-friendly areas set up by states to encourage export industries, often close to national borders. Businesses have relocated to developing countries to take advantage of cheap labor, and often unskilled and semi-skilled women are employed in industries such as apparel, data processing, and assembly in casual or insecure jobs.[28] Sponsoring states frequently promote deregulation in order to spur development. Employers often perceive women workers to be more docile, and they actively work against labor unionization or factory regulation. Moreover, the informal work sector has grown tremendously. This is where people take work into their home and are often paid by the amount they produce. Under this system employers are not required to ensure that there are safe and decent working conditions.

In much of the developing world, women have had primary responsibility for local agriculture; it is estimated that women subsistence farmers produce food for the majority of the world's population, especially in Africa and Asia.[29] Globalization initiatives have encouraged the development of larger farms, commercialization, and emphasis on crops grown for export, and the United Nations reports that women who previously worked in sustainable agriculture now have to seek seasonal employment.[30] The move from sustainability on traditional lands to paid employment has been a hallmark of many developing countries but may also have contributed to what has been termed "the feminization of poverty." Commentators have also noted that women in developing countries have relatively less access to capital, credit, technology, and property rights and so become systematically disadvantaged

[27] J. Oloka-Onyango and Deepika Udagama, "The Realization of Economic, Social and Cultural Rights: Globalization and its Impact on Full Enjoyment of Human Rights," United Nations Economic and Social Council, No. E/CN.4.Sub.2/2000/13 (June 15, 2000).

[28] Riham el-Lakany, "WTO Trades Off Women's Rights for Bigger Profits," *Women's Environment and Development Organization News and Views*, 12 (November, 1999), p. 1.

[29] Silvia-Federici, "Women, Land Struggles and Globalization: An International Perspective," *Journal of Asian and African Studies* (January 1, 2004), pp. 47–62.

[30] United Nations, *1999 World Survey on the Role of Women in Development: Globalization, Gender and Work*, No. E.99.IV.8 (1999).

when the political system moves toward free markets. Once again, nominal conditions for emancipation, such as an expanding free market, may lead to further disadvantages for women, unless there are some political safeguards in place.

## Summary

Allison Schieffelin was undoubtedly treated badly by Morgan Stanley, her employer. However, we have seen that the effects of gender bias extend far beyond isolated cases of harassment and may have global implications. It is not, in Allison Jaggar's phrase, a case of business coping by "add women and stir." Feminist philosophers offer us insights that challenge both the way women are treated in business and perhaps the very way business is structured, and they prompt us to reexamine some of our foundational philosophical assumptions about fairness and impartiality. A continuing challenge to be solved is for us to work out how to treat men and women equally despite their unique life experiences.

## General issues for discussion

1. Do you think being a business manager is harder for a man or woman, and what specific challenges do both face in the contemporary workplace?
2. What do you think would be a solution to the problem of there being few women role models for senior executives? Would a program of accelerated promotion be appropriate?
3. Would you agree that the business world is based on a template of male experience? What examples can you think of to support your view?
4. Do you think globalization may threaten the welfare of women? What would mitigate the potential dangers?

## Case – time off or time out?

Margaret Roberts works as an administrative assistant in a regional sales office. Her work group consists of three assistants (all women), two mid-level managers, and a senior manager. The office handles routine correspondence, planning, expenses for field sales staff, and quarterly reports for the national office. Margaret is married and has a two-year-old son who has been in day care from the age of three months.

In the last few months there has been rising tension in the office caused by Margaret's frequent absences. Sometimes she leaves unexpectedly during the day, and other times she calls in at short notice to say that she will not be coming in at all. The apparent reason is that her son, Matt, has medical issues that cause repeated visits to the doctor. One of the manifestations of his condition is a behavioral problem – he tends to lose his temper easily and hurt other children. He has been given medicine, but there are problems in calibrating the appropriate dosage. This means that the day care provider sometimes calls and asks Margaret to take Matt home.

The work team has tried to accommodate Margaret as much as it can: she has a company laptop and a network connection that allows her to work from home. She is formally on a flextime schedule so that she will be paid as long as she completes the required number of hours a week. However, there are some times when she is needed in the office, especially when the quarterly reports are being prepared, and her coworkers are disturbed by the unpredictability of her absences. She is less productive than she used to be, and the two other assistants feel that the extra burden has fallen on their shoulders. They feel they have "bent over backwards" to assist her as much as they can but now believe their good will has led to them being exploited. They have appealed to the office manager to resolve the situation so they are not unduly disadvantaged by the situation.

## Some questions from the case

1. Should management make any accommodations for Margaret? If so, on what basis?
2. Is the current model of employment responsive to the needs of workers? If not, how could it be changed to be more fair or just?
3. Would your position on the issue be changed if it seemed to be temporary?
4. How much time is reasonable for an employer to give to an employee in need?
5. Does Margaret's rank at the firm make any moral difference? Would you alter your view if the situation involved Matt's father rather than his mother?

6. What is the role of the state in regulating employer/employee relations in this case? Do you feel the state has any responsibility for supporting the employee?
7. How do you think Margaret's coworkers would feel if they were men instead of women? Do you think women are more or less sympathetic to women's work conflicts?

# 5    Responsibility

Businesses are often held responsible for the goods and services they provide and the conditions under which their products are made; they are said to be responsible for their employees and the environment. They are encouraged to act like responsible citizens and members of the community. There are master's degree programs in responsibility and business practice.[1] We also have investment programs that limit purchases to "socially responsible" vendors. The term *responsibility* is commonly used in business ethics, and properly understood, it will help us shape the discussion of the scope and limits of appropriate corporate action. However, before looking at the various applications, it is useful to look at some real cases to distinguish some of the various ways the term could be used.

## The *Herald of Free Enterprise* ferry disaster

The *Herald of Free Enterprise* was a large ferry that capsized in the early evening on March 6, 1987, just moments after leaving the Belgian port of Zeebrugge on its way to Dover in England. In addition to its regular load of cars and trucks, a British national newspaper had offered its readers an inexpensive day abroad through Townsend-Thorensen lines, the ferry's owners, and so there were many more day trippers on board. The 7,000-ton ship rolled on its side, and over 190 people died, from either catastrophic injuries when the ship tipped, drowning, or hypothermia when they were trapped inside surrounded by freezing water. Over 400 others were rescued,

---

[1] For example, the M.Sc. in Responsibility and Business Practice at the University of Bath, UK.

many of whom survived by smashing portholes and climbing onto the side of the ship.

The tragedy took place in calm conditions and only 100 meters away from the shore. The ferry came to rest on a sandbank and held steady on its side. If it had been any further out to sea, it would likely have sunk completely. Initial reports speculated that the ship must have hit an uncharted object, but soon it was known that the bow door was left open, allowing tons of seawater to flood the car deck as soon as the ferry left dock and picked up speed. The captain, David Lewry, had no time to send out an SOS, but luckily there were ships and rescue equipment nearby.

The ferry was designed as a quick turnaround "roll on, roll off" (ro-ro) vessel. Essentially, it was a floating platform with massive doors at the bow and stern, which were lifted when it was in port. Drivers could drive right onto the ferry, and at the destination, they could drive off again in the same direction, since the other gate could be lifted. It also had a ballast system that could raise the ship out of the water to the appropriate height for easy access to dockside ramps. The old pumps on the ballast were slow, and this meant that the ship could not get onto an even keel and have the doors clear of the water until it was out to sea. The design of the stern also meant that water would not have rushed in if the ship had been going slightly slower, but because the captain had ordered 18 knots, a wave built up and swamped the opening.

Townsend-Thorensen had recently been acquired by the P&O firm and was undergoing a change in management styles. The seaman's union had complained that there was a manpower shortage because of recent layoffs. Some crewmembers were also pulling double shifts, with the attendant risks of exhaustion and sleep deprivation.

The ferry did not have a warning system to indicate that the bow door was not closed. In effect, the safety designs were built around the assumption that all was well unless there was a positive indication of something wrong. The captain was unable to see that there was a problem from the bridge, and although the bosun in charge of closing the bow door was asleep in his cabin, his superior officer had seen him on the car deck earlier and so assumed that he had completed his duties. When the ferry left the dock, the first mate, who was usually by the bow door, had been called away to do other work.

## Meanings of responsibility

Consider the following set of claims about the disaster:

1. Captain Lewry was a responsible person.
2. Captain Lewry was a responsible seaman.
3. Captain Lewry was responsible for the loss of the *Herald of Free Enterprise*.
4. Captain Lewry was responsible for his actions on the day the *Herald of Free Enterprise* capsized.
5. Captain Lewry was not responsible for the loss of the *Herald of Free Enterprise*.
6. Captain Lewry was held responsible for the loss of the *Herald of Free Enterprise*.
7. The P&O line was held responsible for the loss of the *Herald of Free Enterprise*.[2]

Captain Lewry was a respectable member of his community, had no criminal record, and had fulfilled his civic duties such as paying taxes. In that sense the first claim – that he was a responsible person – is true. In the second sense of the term, he was also a capable seaman who had gained steady promotion and senior rank. There are various obligations that apply uniquely to sailors (such as power vessels giving way to sail boats), and he no doubt upheld them well, which allows us to describe him as responsible as a ship's captain. He had special authority by virtue of the uniform he wore and the rank he held. He could, for example, have a passenger confined against his will if he felt it necessary – for example, if the person was inebriated and violent. He could change the speed and course of the vessel, deny boarding if he felt it had reached its carrying capacity, and finally issue orders to abandon ship. The authority also meant that he had more duties than other seamen on board, for instance, the bosun or first mate, and, not surprisingly, he was paid substantially more than other members of the crew.

The third sense can be taken to represent a doctrine that says the captain of a vessel or the pilot of an airplane is ultimately responsible for everything

[2] This analysis draws on H. L. A. Hart, "Varieties of Responsibility," *Law Quarterly Review*, 83 (1967), pp. 346–364; Kevin Gibson, "Going Beyond Intuitions: Reclaiming the Philosophy in Business Ethics," *Teaching Business Ethics*, 6.2 (May, 2002), pp. 151–166.

that happens on board, whether or not he or she is directly involved. The same might be said for a military commander or university president: while they may be ignorant of what is going on, they are held responsible by virtue of their rank. Hence when Japan Airlines lost a flight with 520 passengers in 1985, the company president Yasumoto Takagi took responsibility, asked forgiveness from the relatives, and offered to resign.

The fourth point – that the captain was responsible for his actions – changes the perspective to say that the captain was not delusional or ill and so cannot be excused. He did not order excessive speed because he heard voices in his head commanding him to or because he was chasing phantom ships. He was in his right mind and firmly in command.

The paradoxical claim of the fifth sentence – that he was not responsible for the loss – reflects a causal approach that looks to the immediate sequence of events. It was not the captain's job to close the bow door, and he had nothing to do with the design flaws of the ship. Indeed, senior Townsend officers had requested alarm systems that would warn of open doors after an earlier incident, and repeatedly requested upgraded ballast pumps. Moreover, Captain Lewry issued the appropriate sequence of commands on leaving port, and if his orders had been complied with correctly, it is unlikely the tragedy would have ensued.

Despite these facts, we can imagine that a legal inquiry might look at all the factors leading to the tragedy including those that might have prevented it. The captain had ordered the vessel to sea and set the speed of the vessel. Perhaps most importantly, the bosun was asleep in his cabin and had not secured the bow door. If not for those key human factors, the other elements probably wouldn't have mattered. At the same time it would be difficult to have these two individuals pay adequate compensation, which creates the natural desire to place the fault at the feet of the corporation, an entity with the potential to mitigate the harms involved. As the official report on the accident stated:

> All concerned in management, from the members of the Board of Directors down to the junior superintendents, were guilty of fault in that all must be regarded as sharing responsibility for the failure of management. From top to bottom the body corporate was infected with the disease of sloppiness.[3]

---

[3] Sheen Report, Department of Transport, Report of the Court No. 8074, *Formal Investigation of the MV Herald of Free Enterprise* (London: HMSO, 1987).

What we find, then, is that there are a number of ways to understand the concept of responsibility. Responsibility may be used very generally – the captain was a responsible man – or in very specific ways – the bosun was responsible for ensuring the bow doors were closed. A common view is that we are accountable as people, and we should expect a certain level of decent behavior and participation in society; thus a responsible person has characteristics, including, but not limited to, self-control, awareness of potential consequences for our actions, and some consideration for others. The law will not prosecute those who lack these capacities – for example, the insane, incompetent, or very young – based on the assumption that they do not have the wherewithal to frame accurate intentions or make proper judgments about potential outcomes. Thus a young child that takes candy on impulse from a display at a supermarket check-out probably does not understand the concept of property in the same way that an adult does, and we would expect a grownup to be able to withstand impulses for immediate gratification.

## Role responsibility

Another view could be termed *role responsibility*. The illustration of the ship's captain is useful here, since there is a doctrine that suggests that the captain of a ship or the pilot of an airplane is responsible for everything that happens on the craft, whether or not he or she was personally involved or aware of what was going on. Thus by virtue of rank, there is an associated mantle of responsibility that embraces everything that happens under the purview of the role. Because the captain has greater power – for example, he could order the ship to divert to a different port, something that the assistant mate could not do – he has a correspondingly greater benefit or burden of responsibility. Hence we might also say that managers cannot abdicate moral responsibility just because they were not personally involved.

From this perspective, role designation in an organization yields the scope of individual discretion in making decisions and informs employees of corporate expectations. The organizational chart provides a guide as to who reports to whom and whose actions are under an individual's control. Hence, using the "captain of the ship" doctrine, one avenue for assigning responsibility would be to examine the corporate structure and pinpoint who controlled the division involved.

Some roles may arise from special relationships: parents have responsibility for their children, for example. In business there are formal and informal relationships with various stakeholders, each implying special duties. Thus in some cases agents have what is termed a *fiduciary relationship*, which means that they have been entrusted to promote the interests of others as their own. An example would be a stockbroker who works to maximize the portfolio of investors or a corporate executive who is charged with directing the company to provide the maximum yield to its owners, the shareholders.

We can see that there may be times where the decision-makers in business have multiple layers of responsibility, and some responsibilities may even be incompatible. Thus when the chairman of P&O, Lord Sterling of Plaistow, was quoted as saying, "My first responsibility is to the shareholders of P&O, and profit is what it is all about," we should not necessarily see this as reflecting his personal view or that he did not care about the victims.[4] Instead, we should take the statement at face value, where the fiduciary for the investors in a company is simply stating that he has a hierarchy of duties to his stakeholders, and in this case their interests should be held paramount.

The difficulty in balancing responsibilities has been addressed in several ways. Some commentators such as Milton Friedman have held that businesses have the sole responsibility to maximize profits.[5] This does not mean that managers should be blinkered to other concerns, but rather that they should recognize all the factors that go into a profitable concern, including reputation and goodwill. As we have seen in chapter 2, others like R. Edward Freeman will take a deontological view that suggests we ought to treat all stakeholder interests equally, or following Ross, we have to be more responsive to some because of factors such as reciprocating benefits or compensating for harm.[6] Thus although a business may face competing claims from a range of stakeholders – including the community, shareholders, customers, and suppliers – it could discriminate among them based on

---

[4] Stuart Crainer, *Zeebrugge: Learning from Disaster – Lessons in Corporate Responsibility* (London: Herald Families Association, 1993), p. 17.

[5] Milton Friedman, "The Social Responsibility of Business is to Increase Its Profits," *New York Times Magazine* (September 13, 1970).

[6] W. M. Evan and R. Edward Freeman, "A Stakeholder Theory of the Modern Corporation: Kantian Capitalism," in T. Beauchamp and N. Bowie, eds., *Ethical Theory and Business*, 3rd ed. (Englewood Cliffs, NJ: Prentice-Hall, 1987), pp. 97–106.

what they have done for the company in the past and on claims to justice. If, say, the community had attracted the company to the area through generous tax breaks, then we could censure the company if it moved operations overseas without offering some form of compensation. Similarly, a transportation company could justify giving priority to maximizing shareholder returns, but it could not be absolved from its responsibility to provide safe passage or to make reparations if it causes harm.

## Legal liability and moral responsibility

Legal liability is not the same as moral responsibility, but it provides a useful starting point to discuss the nature and extent of a company's duties to its stakeholders. Adopting the legal framework, we could characterize responsibilities as both positive and negative. A positive responsibility is one that requires action, say, providing sufficient lifeboats or compensating victims. A negative responsibility is one that is fulfilled simply by not doing any harm. Many would argue that moral responsibilities are more demanding than the legal threshold and that businesses are wrong to judge their duties to stakeholders by looking at the minimum legal requirement alone. Nevertheless, the language of the law gives us a way of approaching the issue of responsibility in business.

The legal notion of liability defines a number of relationships where responsibility may be transferred or avoided because of the formal relationships involved. This goes by the general name of *vicarious liability*. In rather old-fashioned language, one of the main ones is known as the "master–servant" relationship, where a business may be held responsible for any and all actions of an employee at work. This means firms cannot distance themselves from wrongdoing by their employees. So if a stocker in a grocery store sexually harasses a customer during the workday, the store will be liable. It also means that an unscrupulous manager cannot avoid blame by delegating questionable acts to subordinates and then claiming ignorance.

A related doctrine is *strict liability*. Here *all* responsibility rests with the manufacturer of a product without regard for fault. It is easiest to understand in ultra-hazardous cases. If a firm makes high explosives or a person keeps wild animals, they will be responsible for any and all consequences where harm results. In other cases, making a firm pay for something not directly under its control may initially strike us as unfair, yet the practice sends a very clear message to producers and ensures that compensation will be paid by the entity with the deepest pockets. For example, a country may have legislation that automatically charges a milk producer if a shipment is tainted on arrival. Although there may be a number of causes for the contaminated milk, this approach is economically efficient and gives every incentive for all producers to maintain the highest possible standards.

When society applies the doctrine, it tells companies that they need to give paramount concern to certain interests by imposing legal liability without moral responsibility – that is, an agent who is blameless nevertheless may still have to foot the bill.[7] Thus a firm could have a strict policy about environmental dumping, hold seminars for employees, post procedures and rules all around the factory, and place reminders on the sun visors of all its vehicles. Yet if an employee disposes of a can of used oil in a stream because he is running late to his child's soccer practice, the company will still be held liable. Although the company may say that it had done as much as it could, the economic signal that strict liability sends is that there will be absolutely no tolerance for any wrongdoing at all, and thus the firm should work to prevent every eventuality, however unlikely. In this case, perhaps having two workers in each truck would mean that every action was monitored and the man would not have dumped the oil.

Often several different manufacturers share in putting a good on the market. The legal doctrine of "joint and several liability" means they may all be held liable even though they are only partially involved. Thus if someone were injured because of a defective bicycle, she could sue the store that sold it to her, the bicycle manufacturer, and any subcontractors, such as the firm that made the brakes. The doctrine means that the injured person does not have to go through the details of allocating percentages of blame but can recover from anyone involved who is solvent. Similarly, if a number of pharmaceutical companies have all produced the same drug, and patients suffer ill-effects, these patients can sue all the manufacturers.

## Cause

As we have seen, a key meaning of the term *responsible* is that an agent is the cause of an outcome and therefore deserves appropriate praise or blame,

---

[7] See G. Bernkert, "Strict Products Liability and Compensatory Justice," in Beauchamp and Bowie, eds., *Ethical Theory and Business*, 5th ed. (Englewood Cliffs, NJ: Prentice-Hall, 1997), pp. 210–215.

and the associated financial rewards or liability. Therefore we should briefly look at the notion of *cause*. The philosopher David Hume investigated the nature of cause, and drew the conclusion that we infer the cause based on three factors: contiguity, temporal precedence, and constant conjunction. *Contiguity* refers to how near one event is to another, *temporal precedence* to the fact that causes precede effects, and *constant conjunction* to the idea that one state of affairs is always present when the other occurs.[8] He maintained that causality is a function of human reasoning in that we are the ones who make connections that describe the phenomena we perceive. So if someone presses a switch and a light comes on, we might say that she turned on the light, although there is a whole range of intervening actions that are taking place – the flow of electrons and so forth. It might be more accurate to say that she initiated a chain of events that resulted in the light coming on. Moreover, our accounts of cause can be mistaken, so it is plausible that the switch is defective and stays in the on position constantly, and a loose wire arced at the same time as she pressed it, giving the impression that she caused the light to go on, when in fact it turned out to be a coincidence.

In the same way, we want to avoid attributing cause to mere correlation. Although geese fly south in the winter, and snow often follows, it does not mean the geese cause the snow. This kind of false attribution has the technical name of "post hoc, ergo propter hoc," which translates to "after which, therefore because of which." A contemporary example of this may be found in the chemical company Dow Corning, which produced silicone gel breast implants. A number of women who received the implants subsequently became sick, and juries awarded millions in compensatory damages, resulting in Dow Corning going bankrupt. However, the latest scientific evidence suggests that the implants were safe all along. Juries saw a powerful, rich company and a woman in obvious distress and were told that she was well prior to having the implants and later became ill. They tended to side with the apparent victim despite the paucity of scientific data causally linking the two events.[9]

Another issue in assigning cause and consequent responsibility is our tendency to isolate a single factor when faced with large amounts of

---

[8] David Hume, *An Enquiry Concerning Human Understanding* [1748], ed. L. A. Selby-Bigge and P. H. Nidditch (Oxford: Oxford University Press, 1975), section vii.

[9] A. Gianturco, "Breasts, the Media, and Boobs: The Implant Hysteria," *Johns Hopkins Newsletter* (October 14, 1999), available at http://www.jhu.edu/~newslett/10-14-99/ Opinions/8.html, accessed December 21, 2006.

information. One researcher, Christopher Roux-Dufort, commented about the *Herald* case:

> Almost every manager in the company itself and in other ferry companies was convinced that the ferry sank for one simple reason: because one of the crewmembers was sleeping in the cabin and left the loading doors open. For a researcher, this conclusion is striking and contradicts some of the major findings in crisis management research . . . crises are characterized by the ambiguity of their causes and consequences . . . Systemic analysis of crises usually highlights the dynamics of a crisis, delves into its historical roots and multiple consequences, and discovers the many relations linking diverse stakeholders and issues.[10]

Thus in any given case, we should be cautious about pointing to any one cause without considering the constellation of other factors at work.

Philosophers use the term *sufficient condition* to describe elements that are causally efficacious. Another way of putting this is to say that there are "but for" conditions involved. It might be true, then, that *but for* the doors being left open, the ship may not have capsized. However, as Roux-Dufort notes, this should not preclude us seeking out others – so the truth about the bow doors does not mean it isn't also true that *but for* the decrease in manpower and extra duties placed on the crew, the bosun might not have been asleep while on duty, or similarly, *but for* the quick acceleration a bow wave might not have developed. One effect of our tendency to look at simple and easily identifiable causes is that we may miss the larger forces at work, such as management philosophy or lax government oversight, which are more difficult to assess and correct.

Joel Feinberg described three types of search for cause that depend on what we ultimately want. First is a "handle," which is a causal explanation that looks to the immediate factors that led to the incident; by understanding these factors we may prevent similar occurrences in the future. In this case, the causal explanation is described in engineering terms – the open door – and the solution is obvious: setting up positive alarms when the door is not closed. Second is a "lantern," shedding light on the broader, more systemic causes that led to the immediate problem. Hence, while acknowledging that the open door was the prime factor, it examines what led up to

---

[10] Christophe Roux-Dufort, "Why Organizations Don't Learn from Crises: The Perverse Power of Normalization," *Review of Business*, 21.3 (2000), pp. 25–30.

that happening, both in the management decisions and in the physical and system designs. However, one of the prime motivators for defining cause is to apportion fault and garner compensation. Feinberg calls the third type of analysis the "stain" that seeks out the factors that we can ascribe to human error and pave the way for legal action.[11]

We can see some of the complications involved in ascribing responsibility in the case of the world's deadliest oil spill that occurred in 1989 when the Exxon tanker *Valdez* ran aground in Prince William Sound, Alaska. The captain had apparently been drinking vodka all day and relinquished command to a junior officer while he went to his cabin. The ship had been rerouted from the usual course and shortly after hit a reef. The resulting gash leaked an estimated 11 million gallons of crude oil. The captain was found guilty of negligently discharging oil, and eventually Exxon paid over $900 million in damages and $2.2 billion in cleanup costs. Initially it might seem that the captain was the direct cause of the crash, and his employer ought to bear the moral and financial responsibility. However, the Alaska Oil Spill Commission report did not lay the blame solely on the captain or consider it a freak incident. They concluded the crash and inept cleanup were part of a much wider pattern, "simply one result of policies, habits, and practices that for nearly two decades have infused the nation's maritime oil transportation system with increasing levels of risk."[12]

After the spill there were recommendations that large ships should have a double hull to minimize spills, something an international convention has demanded be in force, but only by 2015.[13] Additionally, although there was a public outcry against the resulting pollution and devastation to marine life, there were few boycotts of Exxon products by the public. Both these factors suggest there is a lack of public support for immediate action, and the signal that the failure of effective boycotting sends to Exxon is that consumers value cheap oil over marine animals. Moreover, a spokesman for the International Association of Independent Tanker Owners noted that

[11] Joel Feinberg, "*Sua Culpa*," in *Doing and Deserving* (Princeton: Princeton University Press, 1970), pp. 204–205.

[12] Alaska Oil Spill Commission, *Spill: The Wreck of the Exxon Valdez* (Junean, AK, 1990).

[13] International Maritime Organization, International Convention for the Prevention of Pollution from Ships, 1973, as modified by the Protocol of 1978 relating thereto (MARPOL 73/78), available at http://www.imo.org/Conventions/contents.asp?doc_id=678&topic_id=258#2, accessed March 11, 2006.

most of the oil pollution in the sea comes from the land, not from tanker spills, which only account for 11 percent. "More oil enters the sea from motorists draining their sump oil into the town drain that from all the world's tankers."[14] Thus the *Valdez* was a dramatic incident that highlighted concerns, but we often focus on the immediate and personal causes rather than the wider, more institutionalized problems. While it is undoubtedly true that the crew should take some responsibility, we should also consider the wider context including consumer preferences when determining moral responsibility in this case.

There may be some simple cause and effect cases, but frequently there are a host of conditions, some involving wider systemic issues and some illustrating that events are often a result of many factors and are part of a causal chain. A company may cause harm through its acts, omissions, the situations it creates, or a set of events it initiates. In these cases, we tend to equate the company having *responsibility* for the harm with the company *causing* the harm.

"Monday morning quarterbacking" refers to another factor in the way we assess situations and allocate blame after the fact.[15] When we consider the notion of responsibility, it will make a difference if we are looking ahead of time or if we are looking retrospectively.[16] Beforehand it is very hard to see issues that look obvious in hindsight. It also matters if things go well or badly: if they go well, everyone will want to take part of the credit (and rewards) for any good fortune that a company has, whereas if something has gone wrong, there is a significant retrenchment and avoidance of the blame.

## Corporations as moral agents

At this point we may again raise the issue of corporate personhood. Was P&O acting as a responsible company when it operated the *Herald of Free Enterprise*? Does it make sense to say that the company had moral as well as

---

[14] Quoted in Alex Kirby, "*Exxon Valdez*: Tip of an Oily Iceberg," BBC News (March 23, 1999), available at http://news.bbc.co.uk/2/hi/science/nature/299621.stm, accessed March 11, 2006.

[15] Another version has it that "Hindsight is 20/20 vision."

[16] For a detailed examination of the topic, see Michael Zimmerman, *An Essay on Moral Responsibility* (Totowa, NJ: Rowman and Littlefield, 1988).

legal responsibility to all the stakeholders involved? The families of many of the victims felt that it did, as they did not press for charges of the individuals involved but rather wanted the company Townsend Car Ferries (a subsidiary of P&O) to be charged with corporate manslaughter.[17]

Corporations are considered persons in a legal sense: they can make contracts and be sued just like individuals. On the other hand, they obviously do not have the animal properties of humans, and do not exist in the way that people do. As Edward Coke famously said in the sixteenth century, "Corporations cannot commit treason, nor be outlawed, nor excommunicated, for they have no souls."[18] The difficult question is the intermediate position of whether they are moral entities, that is, can they operate to cause harm or good?

Some commentators have taken what might be termed a *reductionist* approach. This suggests that corporations are composed of people, and hence when we ascribe moral terms to the corporation, it is, in effect, an abbreviated way of talking about the individuals involved. It suggests that having a moral sense is a uniquely human characteristic, and thus it would be a mistake to ascribe human-like qualities to a corporation or other artificial entity. So if we say that the company, Exxon, did something wrong when the *Valdez* tanker spilled oil near Alaska, this is shorthand for the actions of the human actors involved: the captain, the helmsman, the cleanup crews, the corporate executives, and so forth. This approach reduces the moral debate to one about individual behavior alone.[19] It has the benefit of being straightforward in that it focuses on the people who are morally culpable and assigns blame accordingly.

The contrasting view suggests that corporations and institutions can be moral agents over and above their component members. It says that there are times when an analysis of the moral acts of a corporation cannot be reduced to its members without residue, without some remaining responsibility that doesn't belong to any individual actor. To understand how this might work, consider an organization that has a strong identity, perhaps a long-standing corporation such as IBM. There is a corporate culture that

---

[17] C. M. V. Clarkson, "Kicking Corporate Bodies and Damning Souls," *Modern Law Review*, 59.4 (July, 1996), pp. 557–572.

[18] *Case of Sutton's Hospital*, 10 Rep. 32.

[19] Manuel Velasquez, "Why Corporations are not Morally Responsible for Anything They Do," *Business and Professional Ethics Journal*, 2 (1983), pp. 1–18.

reflects values shared by employees. Those who align themselves with the values succeed better than those who ignore them. Some of these values are written down, for example, in codes and policy statements. Others, though, take the form of shared understandings that are passed along. This kind of corporate identity persists despite the coming and going of any particular individual. Plausibly, someone could return to the company after twenty years and find that there had been a complete turnover of personnel, find that the buildings had been razed and rebuilt, and yet the way that the company does its business is instantly recognizable. The effect of this corporate culture is that there may be cases where no one person can be found responsible for an action, yet there is an understanding that a given behavior is acceptable or appropriate. That is not to say that a wrongdoer would be excused: if there were evidence that pointed to an individual, then he or she would be held to account. However, what this approach allows us to do is to treat a corporation as a moral agent in its own right. Thus in the case of the *Herald of Free Enterprise*, the inquiry faulted the company for its overall complacency. Individually, management and employees might not have done anything that could be pinpointed as wrong, but this view lets us judge the organization as a whole as well. In fact, the assistant bosun, the bosun, the captain, and four members of management were eventually charged with manslaughter. However, early in the trial the judge dismissed the case on the grounds that there was insufficient evidence to convict any single person.

The risk of relying on individual responsibility is that if no one can be named, the responsibility evaporates. If a company's corporate ethic is to beat Wall Street analysts' expectations every quarter by whatever means necessary (as was the case at WorldCom before its dramatic and scandal-ridden collapse), we would expect to find employees engaging in morally questionable activities, although there is no written policy or paper trail that makes the expectation an explicit demand. In another financial scandal, HealthSouth was able to avoid government audits for a prolonged period of time because book entries were altered yet nevertheless managed to stay below the threshold amount necessary to trigger reporting requirements. The practice was routine and pervasive in the company, but could not be traced to any specific individual or directive.

The view that a corporation is sufficiently like a person to have moral responsibilities is not without difficulties, though. Responsibility, as we have seen, requires the capacity for framing intentions. Some commentators, notably Peter French, have suggested that the corporate organizational structure provides us with a way to assess a "corporate internal decision" (CID).[20] He believes that the CID can show us the workings of a firm, and in many cases the intention of a firm will be more transparent and rational than those of individuals: firms have mission statements and explicit policies and procedures that give us a fair indication of their moral climate. Moreover, in many cases their cultures are evident. If the CEO of the ferry line emphasizes profit as the paramount concern, it would not be surprising to find a corporate culture that stresses quick turnaround times and maximized carrying loads while downplaying safety concerns, regardless of whether there was a written policy encouraging such practices. Still, critics claim that French and his followers avoid a difficult ethical issue by creating fictitious entities rather than chasing down the real, but often elusive, culprits.

The principal issue in corporate personhood amounts to whether members of an organization (or adherents or the entire business operation) are tainted by the actions of others. If the disaster at Zeebrugge were due to the unfortunate actions of, at most, seven individuals, then the solution would seem to be to separate and punish them appropriately without any other significant changes. However, if we consider that the total corporation is morally accountable, then the repercussions would be wide-reaching. For example, in the Exxon case, if the spill were the result of careless actions by the captain, then there is no real stain on other members of the company. However, if employees feel they are associated with an organization that has engaged in morally questionable activities because of its culture or standards, then any remedies would have to be widespread, since many more people would be implicated in any wrongdoing. In essence, the entire company would have to reassess its values and practices.

The corporate personhood debate also affects how we view the role of top executives. Many CEOs strongly influence the ethical climate of a company, so the ethical posture is very much "top down." There is considerable anecdotal evidence that the charismatic leadership of characters such as Bernie Ebbers at WorldCom, Ken Lay at Enron, or Richard Scrushy at HealthSouth set the moral climate for their followers. Conversely there are moral heroes,

[20] Peter French, *Corporate Morality* (New York: Harcourt Brace, 1996).

such as James Burke of Johnson & Johnson, who effectively steered the company through an ethical crisis when someone tampered with their Tylenol product by lacing it with the lethal poison cyanide, and P. Roy Vagelos, the chairman of Merck, who dedicated the company's efforts to eradicating river blindness by providing impoverished victims with free drugs. While these individuals undoubtedly had a significant effect on corporate practices, a reductionist would claim that we could attribute the moral climate to only very specific people. On the other hand, someone maintaining that corporations can have personhood would certainly admit that although powerful figures in an organization can have a dramatic effect, and any dealings directly linked to them should merit the appropriate praise or blame, there is still the corporate community to consider because in their view responsibility cannot rest on just a few key individuals alone.

## Inalienable responsibility

Legally, there are times where we can avoid liability – for instance, by buying an insurance policy that indemnifies us. However, moral responsibility often lingers even though we may believe we have absolved ourselves.

In the New Testament story, a crowd is demanding the death of Jesus. The verse relates:

> When Pilate saw that he could prevail nothing, but that rather a tumult was made, he took water, and washed his hands before the multitude, saying, I am innocent of the blood of this just person: see ye to it.[21]

Nevertheless, it was Pilate who authorized Jesus' crucifixion, and he is commonly described as the person who had Jesus killed. The ritual hand washing did little to excuse him by transferring the blame to the crowd, although it may have had the formal effect of implicating them as well. The issue that the incident brings up is whether individuals or corporations can ever disassociate themselves from their actions or whether they remain accountable in some form even though they have disavowed responsibility. This could be termed *inalienable responsibility*, since it adheres to the agent involved.

In Stanley Milgram's famous experiment dealing with individual obedience to authority, he set up subjects to be functionaries in an experiment

---

[21] Matthew 27:24, King James version.

that apparently gave "learners" electric shocks, although the learners were confederates of the psychologist. The subject was in control of a shock generator, and administered the shocks at the command of an apparent researcher in a white coat. Although posed as an experiment about the relationship between learning and punishment, it was, in fact, looking at how far individuals would go in obeying orders, even at the risk of hurting, and indeed torturing, other people. Milgram found startling deference to authority, so although the subjects were often conflicted and reluctant about continuing to give ever-greater shocks, they nevertheless complied.[22] Milgram gives the transcript of one session:

SUBJECT: I can't stand it. I'm not going to kill that man in there. You hear him hollering? . . .

EXPERIMENTER: The experiment requires that you continue, Teacher.

SUBJECT: Aaah, but unh, I'm not going to get that man sick in there . . .

EXPERIMENTER: Whether the learner likes it or not, we must go on through all the word pairs.

SUBJECT: I refuse to take responsibility . . .

EXPERIMENTER: I'm responsible for anything that happens to him. Continue please . . . (Learner gives wrong answer; the subject gives a 285-volt shock, and screams.)

SUBJECT: Something's happened to that man in there. You'd better check on him. He won't answer or nothing.

EXPERIMENTER: Continue. Go on, please.

SUBJECT: You accept all responsibility?

EXPERIMENTER: The responsibility is mine. Correct. Please go on. (Subject works through to 450 volts, the end of the board).

In the post-experiment interview, when it was revealed that the shocks were actually fake, the subject was asked about his reaction to causing pain. He admits that he was anxious and wanted to stop but felt the experimenter would not let him. Milgram asks him directly who was pushing the switches on the generator, to which he responds that he was, but that he always wanted to discontinue.

The experiment is instructive because it illustrates the way that we can easily drift into the role of a minor assistant and feel that we are not in

---

[22] Extracts taken from Stanley Milgram, *Obedience to Authority* (New York: Harper & Row, 1974), pp. 73–76.

control – and hence not responsible – for our behavior. However, in many cases moral responsibility is not a commodity that can be exchanged or a liability that can be avoided. It is more like a signature that is carried forward from the time we do the initial act.

## Reluctant agency and omission

Responsibility is intimately tied to acts that we take. It would seem natural to think that we should not be accountable for actions we do not take or even actively avoid. However, this line of reasoning only works up to a point. To illustrate this dynamic, consider the case of vaccination, where many parents will be reluctant to inoculate their children even in the face of statistics that show a child is more likely to die from the disease than potential side effects of the injection. In technical terms, the parents are not being fully rational. However, we have to recognize a very real psychological dynamic: in one case, getting sick is a fluke of nature, whereas if there are any side effects, we are the ones who are the agents of harm.[23]

Generally the law punishes a positive act but does not require intervention to prevent harm, especially if it involves risks. Yet in moral discussions this is often a weak distinction. Choosing not to act is itself a moral decision, and therefore the intentions and consequences that follow from that choice have moral ramifications. A recycling company that is aware of the growing number of used hypodermic needles in the trash and fails to warn its employees or take precautions might be seen as just as culpable as someone who deliberately stabs an employee with a hypodermic because of the equivalence of the resulting harm. Similarly, a firm that buys extra insurance because it learns that a building it owns is in an earthquake zone but does not tell the workers is making a conscious decision not to act and cannot avoid moral censure by pointing out that it did nothing. The question at hand is how much a reasonable person or firm should be aware of and whether ignorance constitutes a valid excuse. In the *Herald of Free Enterprise*, the company was aware that the ballast pumps were weak, but considered the replacement cost of £25,000 to be too expensive. The company might still have been at fault, perhaps, but have been more morally defensible if no one, including the experts in the field, had any idea that the pumps might constitute a safety hazard.

[23] Jonathan Baron, "Blind Justice: Fairness to Groups and the Do-No-Harm Principle," *Journal of Behavioral Decision Making*, 8 (1995), pp. 71–83.

In the law there is a similar distinction to commission and omission, framed as the difference between intentional acts and negligent ones, and the penalties are generally more severe in cases where harm is the result of someone deliberately trying to hurt someone else. Thus, if Jack deliberately aims his car at a pedestrian with the intention of causing grievous harm, the charges will be more severe than if Jack had accidentally run someone over while searching for a map on the passenger seat. Nevertheless, the consequence is often identical, and intentions are hard to establish. Furthermore, perhaps we should consider driving without due care and attention as equivalent to attempted battery, with the only significant difference being that the victim is not known ahead of time: the attribution of intentions may simply serve to cloud the issue. That is, part of our moral assessment may be socially constructed, in that we accept carelessness, sloppiness, or negligence as an excuse in some settings although there is nothing necessarily less culpable in the act. A society could, for example, decide that any drivers causing deaths from being distracted by their cell phones should be charged with murder.

In the business context, clearly manufacturers do not set out to deliberately hurt people through their products and services. Still, if a car producer is aware of a design flaw that will inevitably lead to injuries and deaths (as seems to be the case of the Ford Pinto with a gas tank that sprayed fuel in a collision, or the known tendency of some sports utility vehicles to overturn when swerving), we might question whether the difference between positive acts and failure to take steps is as sharp as it initially appears in discussions about moral responsibility.

Another example is the export of blood-clotting medicines by American companies to Asia and Latin America in the mid-1980s. The blood agents that help create clots for people with hemophilia were drawn from thousands of individual donors, any one of whom could have infected an entire batch of the medicine with HIV. Cutter Biological, a subsidiary of Bayer Pharmaceuticals, apparently sold off their stockpiles of old drugs for hemophilia that carried a high risk of transmitting HIV/AIDS while delivering a safer heat-treated product to their markets in the West.[24] Internal company documents purportedly show that the company had a number of fixed-price contracts

---

[24] Walt Bogdanich and Eric Koli, "2 Paths of Bayer Drugs in the 80's: Riskier Type Went Overseas," *New York Times* (May 22, 2003), available at http://query.nytimes.com/gst/fullpage.html?sec=health&res=9A00E4DA1F3EF931A15756C0A9659C8B63

and thought it cheaper to offload drugs that they had voluntarily withdrawn from America, while assuring Asian customers that it was "the same fine product we have supplied for years." The company failed to tell distributors and hospitals that they had reached an agreement with the FDA to take the drug off the American market before it was made mandatory. In this case, the deliberate omission turns out to be a positive act, and therefore, almost paradoxically in moral terms, we can still consider it an act of commission.

The other distinction we see in the vaccination case arises when people claim that the deaths from the disease are natural, whereas we are killing people who otherwise might not die if they had the vaccine. This claim has some force but needs to be seen in the context of what humans do all the time. We fertilize the land, use medicines in case of sickness, and build shelters for ourselves. Seen in that light, all human actions are a function of nature and thus "natural." Appeals to the natural can also have a pernicious side if taken to an extreme, for example, the Nazis appealed to a "natural order" to justify some of their genocidal acts. This is not to say that we cannot meaningfully distinguish between, say, man-made artifacts and a pristine environment: clearly there is a distinction between a concrete car park and a stand of old-growth trees. Instead, we need to question the moral defense that humans choose not to act in some cases because they believe non-interference is a preferable course of action even in the face of harms that could easily be mitigated.

There is a tendency not to want to get involved in some issues since once we do we become associated with them, often at some personal cost. Thus a witness to harassment in the office may find it easier to say nothing than to report it to the appropriate authorities, or a firm that has heard reports of destruction of rain forest by one of its subcontractors may believe that it is best not to look too closely so that it can disassociate itself if necessary. However, moral responsibility is a function of both our actions and our failures to act, and we must recognize that our personal reluctance to become a direct agent of change does not necessarily absolve us of moral responsibility.

## The doctrine of double effect

A traditional philosophical doctrine, derived from St. Thomas Aquinas, is called *double effect*.[25] In these cases, the goal is a good outcome, but there

---

[25] Thomas Aquinas, *Summa Theologica*, II–II Qu. 64, article 7, in *On Law, Morality and Politics*, ed. William Baumgarth and Richard Regan, S.J. (New York: Hackett, 1988).

will be at least one unintended but foreseeable bad effect as well. This would approximate so-called collateral damage in wartime, where it is evident that there will be innocent casualties, but as long as they are not deliberate, not a means to the good, and the harm caused is less than the good produced, then the action may be acceptable.[26] The doctrine has often been employed in medicine, where, for example, a doctor might administer pain relief to a terminal cancer patient, realizing that this may hasten death. Proponents of the view would suggest that such action is acceptable because the intent is to lift the pain, not euthanize the patient.

By this way of thinking, we might consider that some business decisions are less culpable if there is a benign intent. For instance, it is clear that if you make cars, then people are likely to die as a result of driving them, or if you make aspirin, you can be reasonably sure that someone will abuse the product and be injured. However, if your intent is to provide affordable transportation or beneficial over-the-counter drugs, then you need not be held responsible for any and all consequences of the product being used even though they are foreseeable. Critics of the doctrine suggest that the stress on intentions does not absolve the agent from being tainted by the act. They maintain that although the harm may come indirectly, it is still harm and the agent is still involved. In a layoff, for example, we can imagine that the survival of the firm and continued production of its goods is an overall benefit, and perhaps in order to preserve the firm its executives believe they need to trim surplus overhead by shutting a factory. Their aim is all for the good of the company, its investors, and its customers, yet some employees will lose their jobs and suffer distress as a result. The doctrine remains somewhat controversial, but those who find it persuasive can apply it extensively in discussions about responsibility.

## Codes and compliance

In general terms, we can think of behavior at work as having three layers: initially there is a bedrock of legal compliance, which means that all parties share a commitment to a common set of values reflected in the law. Although there are dramatic instances where the law is broken and people try to find loopholes, the fact is that the law forms a threshold of acceptable practice, routinely followed by most people and corporations, and this is why

---

[26] *New Catholic Encyclopedia* (Washington, DC: Catholic University of America, 1981), p. 1021.

legal wrongdoing is newsworthy. An example in business law is prohibitions on insider trading. In response to a series of scandals in the 1990s, the United States government enacted regulations that tightened up personal account-ability in the form of the Sarbanes-Oxley Act of 2002. In ethics, following the law is a minimal requirement, although given that the government cannot legislate morality, the oversight provided by the Sarbanes-Oxley Act was the most straightforward response available to lawmakers.

Beyond legal observance, we have codes of conduct for both companies and professions. Sometimes the law demands so-called compliance, and this usually means compliance not only with the law but also with any applica-ble code of conduct. These are typically voluntary sets of policies and proce-dures that apply to specific groups. Companies often have written codes and require new employees to become familiar with them. A code of conduct is one of the hallmarks of professions, too, and there may be crosscutting requirements in the sense that many managers also have allegiance to their professional organizations in accountancy, engineering, or the law as well as to their employer. One government initiative, the 1991 Federal Sentencing Guidelines, aimed to encourage proactive moral organizations. A company convicted of a federal crime in America, say illegal pollution, may have its fine reduced if it can show that it has a well-formed code of conduct that is updated regularly, closely monitored, and strictly enforced. Conversely, the fine may be increased if it has paid little attention to developing a code of conduct and to actively promoting it. The goal has been to give firms an incentive to create an overall ethical culture rather than dealing with problems as if they were isolated incidents by corrupt individuals.[27]

Codes usually have several parts. First, they give minimal standards of conduct. Companies lay out what behavior is expected and what is pro-hibited. For professionals, these standards amount to a minimum level of competence for practitioners – for example, an accountant who borrows a client's money can be sanctioned. Second, codes may have an aspirational element, which suggests what the ideal standard would be and the level to which members should aim. Although such standards may not always be attained as a practical matter, they present worthy goals that may guide discretionary acts. For example, a code might say that the firm expects that

---

[27] See, for instance, the American 1991 Federal Sentencing Guidelines, available at http://www.ussc.gov/orgguide.htm, accessed March 9, 2006.

its employees will treat all its customers equally and with respect and good humor. Despite the fact that we may not be able to fulfill this ambition, it still has value as an ideal.

Codes may often illustrate issues that are specific to the business enterprise so that workers are sensitive to their enhanced responsibilities in their role. For instance, a firm may be legally liable if a delivery van driver wolf-whistles at a female customer. Outside the workplace this kind of behavior might cause individual offense but would not necessarily rise to the level where intervention is appropriate. However, because of particular circumstances of the workplace, employees might have additional duties. The same might be true of issues such as receiving gifts or preventing minor harm to others that may be incidental in everyday life but become important in the context of work.

Notably, codes are elaborated not only for employees but also for the general public, in that they announce the operational standard of behavior for the company: that is, as a moral minimum we might expect a company to hold to their announced standards, and hold them culpable if they fail to adhere to them.

Employees and the public cannot expect that codes of conduct will provide simple algorithms for ethical conduct. The nineteenth-century philosopher John Stuart Mill expressed the same point when he said:

> It is not the fault of any creed, but of the complicated nature of human affairs, that rules of conduct cannot be so framed as to require exceptions, and that hardly any kind of action can safely be laid down as either always obligatory or always condemnable . . . There exists no moral system under which there do not arise unequivocal cases of conflicting obligation. These are the real difficulties, the knotty points both in the theory of ethics and in the conscientious guidance of personal conduct. They are overcome practically, with greater or less success, according to the intellect and virtue of the individual.[28]

So while codes can give us considerable guidance, in order to help employees in difficult or discretionary cases they typically need to be supplemented with reference to undergirding values and to be made real by reference to everyday examples.

---

[28] John Stuart Mill, *Utilitarianism* (New York: Bobbs-Merrill, 1957), p. 33.

## Moral censure

Earlier we saw that individuals may be held morally responsible for acts when they are aware of what is going on and have the capacity to see how their acts will affect others for good or ill. In a wider sense of responsibility, individuals acting in a role may have additional duties – often spelled out in policies, procedures, or a code – and failing to live up to those expectations may be grounds for moral censure.

Analyzing business in terms of responsibility allows us to consider a wide range of topics, but it is also helpful in establishing views about the nature of corporate personhood, cause, and role morality. Broadly speaking, we can divide corporate responsibility into consideration of its behavior and then the effects of its goods and services. For example, a company may make an economic decision to close down a unit or outsource the work. Local employees will lose their jobs as a result. In one sense the company is causally responsible for some of the distress that will follow, since if it had not closed, then things might have continued as before. Still, we can already see that the analysis has to be more sophisticated: the "but for" condition has to be qualified – perhaps the workers were less efficient than they could have been, or the industry had failed to adapt to changing times (perhaps the factory made typewriters and its once-thriving market has disappeared). The company is morally responsible for those conditions that are under its control and could be foreseen. Still, other agents, such as the workers themselves, may share the responsibility, depending on the exact circumstances that led to the unprofitable situation.

Another factor in our moral assessment is the standards that the company has published in light of its mission statement. If, for example, senior executives have publicly declared that their main aim is to maximize returns to the shareholders and everything else is secondary, then it would be a mistake to hold the firm responsible for not maintaining standards above the bare legal minimum. On the other hand, they can be held culpable if they have been negligent in the sense of failing to meet basic threshold standards of care or diligence. Moreover, while the economic forces driving the closure may ultimately be beyond the control of the firm's executives, they nevertheless can determine the way it is handled and are responsible for those decisions.

## Three dimensions of business responsibility

Finally, consider three cases where responsibility is a crucial feature of the analysis. In the first, the company appears to have taken away fundamental rights to health and safety in the workplace and hence is morally responsible for the consequences. In the second, the company seems to have withheld information about a defect that would have enabled consumers to make a conscious choice in their purchasing decisions. The third deals with whether a company is obligated to follow-through when its products are being misused.

In 1991, Imperial Foods chicken processing plant in Hamlet, North Carolina, caught fire. In order to make large batches of chicken nuggets it had vast open fryers. A maintenance worker had shortened a hydraulic hose so that people wouldn't trip over it, but the new fitting burst under pressure and sprayed liquid around the kitchen. The hot oil created a fireball and dense noxious smoke. As the workers ran to the exits, they found the doors blocked by delivery trucks or padlocked from the outside, an apparent attempt by management to minimize employee pilfering. Of the ninety workers that day, twenty-five died, and fifty-six were injured.[29] While we may say that management did not deliberately intend to cause those deaths, clearly they have to take the responsibility that stems from chaining fire exits closed.

In the second case, the firm is responsible because it interfered with the choice of the customer through deliberate omission. With the rise in popularity of sports utility vehicles (SUVs), manufacturers began to make special tires that were supplied as original equipment. During the mid-1990s reports began to surface in the media that Ford Explorer models were prone to crash at speed, often rolling over. Many of the crash reports indicated tire tread separation was involved. The main culprit seemed to be the Bridgestone/Firestone (BF) ATX and Wilderness AT tires, most notably those made at the plant in Decatur, Illinois. According to the government investigation, Ford was aware of tire problems and had issued recalls in the Middle East, Venezuela, Malaysia, and Thailand in 1999 but had not taken action in the United States, believing it was BF's responsibility. Furthermore, BF had been

---

[29] Wil Haygood, "Still Burning: After a Deadly Fire, a Town's Losses Were Just Beginning," *Washington Post* (November 10, 2002), p. F01.

aware of the problem, starting in 1994, and documents from 1996 showed almost half of the tires tested from the production line failed high-speed tests.[30] As a rising number of complaints were made to government agencies and outside investigations began, Ford and BF issued a recall notice in August 2000 for over 6.5 million tires. Estimates put the cost to BF at over $300 million.[31]

The third kind of issue about responsibility presents the question of whether a company can ever be acquitted of responsibility for its goods, especially if the product is abused in some way (as most can be). There are legal minimums that the firm necessarily adheres to, but then we should ask whether the firm is obliged to test the product more thoroughly than the law requires or to advise consumers of its potential hazards. Furthermore, there may be a point at which the producer's moral responsibility is released – whether by its actions, by time, or by some other party taking on the moral burden. It is well known, for example, that some aerosol products can be abused when they are deliberately inhaled in confined spaces. Falcon Safety Products, one of the world's leading producers of computer cleaning sprays, prides itself on its proactive stance against abuse, as it prominently displays warnings on its products and has partnered with United States government agencies to promote awareness of the dangers of misuse through public service announcements on television and providing educational materials for parents and educators.

H. B. Fuller, an international producer of adhesives, sealants, and paints has also taken a strong stand against abuse, but nevertheless found itself implicated in inhalant deaths in Central America. There, street children are able to obtain solvent adhesives, generally known by Fuller's brand name Resistol, which they inhale to get a feeling of warmth, stupor, and stem hunger pangs. Unfortunately, sniffing the products also leads to organ damage and death. When Fuller became aware of the problem it attempted several remedies, including reformulating the product and increasing the price. The company also suggested that the reasons behind the abuse were social ills such as rampant poverty and homelessness, that their product

[30] National Highway Traffic Safety Administration, "Bridgestone/Firestone Recall" (2002), available at http://www.nhtsa.dot.gov/cars/rules/rulings/UpgradeTire/Econ/TireUpgradeI. html, accessed March 11, 2006.

[31] John O'Dell and Edmund Sanders, "Defective Firestone Wilderness Tire Recalled," *Los Angeles Times* (August 10, 2000).

was an incidental factor in the overall picture, and that withdrawing Resistol would do little to solve the problem. Fuller has since taken it upon itself to support UNICEF and other agencies in addressing some of the wider issues.[32]

We can also see the range of corporate voluntary responsibility in the way companies vary in their response to so-called "Robotripping." Dextromethorphan, or DXM, is an ingredient of cough syrups, notably Wyeth's Robotussin and Schering-Plough's Coricidin brands. Taken in large quantities, these products cause hallucinations and euphoria. Some legislators have proposed banning the products altogether.[33] Wyeth's stance has been to rely on the conscientiousness of consumers. A spokesperson is quoted as saying: "The vast majority of people take [medicines] responsibly . . . It works hands-down, so we want people to be able to use it if they need it." Still, Wyeth has altered the packaging to make it more difficult to stash in a pocket or backpack, and it has decreased the individual dose sizes.[34] The makers of Coricidin have produced fact sheets about abuse for parents and pharmacists, but maintain that the product is safe and effective when used as directed and should not be restricted. In contrast, some pharmacies have taken more active steps, by moving DXM products behind the counter so that they are less accessible, prohibiting sales to minors, and limiting the amount that customers can purchase.

## Summary

The concept of responsibility underlies much of the discourse in business ethics, but it is a complex notion that is used in a variety of ways and often not well understood. Yet, when we look at it more closely it we can see that it is a very powerful and persuasive tool in working out the nature and extent of moral accountability in the business world, as well as telling us the duties we can expect. The families of the victims of the *Herald of Free Enterprise* were outraged that the company was not held liable for the

[32] Paul McEnroe, "Latin America Glue Abuse Haunts H. B. Fuller," *Minneapolis Star Tribune* (April 21, 1996).

[33] "Retailers, Suppliers Rethink Approach to Cough/Cold," *Chain Drug Review* (July 25, 2005).

[34] Chuck McCutcheon, "Abuse of Cold Remedy Spreading Quickly: Drug Industry Works to Limit Access to DXM," *Newhouse News Service* (April 18, 2004); Donna Leinwand, "Youths Risk Death in Latest Drug Abuse Trend," *USA Today* (December 29, 2003).

harm to their loved ones, and we can understand their anger. As our survey suggests, a business' responsibility goes far beyond its legal obligations and affects all aspects of its operations. In using a philosophical approach, we can see the root ideas of responsibility that are involved, and then apply them to a wide range of business applications not limited to our current examples. It will also give us a better normative guide as to what how a corporation *should* behave. In the next chapter, we will examine another foundational concept – rights – that will inform us about the demands and limits that we can place on business activity.

## General issues for discussion

1. Do you think strict liability is ever justified?
2. Some products – cars or pharmaceuticals, for example – will inevitably cause harm unintended by the manufacturer. Can a business ever be absolved of responsibility, especially in cases where the firm could have made the product safer?
3. If there are multiple causes for an incident, say an industrial accident that injures hundreds, how do you think we should isolate the key factors?
4. Do you think the "captain of the ship" doctrine should apply to corporate executives? If not, do they deserve high salaries for actions for which they were only nominally responsible?
5. In what ways do you think a corporation may be a moral agent? How do they differ from human agents?
6. What is the role of consumers and the political process in mitigating corporate harm? For example, we could pay more for oil transported in more secure ships, or we could enact laws that would hugely increase fines for spills. How do we create the right balance that will not stifle business while at the same time affording us a high standard of living?

## Case – the aging air fleet

At any given time, there are some 1,200 Boeing 737 passenger jets in the air. Since its introduction in 1968, it has become the world's most successful jet, and there are over 4,000 in service in 115 countries.[35] The first few were

---

[35] "A World of Service for the 737," *PR Newswire* (April 17, 2003).

named 737–100s, and the bulk of production in the 1970s were variants of the 200 models, but since then the aircraft has been continually modified and upgraded. On an average day, one takes off every six seconds, and they have carried over 12 billion passengers during 232 million flights. The latest version is still assembled in the Boeing factory in Renton, Washington, from 367,000 different parts and 36 miles of wire.

At the time the 737 was first put into service, the anticipated lifespan of any commercial airliner was considered to be fewer than thirty years. However, the maintenance protocols for passenger jets require that faulty equipment be replaced, so there is theoretically no limit to how long an aircraft can keep flying. Two incidents prompted extra vigilance, over and above maintenance of the moving parts of the plane, however: the loss of an older jumbo jet in 1996 was blamed on sparks caused by aging wiring in an empty fuel tank, and in 1998 an Aloha Airlines 737 lost part of its fuselage in flight due to structural failure blamed on a crack in one of the joints. Subsequently airlines were advised to significantly revise their maintenance checks on older planes.

Two dramatic crashes of 737s during the 1990s have been linked to defective rudders. The rudder controls the side-to-side direction or yaw of the plane, and at low speeds a sudden shift can cause it to roll into a dive. In 1991 a United Airlines flight approaching Colorado Springs suddenly flipped to the right and plummeted to the ground. Three years later, a US Airways 737 was landing in Pittsburgh when it rolled left, turned upside down, and nose-dived. Suspicion fell on a valve that might have stuck when hot hydraulic fluid was pumped into a cold pipe. Boeing blamed pilot error in the Pittsburgh crash, maintaining that the pilot must have pushed hard right on the controls and kept them there during the final twenty seconds. Boeing also claimed the pilots could have flown out of the situation if they had reacted appropriately by dipping the nose. Apparently Boeing had evidence that 737s with a greater landing approach speed would make an easier recovery in the event of a rudder problem but had not shared that with the airlines. The National Transportation Safety Board (NTSB) recommended design changes, saying the cause was "most likely" a jam in the rudder valve, and gave United States airlines six years to comply. Foreign carriers were expected to make the changes voluntarily.

In 2005 there were five major crashes involving 737s. A Nigerian plane plunged into a swamp shortly after takeoff, and a Cypriot flight crashed near Athens after an apparent in-flight decompression rendered everyone unconscious. A Kam Air flight came down in Afghanistan, and crashes occurred in Peru and Indonesia. The older 737 is a mainstay of budget airlines, and there are concerns that poor maintenance is a major factor in these disasters. A spokesman for Boeing said: "The accident rate across the 737 fleet is very low, and there have been none involving the [new generation] 600s, 700s, 800s, or 900s. I can't comment on individual countries or airlines, but aircraft are like cars in that they have to be properly maintained."[36]

## Some questions from the case

1. How long should a manufacturer be liable for its products?
2. Should a manufacturer be responsible for any and all defects in its products?
3. At what point, if ever, is it appropriate to deem a fatal event as an accident?
4. Should the government intervene to investigate or enforce compliance when there are safety concerns?
5. What is the relationship between the manufacturer and purchasers in different countries with different legal systems?
6. What should be the public's role in setting air safety standards?

[36] James Mills, "*Another 737 Crash: Fifth Disaster in a Year Renews Safety Fears over Boeing's Workhorse of Short-Haul Flights*," *Daily Mail* (London) (October 24, 2005).

Sources for this case include: www.airlinesafety.com; National Transportation Safety Board, Public Meeting, March 23–24, 1999, available at http://alpha.org/submissions/nstb427.htm; Don Phillips, "U.S. Airways, Boeing Trade Words: Airline Says It Didn't Get Needed 737 Data Before '94 Crash," *Washington Post* (February 16, 2000); Michael Paulson, "Rudder Blamed in Two 37 Crashes: Investigators Reject Boeing's Explanations," *Seattle Post-Intelligencer* (March 24, 1999); NTSB Panel Summary, "Aging Aircraft," available at http://www.ntsb.gov/Events/TWA800/aging.htm; "Safety at Issue: The 737," *Seattle Times* (October 31, 1996).

# 6 Rights

## Le Clemençeau

The *Le Clemençeau* was a 50-year-old French warship decommissioned in 1997. In January 2006 the ship set sail from France to be broken up at the Alang works in India, Asia's largest maritime graveyard.[1] Alang is a port north of Bombay where workers, often with few tools and no protective clothing, are paid less than $5 a day to rip apart old ships. However, Greenpeace and three other non-governmental organizations (NGOs) vigorously opposed the move, and they took the issue to the Indian Supreme Court. It agreed with Greenpeace that the ship contained more than 500 tons of asbestos and other toxins and banned the transfer.

Breaking yards are concentrated in four countries: India, Bangladesh, China, and Pakistan. The court ruling was not universally welcomed in India. Shambhu Nakrani, a local Greenpeace activist, believes that his group was mistaken: times are hard in the area, and the people were counting on the *Clemençeau* work. Alang used to account for 90 percent of the world industry, but now only 15 of 173 yards are operational, and 5,000 of the peak 40,000 workers are employed. The yard managers claim that there are special areas, workers, and disposal techniques for dealing with asbestos, and protective gear is available. They pointedly express regret that contracts have gone to other countries where the environmental regulations are looser. Workers believe that the Greenpeace campaign has helped improve conditions, but they also think it is the primary cause of lack of jobs in a once-thriving industry, and anti-Greenpeace graffiti are widespread near the yard.[2]

---

[1] Simon Freeman, "Court Sinks French Plan to Scrap 'Toxic' Ship in India," *The Times* (UK) (February 15, 2006).

[2] Geeta Pandey, "Asbestos Test for 'Graveyard of Ships,'" BBC News (February 10, 2006). Written copy published at http://news.bbc.co.uk/go/pr/fr/-/2/hi/south_asia/4700160.stm, accessed March 11, 2006.

At first glance, it seems that protecting workers is an unqualified good. The government may see nothing wrong with the state of the industry, perhaps comparing it to European conditions at the same level of development a century ago. Yet there is something troubling about the case: regardless of whether or not conditions are acceptable in different societies at different times, there may be a point where the way we treat people is not context-dependent. It may just be wrong to expose unprotected individuals to asbestos and other toxins. Do people have a right to safe working conditions? Can they forgo those rights if they choose to, or is there any amount sufficient to compensate them for the risks they face?

## Rights in the workplace

The market does seem to influence rights in the workplace and the market. Consider the way that some jobs pay "danger money." Some workers on high-rise construction or oil rigs are paid more in recognition of the fact that they are doing something risky. There is a market in labor, and it has found a price where certain workers are willing to face peril. At the same time, we might consider that there ought to be rights that cannot be made into commodities – that is, we should not allow people to put them on the market, even if they wanted to. So, for instance, in the interests of productivity, a meat-packing plant might decide to issue less protective gear to cutters and pay them more to offset the increased risk of harm. Although we can imagine the meat plant using a cost/benefit analysis, it may be wrong to make safety decisions purely on the basis of finances. An entirely economic analysis would suggest that it is acceptable to put a price on the jeopardy in the workplace, and it seems appropriate that a firefighter is paid more than an office worker. Yet at the same time, we want to say that life is infinitely precious, and we should not put a price on it.

The issue comes down to whether we agree that there are areas that are morally out of bounds. For instance, we may have rights of personal safety, so that as a society we order airlines to have minimum levels of maintenance and training, or require that lawnmowers automatically shut off when unattended, even if there is a demand for cheap goods and services from people willing to take the risk of hurting themselves. A manufacturer could put out a dangerous product, perhaps a sports utility vehicle that has a tendency to roll over at high speed, and the information and sub-sequent purchasing choice would only be available to consumers once a number of people had been injured and the data became publicly available. Mandatory testing and regulation serves to discover information and control standards prior to people being hurt. Whether in employment or the production of goods, the market can only find a stable price for compensation after a number of people have been injured, and thus it is a reactive instrument. As a society we may impose pre-emptive regulation that actively protects us so that a market in human risk does not have a chance to evolve.

Similarly, the fact that compensation alone does not give people a sense of justice is a clue that there are areas – such as privacy, safety, or freedom of religion – where the market simply should not apply. An individual who loses a finger or is spied on in the restroom at work may go to court and get some payment, but that is not usually a trade the person would have made, given the choice, and very few would accept money in exchange for changing their religion. So, for example, if Joe breaks his leg but wins the lottery in the same week, we might ask how much Joe would have to win in order to say that it was not such a bad week after all. We can then say that a value has been placed on the broken leg. Yet we should realize that although this tells us how much compensation might be appropriate in any given incident *after* it has taken place, many people would say that they would rather avoid the experience for any amount of money if they were offered the trade ahead of time, especially when the issue is about infringing rights.

Rights can conflict with maximizing utility. For example, a firm and many of its employees may do well by blaming poor performance on an unwitting branch manager overseas, or a woman might be unknowingly hired as "eye candy" for her male manager. However, at some point an appeal to rights "trumps" all, a term from playing cards that signifies that one card wins out no matter what the other players hold.[3] A trump claim might suggest, for example, that it is wrong to objectify a woman without her consent, or that we cannot force a tribe from its native lands in order to graze cattle whatever the potential rewards might be. Another way of putting this is to

---

[3] Ronald Dworkin, "Rights as Trumps," in Jeremy Waldron, ed., *Theories of Rights* (Oxford: Oxford University Press, 1984), pp. 153–167.

use Robert Nozick's terminology of *side constraints*, which prohibit certain actions that violate personal rights. As he says, it is wrong to use people for the benefit of others unless they are aware of the dynamics and get some benefit from their sacrifice. He would object to workers being subjected to mandatory overtime or hazardous duty unless they freely consented and were appropriately compensated.[4]

## Positive and negative rights

The language of rights is pervasive in business ethics. Initially we need to make two major sets of distinctions that underlie the discussion. The first echoes one we encountered with responsibility, where rights can be described as positive or negative. One way to think about these is to draw on the Miranda warning that police in the United States give when arresting a suspect. They use words along the lines of: "You have the right to remain silent. Anything you say can and will be used against you in a court of law. You have the right to speak to an attorney, and to have an attorney present during any questioning. If you cannot afford an attorney, one will be provided for you at government expense."[5] There are two different kinds of rights asserted in the warning. The right to remain silent is a negative right, in that no one has to do anything to uphold it. In other words, it is an immunity or shield from outside interference. In contrast, the suspect will be provided with an attorney, even at state expense. It is a positive right because it takes action for the right to be preserved. In that sense, it is a claim or entitlement that can be made on other people. Thus the right to free speech may be seen as a negative right, since it means that authorities just have to refrain from censorship, whereas the right to adequate shelter may require some agency to actively provide housing. Historically, the United States at the time of the American Revolution largely concentrated on rights keeping the government out of local affairs, and so the stress was on negative rights. Over the past hundred years or so, however, the discussion of rights has widened to include notions of entitlement.

---

[4] Robert Nozick, *Anarchy, State and Utopia* (New York: Basic Books, 1974), p. 32.

[5] Text and history of Miranda is available at http://www.usconstitution.net/miranda.html, accessed March 23, 2006.

## Rights and privileges

The other major distinction between sets of rights is between what are sometimes called basic or natural rights, and privileges. A long tradition maintains that we have rights by virtue of being human, so that, for instance, it
is wrong to torture or enslave people, simply because they are people. Thus
Thomas Paine, an intellectual inspiration for the American Declaration of
Independence, asserted that we have universal rights not subject to state
control – fundamentally, those of liberty, property, and security.[6] The primary focus is on individuals, and the state is an artificial creation that serves
people by promoting their liberty and happiness. As we find in the Declaration of Independence, these kinds of rights are considered "self evident."[7]
The broad term for this approach is *legal naturalism*, since it holds that laws
are an attempt to codify a fundamental threshold of morality inherent in
nature. It rejects the validity of laws that appear to go against basic moral
norms.[8]

The contrasting view, *legal positivism*, suggests that rights only arise within
a legal framework. Jeremy Bentham took issue with natural rights, believing
they were a dangerous and misguided fiction. As he put it,

> In proportion to the want of happiness resulting from the want of rights, a
> reason exists for wishing there were such things as rights . . . a reason . . . is
> not that right – want is not supply – hunger is not bread . . . Natural rights
> is simple nonsense . . . rhetorical nonsense, – nonsense upon stilts.[9]

This is not to say that Bentham thought all rights talk was foolish. Rather,
he felt that we need to recognize that laws are made by humans and ideally
should work toward human happiness, and thus all rights are conditional

---

[6] See generally, Thomas Paine, *Rights of Man* [1791] (New York: Penguin, 1984). The wording
is echoed in the American Declaration of Independence that asserts rights to life, liberty
and the pursuit of happiness.

[7] The Virginia Declaration of Rights (June 12, 1776) asserting natural rights, initially
drafted by George Mason, is considered to be the basis of the American Declaration
of Independence (July 4, 1776), drafted by Thomas Jefferson, and the Bill of Rights (1789),
the first ten amendments to the American Constitution drafted by James Madison.

[8] This is captured in the motto *Lex iniusta non est lex*, "An unjust law is no law at all":
St. Augustine, *On Free Choice of the Will*, trans. Anna S. Benjamin (Indianapolis: Bobbs-
Merrill, 1964), Book I, chapter 5, sect. 33, p. 11.

[9] Jeremy Bentham, "Anarchical Fallacies," in *The Works of Jeremy Bentham*, vol. 2, ed.
J. Bowring [1843] (New York: Russell and Russell, 1962).

upon the societal backdrop. The strongest form of this view would treat all rights as privileges, which are powers we are given that may be withdrawn. Hence the right to drive a car is more properly described as a privilege, since the state sets down the appropriate qualifications and may take them away, if, say, a person is discovered driving while under the influence of alcohol. The question at hand is whether there are any rights that cannot be retracted. For example, although many in the West think that there is a personal right to reproduce, that freedom may really be a function of the society we live in, with nothing special or inherently valuable involved. Rights that derive from a legal system are usually described as *civil rights*, and those that are said to apply universally are termed *human rights*.

Thus we can describe four basic categories of rights: positive and negative human rights and positive and negative privileges. The discussion becomes cloudier when we are talking about rights that are unrecognized or unfulfilled: workers may have a right to associate with others to form a union, but the firm or government may ban any meetings. The fact that workers are prevented from unionizing does not necessarily mean that the right does not exist, only that it is suppressed. Viewed in this way, a legal right is less compelling, since it can be scaled back or rescinded by a legislative body, whereas a moral right would endure across time and cultures.

Another question for discussion is whether we can forfeit rights, and again this is perhaps easier to consider with legal rights. We may have a right to vote, but that can be forfeited if we behave in certain ways – if we are convicted of a felony, for example. The right to vote can also be rescinded on the grounds of mental incompetence, which shows that it is a qualified right. Compare this to, say, the right to bodily integrity, which prevents people from being used for medical experiments against their will and is not surrendered just because people have lost physical or mental capacities.

Another class of rights is termed *inalienable*. We might voluntarily assent to some activities that compromise our rights, like becoming a compensated human test subject for pharmaceutical trials or, less dramatically, being paid at work and not being able to leave whenever we want. We often release rights and give other people powers: a boss might tell us that we cannot take more than an hour's break for lunch, for example, or that we cannot smoke in the office building. However, there may be cases where we are legally prevented from doing something we might agree to, such as selling our internal organs for transplants or putting our citizenship on the market. These are inalienable in the sense that we cannot detach them even if we want to.

## Recent initiatives

Two distinct lines of debate emerge from the philosophical framework. First there is the question of what rights are; second are the issues about who holds the rights, what priority they have, and who has a burden to act as a consequence. Although people often disagree about the fundamental nature of rights, there is considerable consensus around several key features. First, rights are more important than norms and provide a benchmark of minimally acceptable behavior. It may be a norm in Western society to provide free secondary education or three months of unemployment compensation, but to assert something as a right is more compelling and implies duties on other parties to allocate resources or protections. An associated claim is that rights are universal, so that they apply to all regardless of gender, race, nationality, social standing, or other factors.[10]

In response to those who maintain that all rights are legal and local (a strict legal positivist viewpoint), we could look to the precedent of international agreements. For example, the International Covenant on Economic, Social, and Cultural Rights (CESCR) is widely used as a standard for international law. It was developed from the United Nations Declaration of Human Rights and has been ratified by 149 countries since 1976.[11] Among the rights it asserts are freedom from discrimination; life, liberty, and security of the person; freedom of religion; freedom of assembly; freedom from torture; equality before the law; freedom of expression; freedom from arbitrary arrest and the right to a fair trial; privacy protections; and freedom of movement. Notably it has a section on economic rights that includes a right to work at a job of one's own choosing; fair wages; an adequate standard of living; safe and healthy work conditions; rest periods and holidays with pay; and explicitly rights to form unions and strike.

[10] These conditions are drawn from James Nickel, *Making Sense of Human Rights* (Berkeley: University of California Press, 1987).

[11] The Covenant is available from the United Nations High Commissioner for Human Rights at http://www.ohchr.org/english/law/cescr.htm, accessed March 30, 2006.

The latest United Nations initiative is the "Global Compact" that lists ten principles drawn from the Declaration of Human Rights. The UN Secretary General Kofi Annan challenged business leaders to set benchmark standards of practice and offered the resources and facilities of the United Nations to promote them. Launched in 2000, companies signing the Compact are required to "embrace, support, and enact, within their sphere of influence, a set of core values in the areas of human rights, labor standards, the environment and anti-corruption."[12] To date, over 3,000 companies have voluntarily joined the initiative including many of the Fortune 500 top international corporations such as Nike, Royal Dutch Shell, BP Amoco, BASF, and Rio Tinto. The Compact is also open to NGOs, and some that have joined are Amnesty International, Human Rights Watch, the International Confederation of Free Trade Unions, and Human Rights First. The Compact is not binding but announces that a company is willing to be publicly accountable and transparent in its practices, judged against a common baseline standard.

Let's now turn to two cases that illustrate some of the major issues involved in applying a rights-based analysis to business.

## The Niger delta

The Niger delta in the southeast of Nigeria has some of the world's richest oil reserves. The area is home to many indigenous groups, including the Ogoni tribe whose traditional lands are a relatively small but densely populated region about 12 miles long by 14 wide above the oil field. A subsidiary of Shell Oil began drilling in 1958; reports describe pipelines built across farmland, fields churned up by heavy vehicles, widespread leaks that contaminated the soil and water, and constant flaring – a practice of burning off excess gas at the well head that leads to acid rain. The Ogoni traditionally lived off subsistence farms supplemented by coastal fishing, which have both been decimated by pollution.

After a massive spill in 1993, the Ogoni formed MOSOP, or the Movement for Survival of the Ogoni People, to protest environmental and human rights abuses. They publicized the Ogoni Bill of Rights that demanded cleaning up oil spills; reduction in gas flaring; fair compensation for lost

---

[12] http://www.unglobalcompact.org/, accessed April 15, 2006.

lands, income, and resources; a share of profits from locally extracted oil; and self-determination.[13] It sought $10 million from Shell in compensation. It is estimated that Shell earned over $30 billion from Nigerian oil, although it employed few Ogoni and did not engage in social projects at the time. It appears that Shell colluded with the government in quelling protest. Human rights organizations claimed that when Shell requested protection, the police and army reacted swiftly and violently. Some MOSOP activists were murdered, and the police arrested eight other members of the organization, including the internationally renowned poet Ken Saro-Wiwa, putting them on trial for the crime before a military tribunal. They were convicted and hanged on what many considered sham evidence, despite international political condemnation and protests. Shell's reaction at the time was that it could not meddle in the internal affairs of a sovereign nation, although the vast majority of Nigerian revenues came from oil, and a military dictator whose regime was viewed as thoroughly corrupt ran the country.

In recent years, Shell Nigeria has become involved in community development.[14] However, many of the projects lack government backing and have proved unsuccessful. In the words of an NGO spokesman, "Shell built hospitals, but the government didn't provide doctors. It built schools, but there are no teachers."[15] A Shell representative maintains: "Expectations have increased on the role that the oil companies have to play in providing basic amenities, whereas it is rightly the responsibility of government."[16] Peaceful protest has given way to action by militia groups including oil piracy, weapons smuggling, and kidnapping. Oil companies often pay the ransom, and seek to prevent attacks by hiring hundreds of local people for nominal jobs for short periods.

The Organization of African Unity, created by governments on the continent, founded the African Commission on Human and People's Rights, which called for Nigeria to initiate a comprehensive cleanup of lands and rivers damaged by oil operations and required assurances that future

---

[13] Available at http://www.waado.org/nigerdelta/RightsDeclaration/Ogoni.html, accessed April 7, 2006.

[14] http://www.shell.com/home/Framework?siteId=nigeria, accessed April 7, 2006.

[15] Xin Li, "Oil Unrest Grips Nigeria," *The Washington Times* (February 9, 2006).

[16] Renee Montagne and Steve Inskeep "Fight over Oil Money Percolates in Nigeria," Morning Edition, National Public Radio (USA) (9 March, 2006).

development did not negatively impact local communities.[17] However, the main function of the commission is to "collect documents, undertake studies ... organize seminars, disseminate information ... and should the case arise ... make recommendations to governments."[18]

The case illustrates several issues involving rights. The first is whether there are rights that exist apart from, or above, the legal system. If rights can only derive from a legal system, what do you do when the government is corrupt or ineffective? Nigeria, for example, consistently ranks just above last place in Transparency International's corruption index.[19] Most people have trouble with the idea that only those lucky enough to be born in a developed country, with a responsible government, are entitled to clean water or the right to make a living.

It also shows that despite the fact that we often think of rights as a case of all or nothing, it may be useful to consider them in a more graduated way. Thomas Donaldson has developed such a ranking, and additionally he cautions us to be wary of a "one size fits all" approach that might turn discussions about rights into a promotion of cultural imperialism. He maintains that we should cherish those basic human rights such as owning property and self-determination that are the threshold of all business activity. Beyond that he thinks that we need to bear in mind the economic realities in what he calls a fairness/affordability test.[20] Affordability in Donaldson's sense is making sure the most basic rights are given highest priority – for example, we have to recognize that security matters before, say, concerns about working hours. If the country is in anarchy and run by militias, then those issues have to be addressed before we can deal with other rights claims. Further, he suggests we have to be open-minded about local traditions and realize that the cultural context matters in deciding what is right and wrong.[21] His listing suggests that businesses should not deprive people of the right to subsistence, non-discrimination, and freedom of speech and association.

---

[17] Jim Lobe, "Rights-Nigeria: Commission Orders Gov't to Pay Ogoni Damages," Inter Press Service English News Wire, July 4, 2002.

[18] http://www.achpr.org/english/_info/charter_en.html, accessed April 7, 2006.

[19] http://www.transparency.org/, accessed April 7, 2006.

[20] Thomas Donaldson, *The Ethics of International Business* (New York: Oxford University Press, 1989).

[21] Thomas Donaldson, "Moral Minimums for Multinationals," *Ethics and International Affairs*, 3 (1989), pp. 163–182.

In his view, it would be wrong for a company to deny people the chance to provide for themselves, for example, by mining on their traditional lands without adequate compensation. On the other hand, requiring workers to perform a mandatory exercise program in the morning before work would probably not amount to a human rights violation.

Difficulties arise in determining which practices amount to efficient use of labor by a firm with a bargaining advantage, as opposed to a violation of individual rights. Additionally, there are times when it is in the company's immediate interest not to promote some rights, such as the freedom to form unions and to strike. The United Nations' International Covenant on Economic, Social, and Cultural Rights is more demanding than Donaldson, insisting on fair wages and an adequate standard of living. Recall that people may have rights that are ignored or suppressed, and the fact that abuses happen does not refute the argument that workers have certain entitlements.

So far it seems that the duties to safeguard rights primarily lie with sovereign governments. However, in the Nigerian case, it appears that the oil companies have operated jointly with the government to some extent, or at least stood mutely by when they were aware of gross violations. The contemporary philosopher Henry Shue has divided duties to uphold rights into three categories: rights that we should not deprive; rights that we should help protect from deprivation; and finally, rights to bring to the deprived. For example, if a multinational company operates in a host country that abuses rights, then the company will face the issue of whether it should operate by the prevailing standards or, at the other extreme, intervene to provide rights to its workers and the community. Thus it might be more appropriate for Shell to claim that it should not be expected to do what is properly the job of the government when it comes to, say, building schools. Yet it is not as clear that Shell should either ignore or not work to rectify the pollution that destroys the livelihood of the community when there are unmistakable links between its operations and the ill-effects. Therefore it is important for companies to decide what constitute basic rights and at what point they have a moral duty to become involved, whatever the existing norms. Here again, the tricky cases are those where the host nation allows the behavior, which may be traditional or accepted but strikes us as violating individual rights in ways that we would not tolerate in our own society. For example, the local population might be divided along sectarian

lines, and the question then arises as to whether the company should follow the local pattern of discrimination or actively engage in some kind of
affirmative action program.

## Sweatshops

Another topic that benefits from a rights-based analysis is the case of sweatshops. As we have seen in previous chapters, some industries rely on low-
skilled or unskilled workers and often operate on very small margins. These
conditions, together with fierce competition within the economic sector,
lead to a situation where firms can relocate easily and workers are dispens-
able. Employees who take jobs like these usually have few other choices
and are ripe for exploitation. Because employment is only on a casual
basis, there will likely be no benefits or protections for workers. Typical
abuses include low wages, child labor, health and safety compromises, intim-
idation, and harassment. In a typical case, investigators in Los Angeles
found undocumented Thai and Mexican workers kept in a compound surrounded by razor wire, working 20-hour days for a dollar an hour. They
were threatened with rape or beatings if they failed to meet their sewing
quotas.[22]

The television personality Kathy Lee Gifford was embarrassed when news
reports showed that her line of clothing sold at Wal-Mart was often made
by girls as young as 13 in Honduras, working from early in the morning
until late at night. A month later labor activists discovered that women in a
Manhattan factory who were cheated out of their wages were also producing
garments under the Gifford label. While Kathy Lee Gifford encountered a
firestorm of criticism and her husband went to the New York factory hand-
ing out envelopes of cash in recompense, the story illustrates that sweatshop
practices are not confined to developing countries but are a function of prevailing economic conditions, including the powerlessness of undocumented
workers. A second connotation of *sweatshop*, then, refers to systematic violations of worker's rights, and these need not be confined to subcontrac-
tor factories making shoes or clothes. A number of multinationals have
set up monitoring systems to ensure decent working conditions, largely
in response to public outrage when factory conditions are made public.

[22] Rob Howe, "Labor Pains," *People Weekly* (June 10, 1996).

However, Prakash Sethi, an expert on international labor rights, comments that it would be surprising to find that even 10 percent of Western companies charged with abuses have done anything meaningful about labor conditions.[23]

Historically, sweatshops have migrated elsewhere in the face of increasing levels of employee skills and mounting worker activism, and some commentators see this as an inevitable stage in economic development. However, this assumes that workers are allowed to freely associate, whereas in fact many of firms vigorously resist the development of unions, sometimes with the collusion of government agencies.

The language of rights now allows us to make another vital distinction. Whereas we may not condemn factories using low-skilled workers out of hand, nevertheless we have grounds for criticizing a workplace that violates basic rights. Thus it would be wrong to judge clothing by its country of origin alone, since these abuses can happen everywhere. We should also be careful in the debate when looking at pay rates and conditions without reference to the societal context. In order to make appropriate comparisons, we need to be aware of the prevalent standard of living and what constitutes a "living wage" in assessing a situation. Thus workers may be poorly paid, especially by Western standards, yet if they are not coerced to work, have alternatives, and elect to take the job knowing the conditions, their contract would be acceptable under a capitalist model. At the same time, rights language enables us to explain why it is universally wrong to force 8-year-olds to sew soccer balls in harsh factory conditions.

## Rights and accountability

At this point we can make two interim conclusions. First, when discussing rights, it is important to be as specific as possible. A broad-brush accusation of human rights abuse is unlikely to be effective. Instead we should draw on our initial distinctions to see what sort of right is owed to whom and by whom within a particular cultural context as well as considering the level of economic development. Thus discussions about, say, a living wage should be nuanced by reference to prevailing wages and the cost of living. Moreover,

---

[23] Aaron Bernstein, "Special Report: Global Labor: A World of Sweatshops," *Business Week International* (November 11, 2000).

there are some issues that may offend Westerners but, when examined closely, are concerned with a privilege rather than a basic right. For example, the practice of nepotism in hiring is widespread in Asia and seems to go against rights to non-discrimination. However, given the background of significant unemployment, acceptance of the practice within the culture, and its social utility in preserving the family structure, it may not rise to the level of abuse.[24]

Second, we have to think about where the moral onus should lie when it comes to preserving and protecting rights. Four major candidates come to mind: governments, companies, non-governmental organizations (NGOs), and consumers. Governments have the ability to regulate internally and to influence other countries as a matter of political policy. Notoriously, though, some rights abuses are taken much more seriously than others. In the United States, for example, there are garment regulations in place but fewer than 800 inspectors for the 22,000 domestic contractors. The mobility and casual nature of many of these operations also makes it difficult for the authorities to police them. Externally, America has criticized other countries for their human rights records, sometimes imposing sanctions. However, these efforts have not been very successful. After the brutal reaction to the Tiananmen Square uprising, for example, America tried to impose economic sanctions in 1993, but the efforts were thwarted by China's refusal to make concessions and by US business pressure to maintain trade links.[25] Plausibly, transnational bodies could demand sanctions. The UN Human Rights Council created in 2006 could take on this role, although currently its main functions appear to be advisory and symbolic rather than punitive.

Companies themselves may assume the role of protecting human rights. Many major companies now incorporate rights language into their corporate codes of conduct. Additionally there have been initiatives where companies are certified as being in human rights compliance. The AccountAbility network, for example, promotes an assurance standard – AA1000 – that members seek to achieve based on the best practices for all stakeholders.[26]

---

[24] Thomas Donaldson, "Values in Tension: Ethics Away from Home," *Harvard Business Review*, 74.5 (1996), pp. 119–128.

[25] Catharin E. Dalpino, "Human Rights in China," Policy Brief no. 50, The Brookings Institution, Washington, DC (June, 1999).

[26] http://www.accountability.org.uk/default.asp, accessed April 7, 2006.

Similarly, Social Accountability International specifically awards the SA8000 to companies that promote human rights for workers.[27] These are voluntary certifications, yet they have attracted interest from many of the world's major firms.

A third monitoring system comes from NGOs. These are groups that are not directly affiliated with industry or government. They include human rights organizations such as Amnesty International, Human Rights Watch, and Human Rights First, which survey and report on industry practices. Labor unions and their international agencies work to promote the interests of workers. Some movements are centered on a particular industry – the American Clean Clothes Campaign seeks to improve fair trade in the apparel industry, for instance. Sometimes even a specific firm is the focus of a campaign for improvement, for example, the "McSpotlight" website that focuses on the action of McDonald's Corporation. There are also NGOs associated with shareholder groups that want to practice socially responsible investing by avoiding firms with questionable practices, as well as religiously based groups that monitor issues of social justice and welfare.

The fourth candidate for preventing rights abuses is the consumer. Companies may tolerate abuses, but if consumers were to boycott goods that do not have a union-made label, then firms would get a clear economic signal about the values of their customers. Various student groups have recently pressured university authorities to ensure that the $2.5 billion a year university-sponsored clothing sector – so-called logo wear – is made in factories with reasonable conditions.[28] As we saw with Nike earlier, such campaigns have had considerable effect.[29]

## Communitarian challenges

One contemporary challenge to the primacy of individual rights in discussions in business ethics comes from the communitarian movement. Communitarians claim that individual rights have to be balanced with responsibilities to the community. In their view, human identity is based first and foremost on our social nature, as we establish ourselves in families, friends,

[27] http://www.sa-intl.org/index.cfm?fuseaction=Page.viewPage &pageId=472&stopRedirect =1, accessed April 7, 2006.

[28] Liza Featherstone, "The New Student Movement," *The Nation* (May 15, 2000).

[29] Tony Emerson, "Swoosh Wars," *Newsweek* (March 12, 2001).

and communities. Therefore, they suggest that it is a mistake to begin with the idea that we are all individual actors, making isolated decisions out of self-interest; rather, we should emphasize our common bonds. They often use the metaphor of a three-legged stool: our lives are supported by the state and by the free market economy, but we also need a social sector.[30] Seen in this way, there are times when individuals need to look to the good of society as a whole and compromise some individual rights.

Communitarians themselves resist traditional political labels – many from the political right wing would embrace state-sponsored moral education, or enhancing the strength of the family, or limiting privacy rights to boost state security, acts that appear contrary to individualism. In business terms, communitarians claim that corporations are a necessary element in our social fabric, but argue that they should not thrive at the expense of putting stress on family unity, and they have a duty to preserve or enhance social groups and neighborhoods. For example, corporations ought to encourage flexible work time or provide day care for children.[31]

Communitarians would also favor social engineering through programs such as affirmative action that aim at overall societal benefit, even though they might override individual rights in particular cases. Although they would not completely abandon talk about rights, they see individual rights as often falsely framing our discussions in the sense that if we construe an issue by initially focusing on the individual right-holders, then larger questions about societal good and what it means to have a meaningful work and home life may subsequently be shunted aside.

## Insights from Asian philosophy

Some Asian philosophies also emphasize the priority of community over the individual. Watsuji Tetsuro (1889–1960), for example, proposes that we depend on a web of relationships. In fact, the Japanese word for "ethics" is a composite of two characters, *Rin* and *Ri*. Rin refers to companionship, and Ri to reasons or principles. Hence, ethics is essentially a question of examining human relations, and its fundamental assumption is that humans

---

[30] Juan Williams, "Analysis: What is Communitarianism?" Talk of the Nation, National Public Radio (USA) (transcript) (February 5, 2001).

[31] See, for example, Amitai Etzioni, *The Spirit of Community: Rights, Responsibilities, and the Communitarian Agenda* (New York: Crown Publishers, 1993).

are at once both individuals and involved in continuing social interaction. Given that assumption, obligations to one another will not come from the demands of individuals but rather from an awareness of what a true-hearted person would do in the web of relationships. Hence, in a court case, for example, a judge would not simply consider conformity to the law in making a decision without looking at the particularities of a given situation and the wider circumstances. This type of Eastern adjudication is typically less adversarial than in the West. The downside of this view, at least to Western thinking, is that someone with a justified case where personal rights have been violated by, say, unfair treatment by a supervisor, is unlikely to have many avenues for recourse or appeal after a ruling.

Reliance on relationships and community rather than rights affects what we think of as corporate social responsibility. Traditionally, we have looked at businesses as operating in a separate sphere from the rest of society, with a right to make profits, but with the expectation that they have a social conscience about the way they go about it. However, if we see business as intertwined with society, then we cannot disconnect the good of business from what is good for us overall. This perspective expands our range of issues, moving from the specific concerns of, say, worker safety or establishing a living wage to larger concerns about how the business is contributing to the society as a whole. Thus, asserting personal property rights – for instance, the right to own a car in China – may be shortsighted without looking at the wider issues of environmental impact and the state of China's infrastructure, and only then can we tell whether increasing the number of vehicles serves an overall good. Therefore, they suggest it is important to use the widest possible perspective first when we apply concepts of rights in analyzing business practice, especially when other cultures are involved.[32]

## Non-human rights

So far we have discussed rights as belonging exclusively to humans. The justification for this exclusivity relies on humans having special properties that allow them rights. Some philosophers have questioned whether we are using circular reasoning in this argument: we pick some human property,

---

[32] See Daryl Koehn, "What Can Eastern Philosophy Teach Us About Business Ethics?" *Journal of Business Ethics*, 19.1 (1999), pp. 71–79.

say, the ability to use language, and then we say that rights holders are the ones who have that property. Doing so systematically bars any other contenders, which in turn limits our analysis. Thus, for example, if clear-cutting a forest for timber endangers a particular kind of bird, the rights holders would be the humans who care about birds, and the analysis would be in terms of how their interests are hurt.

A number of recent commentators have challenged this view, suggesting that we might consider whether there are other candidates, including non-human animals or even the environment. Perhaps in building a commercial center we would have to disturb a graveyard or some other holy site. It is plausible to think of the area as off limits relying on a rights-based argument, even if there is no longer a direct connection to a living person: the dead may have a right to rest in peace or to be treated with great respect. Similarly we treat various historical locations as hallowed and leave them alone with the sole justification that it is the proper way to act. We might say future generations already have rights – that is, as possible people. Although they do not currently exist, perhaps they nevertheless are entitled to certain rights such as clean air or water on the same grounds as are living people.

Let us take the case of animals used in pharmaceutical research. Chimpanzees have been used extensively in experiments dealing with hepatitis and HIV/AIDS. They are typically bred by for-profit companies and routinely euthanized after they are no longer useful. They rarely get palliative drugs during procedures. If the criterion for being a rights holder is intelligence or the ability to speak, then we can say they have no individual rights. However, some recent philosophers have followed Peter Singer in thinking that historically rights may be seen as an expanding circle.[33] The idea is that originally only the male sovereign had rights, but then they were expanded to the aristocracy, to property owners, and then to men universally, and subsequently the barriers have come down to include women, children, and people of all races and creeds. Singer's significant move is to claim that the material distinction in assigning rights is the ability to suffer, rather than the ability to use language or to reason.[34] If we follow his thinking, then

---

[33] Peter Singer, *The Expanding Circle: Ethics and Sociobiology* (New York: Farrar Straus & Giroux, 1981).

[34] Singer draws on the work of Jeremy Bentham in this regard. Bentham said: "Other animals, which, on account of their interests having been neglected by the insensibility of the ancient jurists, stand degraded into the class of things . . . The day has been, I grieve it to say in many places it is not yet past, in which the greater part of the species,

at least higher animals deserve moral consideration. While this would not necessarily preclude animal experimentation, it would imply that we should ensure that the animals do not have to endure unnecessary distress.

In addition to animal rights, some philosophers and legal scholars claim that natural objects in the environment ought to be given legal standing, so they could be party to a lawsuit even when human parties may not care or cannot afford to make a case. The discussion began when Disney Enterprises wanted to build a ski resort in the area now protected as part of Sequoia National Park. The legal theorist Christopher Stone wrote an influential essay that maintained we should appoint legal guardians for the environment: "We make decisions on behalf of, and in the purported interests of, others every day; these 'others' are often creatures whose wants are far less verifiable and even more metaphysical in conception than the wants of rivers, trees, and land."[35] Some of the judges felt that there needed to be an advocate for the immunity rights of the environment whether or not there was a human who was willing to bring its interests before the court.[36]

---

under the denomination of slaves, have been treated . . . upon the same footing as . . . animals are still. The day may come, when the rest of the animal creation may acquire those rights which never could have been withholden from them but by the hand of tyranny. The French have already discovered that the blackness of skin is no reason why a human being should be abandoned without redress to the caprice of a tormentor. It may come one day to be recognized, that the number of legs, the villosity of the skin, or the termination of the os sacrum, are reasons equally insufficient for abandoning a sensitive being to the same fate. What else is it that should trace the insuperable line? Is it the faculty of reason, or perhaps, the faculty for discourse? . . . the question is not, Can they reason? nor, Can they talk? but, Can they suffer? Why should the law refuse its protection to any sensitive being? . . . The time will come when humanity will extend its mantle over everything which breathes." *An Introduction to the Principles of Morals and Legislation* [1789] The Hafner Library of Classics, no. 6. (New York: Hafner Press, 1948), chapter 17, sect. 1n., pp. 310–311.

[35] Christopher Stone, "Should Trees Have Standing? Toward Legal Rights for Natural Objects," *Southern California Law Review*, 45 (1972), pp. 450–457.

[36] See Justice Douglas, dissenting, *Sierra Club v. Morton*, 405 U.S. 727 at 741–742: "Inanimate objects are sometimes parties in litigation. A ship has a legal personality, a fiction found useful for maritime purposes. The corporation sole – a creature of ecclesiastical law – is an acceptable adversary and large fortunes ride on its cases. The ordinary corporation is a 'person' for purposes of the adjudicatory processes, whether it represents proprietary, spiritual, aesthetic, or charitable causes . . . So it should be as respects valleys, alpine meadows, rivers, lakes, estuaries, beaches, ridges, groves of trees, swampland, or even air that feels the destructive pressures of modern technology and modern life."

## Summary

As we return to the case described at the beginning of the chapter concerning the workers at Alang, recall the negotiation stance of threat advantage, where the party with weaker bargaining power may be put in a position of "take it or leave it." This tells us that the mere fact people have taken a job is no indication of their willingness to forfeit their rights, since the choice can often be substandard working conditions or destitution, and perhaps they – and all workers in the industry – deserve appropriate protection even if it raises costs overall.

In examining particular cases we can see how the language of rights may best be used: that is, by understanding rights generally and criticizing abuses specifically. Rights talk can be profoundly beneficial in broad terms in the sense that it can establish far-reaching norms that may diffuse relativist claims about a given practice's acceptability based on the situation. At times it is appropriate to apply universal standards, say, against physical abuse, regardless of a country's economic development or the particular work context. Furthermore, if we consider human rights within this wide perspective, it is not just a case of businesses trying to squeeze employment conditions to run the most efficient operation possible, whatever the human cost. Rights claims have to be considered in light of the overall place of business, consumers, and government in society. Seen impartially in this way, we ought to expect that people are entitled to certain levels of treatment articulated in terms of rights, whoever they are and wherever they may live, and business actions are only one part of a wider dialogue of what it means to be human and what it takes to have a good life.

The backdrop of human rights thus gives us valuable leverage to examine specific cases. General claims that a country is abusing human rights are less effective than saying that a particular company is going against its own code of practice or prevailing standards. Thus public announcements of standards of practice by companies, transparency, and accountability will all promote ensuring rights for both business and workers, especially in light of transnational norms established by independent bodies such as the United Nations. As we have seen, there may be cases where a company should be prohibited from acting, but we should be conscious of the level of rights that are infringed, the cultural context involved, and the link between the company and the harm.

The problems at Alang would not have been solved if they simply moved elsewhere to a shipyard operating with even more permissive standards. The company could have given assurances that basic rights would be safeguarded and transparency allowed, and perhaps the work could have continued with appropriate protections in place. Yet if we take rights seriously, then we need to see that violations by individual businesses occur against a social and political background. Whatever the conditions at the yard, we should recognize that they occur amid pressures that derive from a poor country actively seeking hard currency as well as impoverished workers desperate to earn a living.

Human rights provide a baseline for deciding what is acceptable in business practice. However, some personal rights are often compromised in our role as employees or consumers. Sometimes the firm imposes restrictions, such as a ban on smoking or dangerous hobbies, and individuals have to make personal decisions about whether they are willing to accept the conditions for the pay. As consumers, there are times when we want to buy goods that could lead to harm, but we are prevented from doing so. Thus there is a balance between the rights to craft our own destiny and the restrictions imposed on us. To help deal with the tension between self-determination and outside constraints, we will turn to the issue of autonomy in the next chapter.

## General questions for discussion

1. What do you consider to be fundamental human rights that are immune to societal changes?
2. Do you think animals or the environment can be bearers of rights?
3. Whose interests ought to be paramount, those of the community or those of the individual? What are the key factors in your position?
4. Whose job should it be to preserve and enforce human rights?
5. Why should people be banned from selling one of their kidneys or eyeballs for cash? When should issues of rights override market concerns?

## Case – human guinea pigs

In March 2006, eight healthy young men were taking part in a drug trial in northern London for a new antibody known as TGN1412 that showed promise in treating some forms of leukemia and rheumatoid arthritis. In a typical short-term residential drug trial subjects are recruited through newspaper advertisements, and are confined to a ward for a week, during which time they may be either given injections, or have topical creams applied, or take oral doses, and a medical team will then monitor their responses. Some participants receive placebos, which are inert substances, so that the researchers will be able to gauge the reactions of the drug against a control group. TGN1412 was developed by TeGenero AG of Germany, while the tests were run by Parexel International of Massachusetts at a facility attached to a hospital in Britain.

The drug had been tested on animals, including monkeys who experienced some swollen glands. The human trials used doses 500 times lower than those given to animals. The drug was administered by injection to the subjects at two-minute intervals. A few minutes after the last dose had been given, the first subject experienced severe pain, nausea, and fever. All of the six who had been given the real drug collapsed in quick succession with convulsions, and four experienced major organ failure. Relatives described massive swelling, and one compared the victim's massive head to the elephant man. The subjects were given immediate treatment, essentially keeping them alive by machines while their blood was replaced. All survived, although at least two lost fingers and toes, and they face a future with compromised functioning of their major organs. There has been no evidence of contamination or that the usual protocols were not followed.

The volunteers were paid £2,000 (roughly $3,750) each for a week's stay at the clinic, and all signed releases before they took part in the study. One, Mohammed Abdalla, was going to send the money back to Egypt. An unexpected result of the massive publicity about the case – and the amount paid to volunteers – was a surge in inquiries to research organizations from prospective test subjects.[37]

## Some questions from the case

1. Should we be able to forfeit rights to health and safety?

---

[37] Sources include: CNN at http://www.cnn.com/2006/HEALTH/04/16/uk.trial.ap/index.html, accessed April 27, 2006; *The Guardian* (UK), http://www.guardian.co.uk/medicine/story/0,,1733287,00.html, accessed June 21, 2006; "Interest Surges in Trials Despite Patients' Plight," *The Guardian* (UK) (18 March, 2006).

2. What sort of rights are involved in this case? Are they human rights, or privileges?

3. How should we develop a market in risk, that is, how would you determine what would be adequate compensation for the subjects?

4. Would you react differently to the plight of the subjects if they volunteered to help research on deadly diseases without compensation?

5. Would it make any difference from your perspective if the test subjects had been volunteer prisoners serving life sentences, or impoverished orphans from an undeveloped country? Is there a point where society could demand that some people are used for drug tests?

6. Many of these tests are conducted for cosmetic products. Would your intuitions change if the drug had been designed for whitening teeth instead of leukemia?

7. It is sometimes said that rights and duties are not symmetrical: I may have a duty to give to charity but the needy have no corresponding right to receive charity, for example. The pharmaceutical industry is large and profitable. Do they have a duty to help out poor people who need drugs? Do people in the third world, for example, have a right to patented drugs at or below cost?

# 7  Autonomy

## CortiSlim

Over a million Americans and Canadians have purchased a product called CortiSlim, which has been widely advertised on radio and television "infomercials."[1] Until restrained by the Federal Trade Commission in October 2004, the promoters claimed that taking CortiSlim caused

- Permanent weight loss of 10 to 50 pounds for virtually all users;
- Weight loss of 4 to 10 pounds per week over multiple weeks;
- Weight loss targeted to the abdomen, stomach, and thighs.

Ads claimed the product worked by restricting the release of the hormone cortisone. Cortisone is released when the body is under stress and can bind proteins and create a feeling of hunger. Thus, CortiSlim's producers argue that stress causes fat accumulation (especially "belly fat") and that by relieving stress, CortiSlim would reduce the body's reaction, thus leading to weight loss.

Although the marketers claimed fifteen years of scientific findings, there is no legitimate research backing the claim that the ingredients of CortiSlim either relieve stress or block cortisone release. The makers, Window Rock Enterprises, broadcast advertisements that claimed persistently high levels of cortisol were the underlying cause of weight gain and retention and that CortiSlim was "the answer." Window Rock also marketed a product called CortiStress in September 2003, saying that high levels of cortisol are the cause of "every modern lifestyle disease that is associated with this

---

[1] This section draws on the FTC press release, "FTC Targets Products Claiming to Affect the Stress Hormone Cortisol" (October 5, 2004), available at http://www.ftc.gov/opa/2004/10/windowrock.htm, accessed January 10, 2006.

fast-paced 21st century lifestyle" and that CortiStress could reduce the risk of osteoporosis, diabetes, Alzheimer's disease, cancer, and cardiovascular disease. In the words of a Federal Trade Commission spokesperson, these claims "fly in the face of reality . . . No pill can replace a healthy program of diet and exercise."[2]

Window Rock used paid programming – infomercials – to promote their products. These 30-minute advertisements are modeled after real television programs, but their purpose is to push a product. In this case, Window Rock went against US television broadcasting rules by making an apparent talk show called "Breakthroughs" and not explicitly labeling it as sponsored by the makers of the pills they were discussing.

The US Food and Drug Administration took regulatory action against CortiSlim in late 2004 and demanded that the product's label and information could no longer make unsubstantiated claims that it "eliminates cravings," "controls appetite," "burns calories more efficiently and naturally through thermogenesis," and "diminishes hunger and stress eating." Three Window Rock executives were fined $4.5 million in September 2005 from charges brought by the US Federal Trade Commission. They were also ordered to cease misrepresenting the efficacy of CortiSlim and CortiStress and were barred from using advertising with a deceptive format. The defendants did not have to admit liability as part of the settlement.

Are we wrong to restrict the sale of goods if people are willing to pay? Is it wrong for us to tell others what is in their own best interest? Would it be more appropriate to let them make their own decisions? The philosophical concept dealing with the ability to make your own choices is known as autonomy, and intervention that blocks autonomous action is called paternalism.

*Autonomy* literally means self-government, and when we use it in reference to people it typically refers to independence or absence of external constraints. It is an important concept in business ethics because capitalism asserts liberty, choice, and personal responsibility as paramount virtues, and hence a number of topics arise from failure to grant or recognize the autonomy of businesses and individuals, whether they are employees, consumers,

---

[2] Consumeraffairs.com, "FTC: Cortisol Claims Defy Reality" (October 6, 2004), http://www.consumeraffairs.com/news04/ftc_cortisol.html, accessed January 10, 2006.

owners, or community members. In this chapter we will first look at the
basic concept of autonomy and then see how valuable it can be by highlighting three different cases where it applies. The first case involves purchasing
decisions, where we hold autonomy to be dominant, and the morality of
advertising, where the craft of the marketers is to get us to choose the product they have to sell. The second case illustrates the tension between the
private life of the employee and the interests of the business with the issue
of drug testing. Finally, the third case highlights the constraints on employer
autonomy by forcing them to follow appropriate non-discrimination guidelines. These cases do not exhaust the concept, of course, but do demonstrate
how a philosophical framework can be applied to a range of topics.

One of the axioms of the capitalist system is freedom: ideally, individuals
are free to allocate their resources as they see fit, and producers are free
to enter or exit markets based on the rewards they anticipate. Similarly,
prospective employees may bargain for the best terms and conditions, while
employers will negotiate for the most efficient and profitable deal they can
get. If consumers want to buy a do-it-yourself tattoo kit, purchase scalding
hot coffee to drink while driving, or eat a constant diet of food high in
saturated fats, then they should not be constrained in their choices. If one
person wants to spend money on poetry or philosophy books while another
buys tickets to mud wrestling competitions, that would be perfectly acceptable. The consumer is held to be sovereign since the system is ultimately
driven by aggregated individual purchasing decisions. In the words of John
Stuart Mill,

> But neither one person, nor any number of persons, is warranted in saying
> to another human creature of ripe years, that he shall not do with his life
> for his own benefit what he chooses to do with it. He is the person most
> interested in his own well-being: the interest which any other person,
> except in cases of strong personal attachment, can have in it, is trifling,
> compared with that which he himself has . . . with respect to his own
> feelings and circumstances, the most ordinary man or woman has means of
> knowledge immeasurably surpassing those that can be possessed by any one
> else.[3]

---

[3] John Stuart Mill, *on Liberty* [1859], ed. Gertrude Himmelfarlo (New York: Penguin, 1982),
pp. 142–143.

## Autonomy defined

We describe a decision as autonomous as long as it fulfills a number of conditions. They include: 1. Intentionality; 2. Understanding; and 3. Freedom from controlling influences.[4] Let us examine these individually.

## Intentionality

To act intentionally means that we frame a plan and purposefully put it into action. We can see a difference between putting goods in a shopping cart at a grocery store and having a can fall into it after we have knocked it while reaching for something else. The first was a planned act, and we willed movements to bring it about. The second was a mere accident. Typically, we place more moral responsibility on the results of intentional acts – for instance, bumping into someone in a crowded shop is considered unfortunate but normal, whereas deliberately jostling someone would be thought inappropriate, and conversely we are much more likely to excuse someone who did not mean to intend harm.

Intentions are not always easy to frame ahead of time, and in fact most often we reconstruct them when looking back, through the process of rationalization. However, we often have a bias that attributes the most favorable intentions to what we did, and so first-hand reports of intentions may be unreliable. Moreover, we usually have mixed motives for doing things, so there may be more than one spur to any given act. Someone who donates to charity may do it out of a desire to do good but also may be doing so out of guilt or a bad conscience, or even something more remote, such as subconscious resentment over a loveless childhood. The issue becomes even more complex in that if we cannot rely on the individual's own report, then we have to look at his or her actions to see if they are consistent with what the person says. In this sense, the hypocrite and the saint may act identically. If we see someone donating to charity, we can ultimately only judge by the act itself, since we do not have privileged access to a person's mind. The same holds true of corporate actions, where we may find it hard to discern the actual operating motives behind any particular decision.

[4] Drawn from Ruth Faden, Tom Beauchamp, and Nancy King, *A History and Theory of Informed Consent* (Oxford, Oxford University Press, 1986).

Sometimes philosophers have used the notion of *authenticity* to examine whether an act was truly intentional. Authenticity in this sense examines whether any given decision is consistent with the general life plans of an individual. Hence if someone with no other bodily decoration enters a tattoo parlor, appears to be intoxicated, and demands to have the name of a new female acquaintance emblazoned across his chest, we might question whether the act is consistent with the general drift of his other life choices. Similarly, a construction worker who voluntarily disdains wearing a safety harness and hard hat may be refusing them impulsively on a dare, thinking it may impress his fellow workers, but alternatively it might be consistent with his other daredevil habits. Generally the closer his actions are to a lifelong pattern, the more authentic his actions and, correspondingly, the more autonomous.

## Understanding

A key assumption in the free market is full information. Sometimes this can be overwhelming to consumers, and therefore we have to rely on the advice of agents or sales representatives who may not always have our best interests in mind. On the other hand, sometimes producers may withhold pertinent information that might deter sales: for instance, some portable music players have a limit to the number of times their batteries can be recharged, thus shortening their life, or the design of some sports utility vehicles (SUVs) means that they are more likely to tip over when doing sharp turns.

Autonomous action requires informed consent, that is, we understand what we are about to do and agree to it. People may fail to grasp information in several ways – for instance, the information may not be available, not be pertinent, inaccurate, or not understandable by a non-expert. Consider computer screens, for example. They may be "interlaced" or "non-interlaced," and the typical buyer will have to do research to find out if this feature makes any practical difference and what the terms indicate.[5]

We might think of information as having two components – one where we are able to describe the nature of an act or decision and the other what the likely consequences of the decision might be. This is not to say that an individual has to be omniscient or always make correct predictions, but

---

[5] Non-interlaced are generally considered superior because they tend to flicker less.

rather the standard speaks to what a reasonable person might expect when presented with the relevant information. Hence someone who chooses to smoke tobacco products is alerted by prominent warning labels about the dangers involved, whereas many household products such as cleaners or paints contain dangerous chemicals that most of us would be oblivious to unless the information were highlighted in some way. Consequently a smoker has made a choice despite the clear dangers, but the person using cleaners is often exposed unknowingly.

Being presented with information is not necessarily the same thing as understanding it, however. For example, to many smokers the risks are distant and abstract, and it is easy for them to discount the warning labels. Educational research suggests that an interactive test would be more effective in getting the message across. However, if we really wanted to inform potential tobacco consumers about the dangers, it might be appropriate to have them tour a cancer ward before being allowed a license to smoke. This would be a similar process to driver's education, perhaps, where being made aware of the potential consequences is more visceral. This leads to the questions of how much information is sufficient and what feedback mechanisms, if any, might be appropriate. For instance, if a consumer buys a powered chain saw, we might imagine that it would come with a code that unlocks the engine only after the purchaser has answered a short true/false quiz and signed an affidavit where he accepts the named risks, similar to many current software agreements.

Many people think that the autonomous individual ought to be able to accept risks by being willingly ignorant. This is perhaps more common than we realize – very often we are faced with contracts, such as those computer software licenses, that have a great deal of fine print, and we are asked to initial that we are aware of the conditions and agree to them. Demanding full disclosure may also have a chilling effect on commerce, and so there is a fine line between requiring consumers to be aware of the material risks and dissuading them from something they want to do. For instance, eating red meat and drinking alcohol are both potentially harmful, and yet we as a society put few restrictions on them. Thus if a pregnant woman asks for alcohol in a bar, the bartender would be unlikely to ask if she is aware of the dangers of alcohol for the fetus, even though such warnings are routinely posted on the labels of alcoholic beverages, and he would probably not dissuade her from drinking.

Information is not necessarily unbiased or readily available. Thus, although we might want to be as informed as possible, there are restrictions on both its reliability and accessibility. The World Wide Web has certainly increased the amount of information accessible to individuals, but its information is unfiltered and largely unchecked. An example of the advantage of the Internet can be seen in the case of the diet pill Fen-Phen, which was popular in the mid-1990s. The combination of two drugs – fenfluramine and phentermine – was available by prescription, and many doctors saw it as a lucrative and beneficial therapy for the problem of obesity.[6] Fen-Phen had only been tested on a sample of 120 people and only for a relatively short while, but it was being prescribed for long-term use. The drugs had no record of causing heart problems individually, but anecdotal evidence started to emerge that in combination, these drugs could be lethal for some people. The government only investigated after there was a flood of Internet traffic exposing the problem. Wyeth, the manufacturer, came under scrutiny for lavishly sponsoring doctors who promoted their version of the drugs, and subsequently Fen-Phen was banned. In this case, the Internet generated sufficient information to create a pattern out of what had initially appeared to be isolated incidents.

Nevertheless, there are other cases where a great deal of inaccurate or misleading information is disseminated on the web. The stimulant ephedra, for example, is promoted as safe and reliable, but it may be deadly to people with heart problems. At the time of writing, under "ephedra" the search engine Google lists a number of articles warning about the dangers on one side of the screen and sponsored links to easy access on the other.

The greater anonymity and impersonal nature of communication made possible by web-based technology also means that it can be more easily abused. Only sites based in the United States can be regulated by American authorities (the same holds true of other countries, too), and regular users are unable to tell how genuine or trustworthy a site may be. Some vendors such as e-bay or Amazon have feedback mechanisms to reflect user satisfaction, although these are subject to manipulation (sellers may post false positive feedback, for example), and most sites do not rate particular vendors. Even legitimate professionals may face temptation when presented

---

[6] Gina Kolata, "How Fen-Phen, A Diet 'Miracle,' Rose and Fell," *The New York Times* (September 23, 1997).

with lucrative rewards and few controls: for instance, some doctors now offer "virtual consultations" over the web, where they review a medical history and prescribe medications (such as Viagra) without seeing the patient in person.

Western societies often use age as a gauge of maturity; for instance, a child has to be 16 to buy a DVD with mature content in New Zealand.[7] However, age is a very rough measure; years of education or psychological profiles would probably be more accurate. If we take the notion of full understanding seriously, then we have to address questions about the reasoning capacity and maturity of the population involved.

## Voluntariness

Although we may feel that we have the freedom to do as we choose, we are in fact constrained both externally and internally.[8] Externally, there are physical limitations to what we can do, and there may be political barriers that control free movement and employment. Government regulations restrict the terms of voluntary contracts in the workplace, so that there are limits on minimum wages and controls on health and safety, for example. Realistically, we cannot talk about the notion of freedom without acknowledging its intimate links with issues of power and liberty. For example, saying that a worker can take or leave a job may be true, but if there are more people

---

[7] http://www.dia.govt.nz/diawebsite.nsf/wpg_URL/Resource-material-Our-Policy-Advice-Areas-Censorship-Policy?OpenDocument, accessed January 9, 2006.

[8] John Locke in the *Essay Concerning Human Understanding* distinguishes between liberty and volition. He suggests that there are times where we may be willing captives to a system, and although we assent to it, it would be wrong to describe ourselves as truly free: "Suppose a man be carried, whilst fast asleep, into a room where is a person he longs to see and speak with; and there be locked fast in, beyond his power to get out: he awakes, and is glad to find himself in so desirable company, which he stays willingly in, i.e. prefers his stay to going away. I ask, is not this stay voluntary? I think nobody will doubt it: and yet being locked fast in, it is evident he is not at liberty not to stay, he has not freedom to be gone. So that liberty is not an ideal belonging to volition, or preferring; but to the person having the power of doing, or forbearing to do, according as the mind shall choose or direct . . . For wherever restraint comes to check that power, or compulsion takes away that indifferency of ability to act, or to forbear acting, there liberty, and our notion of it, presently ceases." John Locke, *An Essay Concerning Human Understanding* [1689], ed. Kenneth Winkler (Indianapolis: Hackett, 1996), Book II, chapter 21, sect. 10, p. 96.

than jobs, and people cannot live off the land, then the power will favor the employer. After all, without the liberty to migrate to a better job market, the freedom to leave a job may translate to the freedom to become destitute. Thus in discussions about the workers at Alang or sweatshops in Cambodia, it is vital to investigate whether the employees made autonomous choices in the sense of understanding what they were letting themselves in for, and whether they had any meaningful alternatives.

Additionally, we are subject to a variety of psychological influences that may encourage us to act against what we would, in a reflective moment, consider to be our best interests: for example, one of the reasons that auctions are successful is that bidders become more focused on winning by outbidding each other than on the objective value of the goods.

Some kinds of influence are more direct than others, and we can list them under three broad headings: coercion, manipulation, and persuasion. Coercion occurs when someone is threatened with consequences so severe that they preclude other choices. Thus a worker whose job is threatened if she fails to wear protective garments when handling food is not literally forced to do so, but the possibility of being fired will outweigh any desire not to. Manipulation is more difficult to describe but usually involves alteration of someone's perceived choices so that the person is strongly encouraged to act in a desired fashion. Thus managers in some firms are urged in clear terms to contribute to favored charities through payroll deductions, and the fact that senior executives have access to lists of the donations effectively makes giving a necessary element for anyone aspiring for promotion.

Persuasion may not strictly offset autonomy, in that it functions by promoting a set of reasons that an individual may then adopt. Hence a manager may change an employee's mind by presenting a case for adopting a certain view. For instance, in the case of the space shuttle *Columbia*, managers considered the available data and successfully persuaded their colleagues that there was no significant risk to the mission, a conclusion that was well reasoned but unfortunately deeply flawed. Still, if those who were undecided chose to adopt one set of arguments as more reasonable than another, their autonomy was not compromised since they voluntarily accepted the case that was made.

Nevertheless, decisions take place within particular circumstances, and when we talk about persuasion we also recognize that there are often elements of coercion and manipulation mixed in. When we think of meetings, an advocate typically tries to convert listeners to a different position and basic facts are rarely presented in an entirely neutral manner. Some facts will be emphasized, and others will be downplayed. The audience also has biases, and we find people with varying degrees of power promoting and defending positions. Elements such as the prospect of future contracts, personal advancement, being perceived as a team player, and many others inevitably come into play and affect individual autonomy.

There may be times when we think that we are in control of our actions, but like the subjects in Milgram's obedience to authority experiment we find ourselves complying despite our initial convictions not to. These influences are significant in philosophical terms because they serve to compromise our autonomy, and sometimes they encourage us to act contrary to our espoused values. Among the dynamics involved is reciprocation, where we are given something and then feel obliged to the donor. This accounts for the success of charities that send uninvited gifts such as address labels to potential donors, because the recipient then unconsciously feels that any gift needs to be repaid. Another is the power of consistency: canvassers will often ask potential donors to sign petitions, and only after doing so do they ask for money, since people feel a natural obligation to demonstrate that their values are consistent.[9]

The upshot of these findings is that we may fall short of our own moral aspirations. The failure may not be due to weakness of the will but to the systematic way that we lapse into ways of thinking that can interfere with our best judgment, and, in effect, take away from our personal autonomy. For instance, many of us do not make the best decisions under time pressure or in an atmosphere of charged emotions, conditions that take away from the voluntariness condition. Therefore, it is useful to be aware that we may be subject to unconscious forces and to make sure that we arrive at decisions that are truly our own.

## Limits on autonomy

There are several morally justifiable reasons to limit autonomy. These include benign paternalism, prevention of harm or offense, and upholding

---

[9] Robert Cialdini, *Influence: The Psychology of Persuasion* (New York: Collins, 1998).

moral standards.[10] *Paternalism*, literally acting like a father, involves interference with an individual's autonomy by a person or institution that has the ability to do so. Paternalism has two aspects: first, it interferes with the liberty of another, and second, the interference usually has a benign intent.

In business terms, a firm may believe that it knows what is best for others and act accordingly. It may require workers not to smoke, or not to engage in hazardous hobbies such as parachuting. It could demand that they keep up a certain level of professional training, or keep to a dress code. None of these may have bad effects, and may actually serve to improve the lives of employees. Businesses may also act to restrain the free choice of consumers by putting conditions on purchase – say, automatically equipping a vehicle with side air bags, or choosing not to exploit a potentially lucrative market such as cheap malt liquor. The moral issue is not whether the outcomes are of some benefit, however, but whether the kind of interference that overrides personal decisions is ever acceptable.

John Stuart Mill suggested that the only justifiable reason to interfere with another's liberty is for self-protection. It would be morally acceptable for the person to engage in risky and dangerous activities as long as those actions posed no hazard to others. He asserts:

> His own good, either physical or moral, is not a sufficient warrant. He cannot rightfully be compelled to do or forbear because it will be better for him to do so, because it will make him happier, because, in the opinion of others, to do so would be wise, or even right. These are good reasons for remonstrating with him, or reasoning with him, or persuading him, or entreating him, but not for compelling him, or visiting him with evil in case he do otherwise . . . The strongest of all the arguments against the interference of the public with purely personal conduct, is that when it does interfere, the odds are that it interferes wrongly, and in the wrong place.[11]

Mill allows restraint, though, where he thinks the person is unaware of the consequences of an act and would want to know that information before proceeding:

> It is a proper office of public authority to guard against accidents. If either a public officer or any one else saw a person attempting to cross a bridge

[10] Drawn from Joel Feinberg, *Harmless Wrongdoing* (New York: Oxford University Press, 1988).
[11] Mill, *On Liberty*, chapter 4, p. 68.

which had been ascertained to be unsafe, and there were no time to warn him of his danger, they might seize him and turn him back without any real infringement of his liberty; for liberty consists in doing what one desires, and he does not desire to fall into the river. Nevertheless, when there is not a certainty, but only a danger of mischief, no one but the person himself can judge of the sufficiency of the motive which may prompt him to incur the risk: in this case, therefore, (unless he is a child, or delirious, or in some state of excitement or absorption incompatible with the full use of the reflecting faculty,) he ought, I conceive, to be only warned of the danger; not forcibly prevented from exposing himself to it.[12]

Thus the liberal approach believes that the individual ought to be self-governing unless there is harm to others. As Mill notes later, warning labels for poison would be appropriate, but he is against undue restriction. He realizes that someone might seek to harm others, and in that sort of case he would allow items to be traceable – for example, the purchaser of a potential poison might have to sign a register, so that there is a disincentive to commit a crime, but he would not go as far as a ban on selling the product.

Consider the case of Viagra, a prescription drug that may increase male sexual potency, but with potentially dangerous cardiovascular side effects. Because the risk is to the person alone, Mill would allow open sales, perhaps with an indemnity clause for the producer. On the other hand, Mill would consider it appropriate to restrict the sale of alcohol to drivers because of the attendant risks to other people.

Most products carry some risks: the widely available non-prescription drug aspirin may cause a reaction in some people and is not recommended for young children. Apparently, a number of people die each year from ballpoint pens (usually swallowing them) as well as from incidents with many other everyday objects.[13] The questions that we must confront are whether a product should carry information about its risks, whether it should come with an explicit warning, and whether its sale and use should be monitored or regulated.

There are also issues about the competence of consumers – should we protect people from themselves? What if a person is quite willing to eat

---

[12] Mill, *On Liberty*, chapter 5, p. 166.

[13] B. D. Bhana, James G. Gunaselvam, and Mahomed A. Dada, "Mechanical Airway Obstruction Caused by Accidental Aspiration of Part of a Ballpoint Pen," *American Journal of Forensic Medicine and Pathology*, 21.4 (2000), pp. 362–365.

nothing but high fat and high sugar fast food, and realizes, at least dimly, that doing so could lead to an untimely death? And what should we do about people subjected to high-pressure sales tactics when they may not have the ability or competence to resist – for instance, young people offered pornography on the Internet or elderly people sold inappropriate life insurance?

Practically speaking, there are few cases where harm is entirely confined to the individual involved. Someone who dies prematurely because of arteries clogged by a fast-food diet may have dependents, may be depriving the workforce of a valuable worker, or may cause health and life insurance rates to rise for the population at large. Some commentators have suggested there is a link between private use of pornography and the individual's objectification of women in general.[14] Both cases serve to illustrate that the line between harming self and others is far from distinct, and arguing for completely free markets is less straightforward than it initially appears.

Society may want to restrict some behavior on the grounds that it goes against morally accepted standards. Pornography or prostitution may be highly lucrative, but society may not want to let the market be the sole arbiter of standards and believe that it is appropriate to restrict individual choices.

The counterargument derives from what we have termed *market morality*. Despite what we may espouse or aspire to, the market shows us what people really value by their purchasing decisions. Therefore, if it turns out that pornography is very popular or that people are willing to support morally questionable products such as radar detectors, potions to defeat drug tests, or pastimes such as cock fighting tournaments, then we have a very practical indicator of what people want, and business is merely supplying the demand. Thus, although many people might think baiting animals for sport is cruel and inhumane, it may not harm the spectators and should be allowed as long as there is a market. If societal values change, then the market will dry up, but in either case there is no warrant for outside regulation of personal liberty.

[14] Helen E. Longino, "Pornography, Oppression and Freedom: A Closer Look," in Laura Lederer, ed., *Take Back the Night: Women on Pornography* (New York: William Morrow, 1980), p. 278.

## Let the buyer beware

One standard of personal liberty that people in business often appeal to is summed up by the Latin phrase *caveat emptor* or "Let the buyer beware." Whereas in strict liability a manufacturer or provider is responsible for all the consequences from a product or service, here the consumer appropriates all liability at the time of purchase. Thus someone buying a car may choose to have it inspected or may just kick the tires, and is free to make any offer based on his assessment of its value. However, once the trade is complete, he cannot complain that he has got a bad deal. The same would hold if someone bought a computer through the Internet or an apparent old master painting at a garage sale.[15]

However, caveat emptor is not unconditional, since some actions breach autonomy. If the seller uses deceit to promote the virtues of the item, or if it turns out to be faulty, then there are grounds for redress. Moreover, the buyer has to be in his right mind and aware of the consequences of the transaction. However, barring these concerns, individuals are generally thought to be capable of making decisions rationally, and so if the deal ends up disadvantaging one side, there are few legal ramifications. Thus if the garage sale painting was a worthless fake, the buyer nevertheless made a free choice and struck the best bargain he could. In essence, he was gambling and lost.

As we have seen, an aspect of consumer autonomy will be that choices are voluntary. Producers spend vast amounts of money on persuasive and pervasive advertising that can successfully influence individual preferences or manipulate our "free" choices. Advertisers and vendors sometimes capitalize on our tendencies to not look too closely at items. For example, two boxes of macaroni come in identical boxes and retail at the same price. One has pasta shaped like a cartoon character. Closer examination shows that the shaped macaroni has only two servings instead of the three in the other box. It takes some effort on the part of the consumer to detect the difference, given the similarity of presentation. Other examples of manipulative

---

[15] See, for example, Mike Lupica, "Yard Sale Table to Sell Big at Sotheby's," ABC Good Morning America (January 18, 1998), which describes a table bought for $25 being sold several years later for $300,000. No mention is made of additional reimbursement to the vendor. Available at http://www.highbeam.com/browse/News-General-ABC+Good+Morning+America+Sunday/January-1998-p1, accessed March 20, 2006.

advertising are spray-on cooking fat that is labeled "fat-free" because the serving size (one-third of a second) falls below the mandated reporting level. Or our example of the soup company claiming that its product now contains 20 percent less sodium, but rather than reducing the salt, the company has merely lowered the recommended serving size from 10 ounces to 8.[16]

The logic of caveat emptor is that the vendor will try to maximize returns and will prey on the gullible. If there is sufficient negative feedback in terms of lowered sales because of a reputation for sharp dealing, then the vendors will change their behavior. We can see this dynamic operating with a number of "no-haggle" car dealers, where customers are willing to pay a premium to avoid some of the traditional gamesmanship when purchasing a car.

Although caveat emptor seems to cleanly remove the seller from responsibility, the reality is more complicated. As we have seen, many deals are not a one-time affair – vendors want their customers to return repeatedly, and so the real cost of avoiding any and all responsibility for sold goods may become significant when it translates into lost potential sales in the future.

## Advertising and autonomy

The language of autonomy gives us a way to assess the morality of advertising. For better or worse, advertising is part of our environment and represents a significant proportion of the stimuli to which we are exposed – think about walking down a street and the number of posters and signs that encourage us to buy products and services, or listening to radio and television regularly interrupted by commercials. Initially we should stipulate that the reason we have so much advertising is that companies believe that it works despite the fact that there are huge problems in scientifically assessing its effectiveness. Nevertheless, US companies alone spent over $50 billion to promote their products in 2002.[17] Research suggests that although we see hundreds of advertisements a day, we register only about seventy and pay attention to less than a third of those.[18] Critics of advertising in general

---

[16] Stephen Schmidt, "Sorting Out Soups," *Nutrition Action Newsletter* (December 1, 1989).

[17] "Advertising and Related Services," US Bureau of the Census, 2002 Economic Census, available at http://factfinder.census.gov/servlet/IBQTable?_bm=y&-NAICS2002=5418&-ds_name=EC0200A1&-_lang=en.

[18] Peter Barrow, "Advertising: Does it or Doesn't it?" *Canadian Manager* (March 22, 1993).

claim that it creates unnecessary demand, manipulates and confuses the market, and creates illusions of the good life for people who will subsequently be disappointed when their consumption fails to make them happy. Proponents suggest that the practice serves to help people make decisions and stimulates competition, leading to a maximally efficient marketplace.

It will be useful to make a couple of distinctions. Advertising is often described as either informative or persuasive. Informative advertising merely announces, say, that a good or service is available, but makes no other claims, and we can consider it morally neutral. Persuasive advertising attempts to influence the audience. The other distinction is between first- and second-order desires.

As humans we have both needs and wants. Needs are those things necessary for us to survive: food, shelter, clothing, and so forth. Wants are things we would like but are not vital. Thus it may be important that we have clothing, but not that we should own designer-label jeans. Within the scope of wants is a general level of goods and services we hope to have – children want toys, people want to be fit and healthy, and we want to have safe, reliable transportation. These are first-order desires. What many advertisers do is to try to get us to fulfill those desires with particular commodities – a Baywatch Barbie doll, a membership to a certain gym, or a given make and model of car. In this sense, marketers have a double job. The first is to promote the general want and then to persuade us that their product is the ideal way to realize it. Sometimes advertisers work from the second order to the first: often we have first-order desires to see ourselves in a certain way, perhaps as a handyman or a sportswoman, and advertisers tell us that if we buy a certain product, such as a particular drill or treadmill, then it will transform us into the person we want to be. The morally questionable aspects of advertising come when it confronts personal autonomy, for example, when it is deceptive, affects vulnerable populations such as children, or appeals to inauthentic desires. In the CortiSlim case, people had a natural first-order desire to be healthy, but there were a number of routes to that end: more exercise, better nutrition, less stress, and so forth. The job of the marketer was to persuade consumers that they could achieve their legitimate goal without making any significant changes to their lifestyle, and they conveyed that message through morally problematic means that affronted autonomy by going as far as presenting a fake news broadcast, with actors pretending to be scientists, as legitimate.

Puffery is a form of advertising that uses subjective, exaggerated, or humorous claims to promote a product.[19] Thus the soft drink Snapple uses the slogan, "Made from the best stuff on earth," and Burger King boosts its food with the claim, "It just tastes better." Often these ads are in the form of a comparative – "faster and more effective" – without presenting a contrasting product, and sometimes they use strained analogies – "solid as a rock."[20] But as long as the advertisement is sufficiently transparent that a reasonable person can see that it is not making a factual claim, it does not offend autonomy.

As we have seen, persuasion has the effect of giving someone sufficiently good reasons that the person adopts them as his or her own, whereas deception, manipulation, and coercion all give bad reasons or force a decision in such a way that it is not really a choice. Thus, if a commercial claims that "the most beautiful women on earth" use a cosmetic, we might regard it as subjective puffery, whereas if it claims that a product is effective in reducing cholesterol and invites the audience to research the claims in scientific journals, that would be persuasion. However, if it seeks to promote the product by suggesting that it is endorsed by the government when in fact it is not, or that failure to respond to a mailing will trigger a tax audit, then it becomes morally questionable.

Many people who have grown up surrounded by commercials approach them with a degree of skepticism, and a reasonable consumer may not take all claims at face value without confirming their veracity. Still, there are some populations that are more easily exploited than others. For example, some financial institutions that cater to low-income groups that have poor credit by offering ready cash actively promote their services but are not always forthright in explaining the details of their short-term loans, or overweight people may consistently purchase diet pills despite evidence that the only effective programs involve regular exercise and restricting calorie intake. Additionally, there may be cases where the product is addictive, like tobacco. The argument would be that only the first few cigarettes are a matter of personal choice, and after that the nature of the addiction precludes autonomy. The moral issue frequently returns to whether the individual has the wherewithal to make a truly autonomous decision.

---

[19] The term arises from a rigged auction where a confederate of the seller would make sham bids in order to inflate or "puff up" the price.

[20] Rogier van Bakel, "Tall-Claims Court: When Does Advertising Puffery Become Customer Deception?" *The Christian Science Monitor* (February 14, 2000).

Advertisers target children. Between the age of 2 and 11 the typical child in the United States watches an average of 21 hours of television per week and half have a television in their bedroom. Children are typically incapable of the kinds of discernment necessary for autonomy. Thus many children cannot tell the difference between cartoon characters in shows and those used to promote goods during commercial breaks, and many associate sugary cereals with the cartoon characters on the boxes.[21] While it is true that most spending is by adults rather than children themselves, studies suggest that "pester power" is highly effective, and parents often buy children specific products to lessen domestic tension.[22] One answer might be to make parents more aware of the effects of advertising on their children. Another is to use the power of government to ban certain types of pernicious advertising, such as tobacco campaigns with cartoon characters that children find attractive. The advertising industry has moved ahead of government in this area and has drawn up codes that discourage certain types of advertising, including those that exhort children to make demands on their parents or take advantage of their credulity.[23]

An interesting development in promotion of products to children has been the increasing sponsorship of educational materials to schools and institutions. Many US schoolchildren watch "Channel 1," a privately produced newscast for students with twelve minutes of news and two of commercials. Critics note that students retain little of the news but are good at recognizing the advertisements, which cost sponsors twice as much as ads on regular television.[24] Many companies provide educational materials directly to schools, and these materials often have a specific bias. Promotions include Revlon lessons in self-esteem that deal with "good and bad hair days" and an Exxon video that downplays the environmental impact

[21] David Schumann, "Using Animated Spokes-Characters in Advertising to Young Children: Does Increasing Attention to Advertising Necessarily Lead to Product Preference?" *Journal of Advertising* (September 22, 2004).

[22] Subir Bandyopadhyay, Gurprit Kindrea, and Lavinia Sharp, "Is Television Advertising Good for Children? Areas of Concern and Policy Implications," *International Journal of Advertising*, 20.1 (2001), pp. 89–116.

[23] See: National Advertising Review Council, http://www.narcpartners.org/; Children's Advertising Review Unit, "CARU Launching Complete Review of Children's Advertising Guidelines," News Release, New York (February 6, 2006); Advertising Standards Authority (UK) at http://www.asa.org.uk/asa/, accessed March 16, 2006.

[24] Chris Bocking, "Corporate Sponsorship," *Teacher Newsmagazine*, British Columbia Teachers' Federation, no. 3 (1997).

of the *Valdez* spill.[25] Schools strapped for money are often willing to accept corporate money and logos to boost their budgets. These practices may not be bad as long as those affected are able to perceive what is going on: some commentators suggest that corporate materials ought to be reviewed for accuracy and objectivity before distribution, and their presence will be an opportunity for students to have a greater awareness and critical assessment of media.[26]

We should also recognize that there might be times when commercials produce a societal good through a breach of autonomy. For example, we could imagine an anti-smoking commercial that is deliberately shocking and manipulative yet successful. These ads raise questions about advertising in general – are its devices only morally suspect when they encourage ends we disapprove of? In the next section we look at discrimination, where autonomy is often trumped by other societal goals.

## Autonomy in the workplace

The very nature of contractual employment restricts personal autonomy. The employer requires a worker to turn up at a given time, demands a level of productivity, and may have further restrictions such as dress codes or limited breaks. Some positions that involve interacting with others often have specific expectations or even a script that employees are required to follow. These restrictions are typically accepted as part of the nature of work. The challenge to autonomy comes when the values of the individual employee clash with those of the company to the point where the company intrudes on one or more of the conditions for autonomous action: the individual employee's liberty may be restricted, the employee may not be given appropriate information, or the employee may be coerced in various ways. Thus moral issues arise if, say, an employee is forced to give up legal activities that have no bearing on workplace performance, is not warned of potential dangers, or is trapped by practices such as debt bondage whereby the person cannot leave the job until the employer is paid off.

The traditional understanding has been "a fair day's work for a fair day's pay" and that what happens off the clock is not the employer's business.

---

[25] John Borowski, "Schools with a Slant," *The New York Times* (August 21, 1999).
[26] Glori Chaika, "The Selling of Our Schools," *Education World* (October 5, 1998).

However, developing technology has altered the nature of the relationship, since measures of success – including ability, motivation, and personality – can be tested with increasing accuracy prior to employment. Moreover, current employees may be monitored for a variety of reasons, chiefly to measure productivity empirically, but also to discourage internal theft and fraudulent compensation claims, to identify troublemakers, and to maintain workplace health and safety.[27] These concerns are not ungrounded. One survey by a monitoring software firm found that most workers repeatedly visited news sites during company time, and a third regularly used their company computer to access auction sites.[28] Companies also feel there are liability concerns if e-mail is used improperly or workers visit inappropriate websites. Some of the ways that employees can be monitored include software that automatically checks keystroke rates and web usage, as well as management eavesdropping on telephone calls and scrutinizing e-mail. Some firms use so-called smart cards that enable employees to be located at any time. The issue of intrusion is more pronounced in the United States where employers pay for the medical benefits of their workers and so have a vested interest in keeping premiums low by hiring relatively healthy workers and discouraging dangerous activities.[29]

## Autonomy and drug testing

We'll now look at three controversial cases: employers can legally discriminate against workers on the basis of drug testing and psychometric assessment, but not on the basis of their own immaterial prejudices. The framework of autonomy will help us make some useful distinctions and analyze the ethical issues involved.

In the case of substance abuse, potentially catastrophic consequences may justify mandatory testing – for example, of pilots, bus drivers, or crane operators. However, in other cases, there are three types of justification that are usually invoked.

---

[27] Rory O'Neill, "Stop Snooping," *Hazards Magazine* (n.d.), available at http://www.hazards.org/privacy/, accessed March 11, 2006.

[28] http://news.bbc.co.uk/2/hi/technology/2278743.stm, accessed March 11, 2006.

[29] The tradition of employer heath coverage in the United States began as social policy through the implementation of favorable tax breaks during the depression as a way of getting around mandatory wage caps.

The first is a productivity claim. Here the contention is that a worker will be less efficient and therefore deprive the employer of his due. It has been estimated that drug abuse drains more than $100 billion from American businesses every year and that substance abusers are one-third less productive.[30] Appropriate testing can weed out abusers and make the workplace safer and more productive. Undoubtedly, there is some truth to the claim. Still, the argument boils down to an empirical one of whether the testing provides the benefits that it purports to. That is, if the test is accurate and reveals one employee out of 200 will test positive, the question becomes whether the deterrent effect and the removal of the worker justify the costs involved. This could be a business decision and from a managerial perspective there need not be a moral component at all.

Some critics have suggested that it would be more effective to test workers for their abilities such as hand/eye coordination rather than their drug use, on the grounds that if performance matters most, then that is what we should test for, given that more workplace accidents are due to fatigue and illness than to substance abuse.[31] Furthermore, many over-the-counter products may have significant effects – for instance, a worker could have taken a common antihistamine and be drowsy, or be suffering from a bad hangover, and both could cause poor judgment and lowered productivity even though they would not be detected by a routine drug test. The claim becomes muddier when we consider that an employer may use legal means to enhance productivity, such as providing unlimited free caffeine and sugary snacks if they promote efficiency, even though they are potentially harmful.[32]

Another line of argument defending drug testing is based on legality. Some drugs are illegal, and an employer has the right to fire a worker for breaking the law, or lying on an application. While this is straightforward, the locus of concern is legality, and therefore it would not, by itself, address issues of abuse of alcohol or other substances.

[30] *Working Partners: National Conference Proceedings Report*, Washington, DC (July 13–14, 1992). Sponsored by the US Department of Labor, the Small Business Administration, and the Office of National Drug Control Policy.

[31] Joan O'C. Hamilton, "A Video Game that Tells if Employees are Fit to Work," *Business Week* (June 3, 1991).

[32] Similarly, a firm might play unavoidable background music: DMX, a major producer, claims that nine out of ten managers say it creates a positive environment and can increase sales up to 40 percent: DMX homepage at http://dmxmusic.com/music_branding.htm, accessed March 14, 2006.

The third position defending testing for drugs and other activities is a moral one. Here the employer disapproves of certain actions, whether they be using soft drugs, smoking cigarettes, or body piercing, and may discriminate on that basis. Discrimination, as we shall see, may be a manifestation of autonomy in that it reflects the capacity to decide between choices, but at the same time some forms of discrimination may be morally unacceptable.

One potential problem with testing is that we have the technology to find out more than an employer needs to know. For example, although body fluids can be tested for the presence of drugs, they also yield information at the genetic level. Most firms confine their tests to illicit substances, but the possibility remains that samples could be screened for health traits that may be hidden from the individual – for example, the tendency to early neurological disease or diabetes. As firms put a premium on productive individuals, and especially when they are involved with health care costs, there will be a temptation to use available information to assess applicants and monitor current employees.

## Autonomy and psychological testing

Another form of compromised individual autonomy can come from psychometric testing. These are usually "bubble tests" that determine a personality profile through such questions as, "Are you happy with the way you look?" Or, "Do you like looking at intricately designed buildings?"[33] They are designed to give employers more accurate insights than letters or interviews and are used by roughly half of the companies in the United States and the United Kingdom.[34] Psychological tests were originally used for military recruitment, and they can be invaluable in selecting appropriate personality types for careers such as police work. In business they can be a useful tool, although the testers usually suggest that they should be used in conjunction with other information. In England the tests gained some notoriety when an 18-year-old, who had just been promoted because of his superior work performance, was fired from his job on the basis of his test results.[35]

[33] Adrian Furnham, "The Truth Will Out," *The Guardian* (UK) (April 24, 2001).
[34] American Management Association, *Workplace Testing: Basic Skills, Job Skills, and Psychological Measurement* (New York: AMA Publications, 2000).
[35] Susannah Prain, "My Week," *The Independent* (UK) (April 21, 2001).

One feature of these tests is that the answers themselves may not matter as much as the patterns that surface. If you have a sufficient sample size of a population with a specific trait, say, clinical depression, and they all answer particular questions in a certain way, those questions can then be embedded in another test; and if a subject's responses correspond with the sample group, it provides evidence that the subject shares the trait. Therefore tests may be used to gauge more than basic characteristics like sociability or attention to detail and they may indicate psychological problems or histories that are not strictly related to the job. If such information surfaces, a prudent employer might err on the side of caution and refuse to hire or move to terminate. Here again, the moral issue involved is whether an employer is entitled to use any and all the data from these tests, even in cases where it may be inaccurate or hard to verify.

## Autonomy and discrimination

Discrimination is not intrinsically bad – we use the phrase "discriminating palette," for instance, to describe someone who has good taste, and one of the jobs of a teacher is to give grades to students based on differing ability. Discrimination is also manifested in a manager's promotion of the most able or qualified candidate for a position. Autonomy would be inhibited if the choice were constrained in some form. Nevertheless, there may be cases where we think that it is appropriate to override an employer's autonomy for the sake of societal justice.

A maxim of proper discrimination is that equals ought to be treated equally. The reason that we may choose one over another is that there is a material difference – that is, some factor pertinent to the decision at hand. Discrimination becomes immoral when it employs irrelevant factors. Thus, all other things being equal, applicants for a job that requires data entry may be screened on the basis of their clerical accuracy, and firefighters need strength and dexterity, but it would be inappropriate to use race or gender as a factor. We license people on the basis of professional qualifications, and so there would be no problem in requiring a dentist or pilot to demonstrate proficiency prior to employment. Moreover, although some classes of people have certain abilities in general, we ought not to look to the class but to the individual. Thus although men usually have greater upper body strength than women, we ought not to exclude all women on those grounds, but look instead to individual qualities.

However, there are two cases where autonomy and discrimination clash dramatically. The first is the case of an employer who, for whatever reason, may prefer to choose employees on grounds not necessarily related to job performance. These may not reflect bigotry on the part of the employer – perhaps female students at a university health clinic prefer women gynecologists, for example, or bank customers in a given neighborhood prefer someone of a similar heritage. In this case, the employer risks business by not catering to the demands of the clients. There may also be instances where there is a demand for a service that many would find morally objectionable – perhaps a restaurant with a beach theme that only employs skimpily dressed young women or one that has an Old South plantation theme where the wait staff are treated as slaves. If there is a demand, and the workers themselves have no issues with working there, are we infringing on their autonomy by imposing values on them? Here again we encounter the claim that the market can decide the issue: if people truly disapprove of discrimination, then they will not patronize those businesses, and the market will react accordingly to align itself with the values people signal through their pocketbooks.

In the United States, the issue has been answered politically instead of relying on the market, largely on the grounds that those who are hurt by discriminatory practices do not have sufficient market power to create the correct signals, and so the government has enacted legislation that prohibits discrimination on certain grounds, including race, gender, religion, national origin, marital status, age (if over 40), and disabilities.[36] In broad terms, the laws are designed to protect traditionally unempowered groups. Thus firms cannot selectively hire only men, or routinely ignore applications from Hispanics, and must make reasonable accommodations for religious observance. There is an important exception, in that there may be jobs where discrimination has to be allowed: for example, a theater hiring for Lady Macbeth is allowed to audition only women, or a police department may require that street officers are physically fit. These conditions are technically known as Bona Fide (in good faith) Occupational Qualifications or BFOQs.

[36] US Equal Employment Opportunity Commission, "Federal Laws Prohibiting Job Discrimination: Questions and Answers," (Washington, DC: Government Printing Office, 2002), available at http://www.eeoc.gov/facts/qanda/html, accessed December 20, 2006. Relevant laws include Title VII of the 1964 Civil Rights Act; the 1963 Equal Pay Act; 1967 Age Discrimination in Employment Act; the 1990 Americans with Disabilities Act; and the 1991 Civil Rights Act.

The protection against discrimination is not absolute, though. There is currently no federal mandate prohibiting an employer from firing someone on the basis of sexual preference, obesity, or political allegiance, for example. Ninety percent of Americans work under a doctrine known as Employment at Will (EAW), which means that both employers and employees may sever their contract for any reason at all, or even without a reason. Nominally, it balances the rights of both sides, although a worker fired with no due process or reason may become tainted when looking for new employment – a new employer will often suspect that someone was let go for a reason even if it was never openly stated, and shy away from hiring that person. An employer may still fire someone from a protected group, say, women or minority group members, for any reason except explicit discrimination, and the onus will be on a member of a protected group to show that there has been a pattern of selective discrimination. The philosophical issue, in contrast to the legal regulations, will turn on whether there are sufficient moral grounds to compromise the cardinal principle of self-determination by an employer in cases where those choices lead to unjustifiable discrimination.

## Whistleblowing

Finally, we should look at one more variation on Mill's bridge analogy: as originally formulated, bystanders should warn the person crossing in order to preserve his autonomy. If we reverse the conditions, so that the individual crossing realizes the bridge is unsafe, he would have a correlative duty to warn anyone else about to cross to maintain their autonomy, too. In plain terms, if a company or employee finds a dangerous or potentially immoral activity, then they have a duty to warn other stakeholders (sometimes called whistleblowing). Thus it was appropriate for Bausch & Lomb to withdraw a contact lens solution from the shelves and publicize its actions once they determined that it could lead to an eye infection, information that consumers might not readily find out.[37] Correspondingly, it was morally suspect that several high-ranking managers in Enron sold their stock before the public found out that the company was insolvent and share prices

[37] "Bausch & Lomb Recall of ReNu with MoistureLoc Contact Lens Cleaning Solution," US Food and Drug Administration News Release, Washington, DC (May 15, 2006).

plummeted.[38] Because the stakes are often very high in these cases – for example, an employee could falsely accuse the company, or there could be an unnecessary recall – it is incumbent on every party to follow regular reporting channels where possible, and make sure the information is correct, timely, and pertinent. Still, if there is risk of great harm or even death, then we may well have a duty to inform those involved, whatever the consequences turn out to be.

## Summary

Autonomy is a powerful claim in human interaction, and in the developed West it is often thought of as a cardinal virtue. However, as we have seen, in a workplace setting individuals are often in the position of shifting their values to align more closely with those of the employer in one form or another, and conversely employer decisions can be overridden if there are compelling societal reasons. The issue of autonomy may, oddly enough, oftentimes boil down to working out the specific situation at Mill's figurative rickety bridge. Recall that if the person is unaware that it is dangerous, Mill says we can only interfere if there is no alternative such as shouting a warning. However, there may be times when we as a society are unaware of the nature and consequences of our actions, and need to be made conscious of the realities of practices such as racial discrimination before we are allowed to proceed.

In the case of consumer choice and the way advertising affects us, it is not immediately clear that there is much harm involved: if someone wants to spend their money on worthless weight loss potions like CortiSlim or other gimmicks, then they will pay accordingly for a lesson in being a discerning shopper. Nevertheless, this is often not the full story, since some products and services may violate the conditions of autonomy to prey on the weak and vulnerable members of society, and there we may have a duty to protect them, just as if the person on the bridge were hard of hearing.

---

[38] Mimi Swartz with Sherron Watkins, *Power Failure: The Inside Story of the Collapse of Enron* (New York: Doubleday, 2003); "Former Enron Chief Executive Officer Jeffrey K. Shilling Charged with Conspiracy, Securities Fraud, Insider Trading," US Department of Justice press release, February 19, 2004, available at http://www.usdoj.gov/opa/pr/2004/February/04_crm_099.htm, accessed December 28, 2006.

The free market gets its name from the ability of consumers and producers to make autonomous choices. Consequently we should take self-governance very seriously, and be clear about the times when the principle may be justifiably violated, perhaps for a person's own good, or the good of society as a whole.

## General issues for discussion

1. What do you consider appropriate grounds for overriding someone's personal decisions? Would you, for instance, prevent the sale of home body piercing kits or child pornography, and if so, on what grounds?
2. Is it morally acceptable for employers to discriminate against the obese or unattractive? Are there reasons that we should force employers to curtail their discrimination?
3. If individuals want to live a life of thrills and indulgence that may lead to an early death – for example, eating fast food and drinking alcohol as a staple diet – should society restrict them? What is the role of the companies who cater to their whims?
4. Do you think employers should see any moral difference between an employee using marijuana at home on the weekends, say, as opposed to abusing over-the-counter medicines, if there is no perceptible difference in work performance? What are appropriate reasons for using drug tests at work?
5. Is it reasonable for companies to sell goods and services using high-pressure tactics to people who are most vulnerable to those techniques? What moral criteria are appropriate to guide company policy in this regard?

## Case – Jodie Brooks

Jodie Brooks was given a portable MP3 player for her fifteenth birthday. Typically these devices are small data recorders that are capable of playing back music through ear-bud type headphones. Unlike larger units that have cups that fit over the ears, these units fit in the ear canal. Proponents enjoy the way they are discrete yet provide excellent sound quality.

About a year later, Jodie woke one morning to a persistent ringing noise in her ears. Doctors advised her that she was suffering from tinnitus, a condition that can be brought on by prolonged exposure to loud noises. In her case, there was no medical treatment except for a device that produced "white noise" to reduce her perception of the constant background buzzing. Although the condition sometimes goes away over time, she was advised that it would likely continue throughout her life. At the time of her exam she was also found to have lost some hearing in high frequency ranges.

Jodie had been particularly fond of rap music with resounding bass notes. She typically would listen to her player for over four hours a day, and sometimes those around her would ask her to turn down her music although she was using earphones. From time to time she would turn the volume way up to overcome background noise, for instance, when using a leaf blower or mowing the lawn.

There were no labels on the unit, although the booklet that came with it had a notice that read:

Warning: Constant exposure to loud noise may lead to hearing impairment.

Some studies suggest that hearing can be threatened at 80 decibels. Many portable music devices can play at 105 decibels, or even higher if used with specialized headphones. A lawnmower averages about 100 decibels, and a rock concert or aircraft taking off is about 120. The decibel scale is exponential, so that each increase represents a much louder noise, or much less time for damage to occur. Hearing is largely a function of tiny hairs that resonate within the eardrum, and some experts have made an analogy to grass – it can be trampled and recover, but with repeated exposure, some of it will never mend.

The European Union has instituted regulations that keep players below 100 decibels. There are no such limitations in the United States or Canada.[39]

## Some questions from the case

1. Who is responsible for Jodie's hearing loss and tinnitus?
2. Is she due any compensation?

---

[39] Adapted from news reports, including BBC News, "*MP3 Users Hearing Damage Warning*," available from http://news.bbc.co.uk/go/pr/fr/-/2/hi/health/4162028.stm, accessed August 18, 2005.

3. Does her age affect your analysis? What role should her parents have taken?
4. Are portable music players a known danger to the manufacturers? To the consumers?
5. Do you believe that young people will continue to listen to music at potentially damaging levels even if they have been warned about the dangers? Should the manufacturer or the government restrict their ability to do so?

# 8    Beneficence

## Wal-Mart

Wal-Mart is the world's largest retailer, and every store sells copies of the biography of its founder, Sam Walton, that expounds his personal philosophy. As he wrote in 1992, Walton believed that it was inappropriate to use corporate funds for charitable purposes:

> We have built a company that is so efficient it has enabled us to save our customers billions of dollars, and whether you buy into the argument or not, we believe it. That in itself is giving something back, and it has been a cornerstone philosophy of our company . . . we feel strongly that Wal-Mart really *is not* and *should not* be, in the charity business. We don't believe in taking a lot of money out of Wal-Mart's cash registers and giving it to charity for the simple reason that any debit has to be passed on to somebody – either our shareholders or our customers . . . By not designating a large amount of corporate funds to some charity which the officers of Wal-Mart may happen to like, we feel we give our shareholders more discretion in supporting their own charities.[1]

The Wal-Mart attitude changed radically in twelve years, and in this chapter we will examine some of the possible reasons why corporations should allocate resources towards the common good. In 2004, Wal-Mart cash donations to charity were the largest in the United States, at over $170 million. It supported over 5,000 reading programs and ran a literacy hotline serving over 40,000 people annually. Wal-Mart awarded over 6,000 college scholarships and honored 3,500 teachers with its "Teacher of the Year" program. The company has received awards for community initiatives and was

[1] Sam Walton with John Huey, *Sam Walton: Made in America* (New York: Doubleday, 1992), pp. 239, 240.

lauded by *Fortune* magazine as the "Most Admired Company in America".[2]
The Wal-Mart foundation aims to help local community organizations such
as Boys' and Girls' Clubs, the YMCA, and local school districts, for example,
rather than making large donations to national charities.[3] It also donated
phone cards to relatives of service personnel serving overseas and gave over
$7 million to victims of hurricanes in Florida and Alabama. Employees are
also strongly encouraged to offer their own time, with the "Volunteerism
Always Pays" program that recorded over three quarters of a million volunteer hours in 2004.

## Degrees of beneficence

In this chapter we examine the notion of beneficence. Acts that bring about
good are beneficent. Beneficence is distinguished from benevolence, since
benevolence is the *desire* to do good, not the actual performance of good.
Philosophers make further distinctions in the concept, suggesting that we
should (a) not inflict harm, (b) prevent harm, (c) remove harm, and finally,
(d) promote the good.[4] The broad principle of beneficence is usually supplemented by norms drawn from ethical theory about the priority of the
elements listed above and how we should resolve conflicts between them.
As a general rule, we tend to think it is more important not to cause harm
than to create the good.

Initially, following Sam Walton's view, there may be no reason for a company that obeys local laws to give anything at all, because successful business
practices benefit society as a whole. As the CEO of Nestle contends, companies should not feel obligated to give back to the community since they
owe nothing: "What the hell have we taken away from society by being a
successful company that employs people?"[5] The investment that occurs and
the wealth that is created within a capitalist system are seen as beneficial:

---

[2] http://www.walmartstores.com/GlobalWMStoresWeb/navigate.do?catg=50, accessed June
30, 2006. In fairness, we should note many also hate Wal-Mart. See, for example, "The
Very Bottom Line," Special Report, *The Economist* (December 24, 2005).

[3] Liza Featherstone, "Wal-Mart Charity Evaluated: Critics Question Company's Motives,"
*The Nation* (November 21, 2005).

[4] William Frankena, *Ethics* (Englewood Cliffs, NJ: Prentice-Hall, 1973), p. 47.

[5] Jennifer Powell, "Nestle Chief Rejects the Need to 'Give Back' to Communities," *Boston
Herald* (March 9, 2005).

corporate activity is the engine that drives modern society, and that in itself should be a sufficient payback. Moreover, firms pay taxes and help provide employment that spurs other economic activity. Still, as we shall see, this view is less widely held that it used to be, and the vast majority of major firms now engage in beneficent behavior of some kind, and several have made it a cornerstone of their mission.

The language used in business ethics discussions in this area may be confusing: *corporate social responsibility* (CSR) is a pervasive term, yet like the parent concept of responsibility it has a wide range of meanings and applications. Compliance with the law is seen as a minimal requirement for the proper operation of business, and CSR is frequently used to describe any action that a firm takes over and above its legal obligations. In the United States the term is often used to refer to the duty of business to pay back to the community, typically in various forms of corporate philanthropy. The European model of CSR is more wide-ranging and suggests that a firm should have a commitment to the overall welfare of society by integrating concerns about the environment, employees, the community, and other stakeholders, as well as moving toward more sustainable business practices. Here we will focus on the practices of philanthropy, community involvement overseas, and affirmative action, using the more specific terminology of beneficence, while recognizing that the term CSR may be used by practitioners in a variety of applications.

## Corporate beneficence

The weakest form of beneficence is non-malfeasance, or not doing harm. While this may be straightforward in discrete personal actions, we have to recognize that most business activity involves some incidental damage, which will lead us to use a proportionality test to balance outcomes.

Sometimes rights act as boundaries for acceptable behavior, and often this notion of non-malfeasance in terms of rights is what firms themselves mean by corporate social responsibility. As we saw in a previous discussion, rights can override utility calculations, and thus for many firms the bedrock notion of corporate social responsibility translates into a company's commitment to upholding fundamental rights. Thus Chiquita, a major fruit supplier, speaks in its report on social responsibility that it is working to make sure that it complies with international standards to make sure that employees have a living wage and do not have to put in excessive hours.[6]

Many companies have publicly adopted the international SA8000 certification of social responsibility. SA8000 is awarded after an independent body inspects a company's practices and demonstrates that it complies with minimum standards regarding child labor, health and safety, collective bargaining, non-discrimination, and bargaining rights.[7] Similarly, the United Nations Global Compact has nine principles of economic, social, and environmental rights that afford protections. These principles tend to cluster around the baseline understanding of beneficence, since they demand that companies avoid harm and be legally compliant, but they do not impose a further obligation to promote the good.[8]

## Motivations for beneficence

When we move away from businesses avoiding harm toward a positive duty to bring about good, the discussion inevitably involves questions of motive, and so we now consider what might cause a company to apportion assets toward that end. After all, upholding human rights can be seen as a minimal ethical threshold, and responsibility for harm can lead to legal liability and consequent payments for compensation, whereas the payoff for doing good is less obvious.

There are four basic reasons why a company may act beneficently.[9] The first is purely instrumental, where a firm's paramount objective is to return wealth to its owners. Therefore if it appears that consumers will patronize a company more if it is engaged in community action, then the company will respond to the market signal. Thus if shareholders express disquiet about various policies, say, not getting involved in arms sales or dealing with corrupt regimes, then the company would only be acting in its own self-interest to respond to those concerns. Beneficence here is a means to an end, and if the evidence shows that the company would be better off by offering cheaper prices and ignoring community involvement, then it will switch its tactics.

---

[6] http://www.chiquita.com/chiquitaCR01/OPerformance/sp_p20_21.asp, accessed June 24, 2006.

[7] www.cepaa.org, accessed May 24, 2006.

[8] http://www.unglobalcompact.org/, accessed May 24, 2006.

[9] This typology is based on Elisabet Garriga and Domenec Mele, "Corporate Social Responsibility: Mapping the Territory," *Journal of Business Ethics*, 53 (2004), pp. 51–71.

The instrumental view relies on evidence, but unfortunately the data may be difficult to determine and may have mixed results. That is, some companies that are committed to beneficent action appear to do well, but that does not necessarily mean that they do well for that reason – perhaps they have the stability and wealth to run community action programs without hurting their profitability.

Although the evidence of a positive correlation between corporate beneficence and profitability is inconclusive, a Pepperdine University study looked at the way companies were affected by negative publicity. They examined the 1999 World Trade Organization (WTO) meeting in Seattle and the effect of the subsequent negative publicity on the targets of protestors. The study took Fortune 500 firms in similar industries and identified those with reputations for exploiting labor and damaging the environment that were highlighted through the protests. In concrete terms, they showed that the firms considered lacking in social responsibility lost an average of 3 percent of their market capitalization – an average of $418 million each. The researchers concluded that there is a "crisis value" in having a good reputation, in that it acts like insurance against poor public perception.[10]

There is little evidence one way or another that companies deliberately engage in beneficent acts to guard against bad publicity, and so it could be a fortunate side effect of a prior commitment to adopt ethical practices. At the same time, though, a strategically minded company might realize that having a reputation for beneficence is a relatively cheap and effective safeguard against bad publicity.

The same sort of claim might be made about companies that are involved in controversial practices or with questionable regimes, since spending a great deal on civic projects and philanthropy may tend to blunt criticism and force observers to at least acknowledge that they are also bringing good into the world. Some commentators have linked Wal-Mart's dramatic increases in charitable giving to widespread criticism about its employment practices, televised news stories about exploiting undocumented workers, and opposition to new stores.[11]

---

[10] Karen E. Schnietz and Marc Epstein, "Does Corporate Social Responsibility Pay Off?" *Graziadio Business Report* (Pepperdine University, Malibu, CA), 7.2 (2004), available at http://gbr.pepperdine.edu/042/responsibility.html, accessed December 21, 2006.

[11] National Committee for Responsive Philanthropy, Washington, DC, *The Waltons and Wal-Mart: Self-Interested Philanthropy* (October 4, 2005).

A second reason for corporate beneficence takes a wider view and suggests that a company's continual growth and sustainability require investment in the overall social welfare of the communities where it does business. This reasoning differs from the merely strategic by seeing that integration in society is a necessary component for its existence. Thus as the president of a business school noted, the next billion personal computers are not going to be sold in the United States and Europe but in the developing world, and companies in that industry have a vested interest in creating a middle class in those countries.[12]

A third reason for business beneficence is grounded in the notion of a social contract. Typically, states or local governments incorporate businesses. The benefits of incorporation include limited liability, so that investors are only responsible for losses up to the amount of their investment, and stability for the corporation beyond the lifetime of its members. From these benefits that the society has bestowed on business comes a sense of reciprocity – that the corporation ought to repay the society in some way. Business has a symbiotic relationship with society, so that each fosters initiatives that ultimately benefit both. Historically, corporations and government have been interdependent, and paying back to the community may be a partial recognition that companies need to maintain good relationships, especially in contemporary times when a number of traditional government functions such as mass transit or security are now increasingly handled by private, for-profit ventures, and companies such as McDonald's or Wal-Mart may be more capable of providing disaster relief than the federal government. This view is often expressed by the term *corporate citizenship*, with the idea that corporations have both responsibilities and privileges, just like other members of society, and they need to act accordingly, or even that corporations have additional rights and burdens because of their greater power and influence.

The vast majority of the world's largest companies have sites on the World Wide Web.[13] When we look at their home pages, there is almost always a statement or link to corporate responsibility or corporate citizenship that

[12] Dr. Angel Cabera, "Corporate Social Responsibility: The Key to Global Business Success," Foreign Press Center Briefing, Washington, DC (March 2, 2005).

[13] This analysis draws on Jamie Snider, Ronald Paul Hill, and Diane Martin's research, "Corporate Social Responsibility in the 21st Century: A View from the World's Most Successful Firms," *Journal of Business Ethics*, 48.2 (December, 2003), pp. 175–188.

echoes a citizenship approach. For example, IBM has a page with links dedicated to "our company," "our people," and "our world." It claims:

> A modern corporation serves many purposes and interests – almost as many as the people with whom it comes into contact. Understanding our business and our relationships is key to understanding IBM . . . In our commitment to communities, our management of environmental concerns, and our advocacy for enlightened policy, we don't just seek near-term results – we also want lasting impact.[14]

In a similar vein, the banking concern Citigroup announces:

> Citigroup has long been committed to making the communities in which it operates better, and at the same time, setting standards for business practices and corporate values that exceed industry norms.[15]

It offers links to a variety of reports, including a fifty-six page report on Citigroup's efforts to enhance the welfare of communities that host its operations. The opening page of General Electric has an extract of a letter from the chairman that says, "We are committed to performance with integrity and to being a good global citizen . . . GE, by virtue of its products and services, and its performance, plays a vital role in both business and society. In fact, I believe that we have the opportunity to make an impact that few companies can."[16] Exxon Mobil also has a banner that goes directly to a page on corporate citizenship and links to subcategories such as education, health, biodiversity, and conservation.[17] The Home Depot site also links directly to a page on corporate responsibility that states: "we seek to be profitable, responsible, and balance the needs of our communities . . . the Home Depot strives to have a positive impact on communities in the U.S., Canada, and Mexico. We also invite the community into our stores to participate in practical and educational programs that benefit children and adults."[18]

These postings are highly significant. They give a clear and consistent message that most of the world's leading companies take corporate social

---

[14] http://www.ibm.com/ibm/responsibility/, accessed October 26, 2005.

[15] http://www.citigroup.com/citigroup/citizen/index.htm, accessed October 28, 2005.

[16] http://www.ge.com/en/citizenship/overview.immelt_letter.htm, "Letter from Jeff Immelt," accessed October 28, 2005.

[17] http://exxonmobil.com/Corporate/Citizenship/gcr_mainpage_categories.asp,      accessed October 28, 2005.

[18] http://corporate.homedepot.com/wps/portal/How_We_Help, accessed October 28, 2005.

responsibility seriously and that ethics plays a large part in their public announcements. Through their language, we can see that corporate
responsibility to a wider community and the environment has been widely
adopted.

Critics could easily charge that these postings represent rhetoric, what
economists call "cheap talk," words that benefit the company but incur no
expense. However, the accusation of hypocritical grandstanding fails under
close scrutiny. If they were solely designed to improve the economic bottom
line, we would expect some clear justification based on potential returns
or their benefits compared to their costs. Instead, companies rarely justify
beneficence at all but assert it as an accepted given for corporate behavior.
The expenditures listed as corporate social responsibility are rarely item-
ized or tracked closely in corporate reports. Moreover, the vast number of
programs and initiatives that companies have funded without precise performance monitoring suggests that they represent a true commitment rather
than an investment in economic terms alone.

The fourth reason for beneficent behavior is that companies naturally
accept that positive ethical duties are embedded in the practice of business,
and therefore responsibility to the community is a normal part of corporate
activity. A strongly normative stakeholder view of the corporation, such as
the one promoted by R. Edward Freeman, suggests that the function of
the firm is to maximize the welfare of all stakeholders, and so a business
would predictably have positive duties to communities, government, and
other constituents such as Non-Governmental Organizations (NGOs) such
as Oxfam, Greenpeace, Amnesty International, and the Red Cross. A recent
concrete expression of this sort of claim is found in the Caux Principles, a
set of aspirations drawn up by a number of influential business leaders. They
suggest that business should be grounded in two basic principles: human
dignity and *kyosei*. *Kyosei* is a Japanese term roughly translated as living and
working together for the common good.[19]

Having looked at the conceptual framework that supports business
beneficence, we now turn to three operational applications: corporate philanthropy, corporate social intervention overseas, and the promotion of
diversity.

---

[19] http://www.cauxroundtable.org/principles.html, accessed May 24, 2006.

## Corporate philanthropy

In the United States at the turn of the twentieth century, several mighty corporations were seen as a powerful threat to society. Partly to improve their public image, these companies began giving considerable sums to charity.[20] Henry Ford initiated health and recreation programs for his workers. J. D. Rockefeller gave away hundreds of millions of dollars, and his funding helped eradicate hookworm in the American South. He boosted the building of the University of Chicago through donations of over $35 million. The wealthy magnate Andrew Carnegie set up an educational fund, the Endowment for International Peace, and founded over 2,000 libraries. Carnegie also wrote a book, *The Gospel of Wealth*, where he publicized his belief that the wealthy have an obligation to help the less fortunate:

> The best means of [the wealthy] benefiting the community is . . . returning . . . surplus wealth to the mass of their fellows in the form best calculated to do them lasting good . . . The man who dies leaving behind him millions of available wealth, which was his to administer during life, will pass away "unwept, unhonored and unsung" . . . Of such of these the public verdict will then be: "The man who dies thus rich dies disgraced."

Notably, like Sam Walton of Wal-Mart, he disdained pure charity: he only believed in giving that would encourage people to subsequently help themselves.

> Neither the individual nor the race is improved by almsgiving . . . He is the only true reformer who is as careful and as anxious not to aid the unworthy as he is to aid the worthy[21]

One legacy from the early days of corporate giving is that very little of current giving is in the form of unconditional handouts, and it typically tries to avoid recipients becoming dependent on charity. As the adage goes, if we give a man a fish, he may eat for a day, but by teaching him to fish we feed him for a lifetime.

---

[20] This analysis is based on Myra Wulfson, "The Ethics of Corporate Social Responsibility and Philanthropic Ventures," *Journal of Business Ethics*, 29.1–2 (January, 2001), pp. 135–145.

[21] Extracts from Andrew Carnegie, *The Gospel of Wealth and Other Timely Essays*, ed. Edward C. Kirkland (Cambridge, MA: Harvard University Press, 1962), p. 29.

Much of today's philanthropy has the deliberate aim of boosting the company image and creating good will. The fastest-growing form of philanthropy is what is called "cause-related marketing," where a firm will donate a proportion of its receipts to an organization. For example, it may say that 1 percent of all profits will be sent to the World Wildlife Fund, or five cents will be given to saving the rainforest for every bottle of a particular brand of beer purchased during a certain period. The practice was started when American Express linked use of its card to corporate donations toward restoring the Statue of Liberty in 1981. According to studies, 54 percent of consumers say that they would pay more for a product that supports a cause they endorse, 75 percent would switch to a brand that is associated with a cause if that were the only competitive difference, and 84 percent believe cause-related giving creates a positive image for the company.[22]

The success of cause-related giving is both astonishing and something of a puzzle. In the wake of Hurricane Katrina, some enterprising car dealerships were offering to donate $100 for each car bought during a certain period to homeless victims. Although the sentiment is well placed, it is economically odd to put an extra $100 premium on a car (assuming that the $100 does not come from dealer profits) and then have the dealer send the money to the appropriate charity. If we wanted to help, say, breast cancer research, wouldn't it make much more sense to donate directly to the cause, rather than have it go through an intermediary level of bureaucracy?

Consumers are attracted to this type of brokered giving for two possible reasons. The first is that the giving is actually a conscience salve for purchasers of luxury goods, since very few of the goods involved are basic staples but rather discretionary purchases. In reality, no one really needs high-fat ice cream, yet it is much easier to justify buying it if we think of it as a way of helping out nut producers in rainforest areas. The action is thus easier to understand as a licensing act that allows us to make a purchase where we previously had misgivings.

Another reason for this type of consumer purchase is that cause-related giving helps people to overcome a psychological impasse in deciding between competing products. In the research, three-quarters of those surveyed would choose an item if giving to a good cause were the only significant difference

<hr/>

[22] Wulfson, "The Ethics of Corporate Social Responsibility," p. 142.

between it and a rival. This means that appeals to our better nature are very effective – more so than brighter packaging or coupons, for example.[23]

Cause-related giving has been criticized on several grounds. For instance, in the United Kingdom, the chain store Tesco promoted a program called Computers for Schools that raised over $15 million. However, consumers needed to spend over $500,000 to generate sufficient vouchers for a $2000 computer.[24] The open question is whether the extra sales spawned by the promotion far exceeded the value of the charitable giving, that is, whether the schools would have been better off asking for direct donations in cash instead of cooperatively encouraging extra spending at the store. A typical response is that it is a "win/win" effect since companies have very large advertising budgets and marketing structures, so charities do well by coordinating their fundraising with a corporation.

A major ethical issue with strategic philanthropy is whether we should just accept that good is brought into the world, even though the motives may indeed be explicitly instrumental. For example, when a company gives money to charity as a marketing ploy, it may end up doing well by doing good, and the charity receives money it might not have otherwise. Once again, the key to analyzing the issue may lie with consumer attitudes – we may be reluctant to give to charity directly, despite the obviously greater efficiency, and it may be that we are more willing to donate when we feel guilty about purchases or want to do the right thing without sacrificing an affluent lifestyle.

However, not all corporate giving is exclusively instrumental. Drawing on our earlier framework, there may be times when a company engages in philanthropy that goes beyond immediate returns: it may be looking at the market with a long-term perspective in order to work out what will sustain the business over time in a global market, or the leadership might consider that corporate giving should be separate from bottom-line concerns altogether. In the United States there are several significant legal cases that uphold the right of a company to make gifts without any concern for maximizing shareholder return. The landmark ruling in 1953 came when a New Jersey court

---

[23] See, for example, Hamish Pringle and Marjorie Thompson, *Brand Spirit: How Cause Related Marketing Builds Brands* (New York: John Wiley & Sons, 1999).

[24] Terry Macalister, "Ads that Make it Add Up," *The Guardian* (UK) (November 25, 2002).

said that a corporation had a right to be socially responsible when it made a donation to Princeton University over the objections of shareholders. A later case in 1991 upheld a $50 million donation by Occidental Oil to construct a museum, without any evidence that the museum would return any profits, based on the vast net worth of the company.[25] The upshot is that there is a tradition of corporate philanthropy as an accepted part of normal business, and as far as law reflects societal policy, investors should not automatically expect an economic justification for giving to worthy causes.

American corporations and corporate foundations currently donate about $25 billion annually.[26] Ted Turner, the founder of the news network CNN, pledged $1 billion in 1997 to the United Nations Children's Fund. In 2004 the largest corporate donors in the United States were the pharmaceutical company Pfizer ($1.2 billion), followed by Merck ($979 million), Bristol-Myers Squibb ($666 million), Johnson & Johnson ($529 million), and Microsoft ($410 million).

Corporate giving surrounds us: many college buildings are named after benefactors, and students often use computers and software donated by private companies. Many of our great cultural landmarks such as concert halls and libraries were funded by large corporate donations. Donations are not always in the form of cash, however. One of the largest donors in the United States has been Mentor Graphics, which gave $100.2 million in contributions in 1994, but of that $100 million was in the form of computer software donated to colleges and universities.[27] A lot of Apple Computer and Microsoft's donations to higher education establishments have been in the form of software, licenses, and grants. Pfizer's giving topped $1 billion largely because it provided low-cost medicine to serve about 2 million poor and uninsured people.

Some of these donations are undoubtedly strategic in the sense that it is beneficial to the firm to promote the use of their proprietary materials in a competitive market, and their charitable donations may attract tax breaks. Staged fanfares when corporate donations are announced also point to a

---

[25] See generally, Einer Elhauge, "Sacrificing Corporate Profits in the Public Interest," *New York University Law Review*, 80 (June, 2005), pp. 733–869. The relevant cases are *A. P. Smith Mfg. Co v. Barlow*, 13 N.J. (1953); *Theodora Holding Corp. v. Henderson*, 257 A.2d 398 (Del. Ch. 1969); and *Kahn v. Sullivan*, 594 A.2d, 48, 61 (Del, 1991).

[26] "Giving USA" site, http://www.aafrc.org/gusa/, accessed October 20, 2005.

[27] Wulfson, "The Ethics of Corporate Social Responsibility," p. 137.

public relations dimension to the act. At the same time, though, there are clearly cases where goods, services, or cash are donated with no evident return on investment, in either the short or the long term.

A litmus test of giving is to determine whether it drops during hard times, in that pure beneficence may imply a disregard of bottom-line concerns. A common vehicle for corporate philanthropy is the foundation, a setup that was created when tax breaks were allowed for corporate giving as part of Roosevelt's New Deal in 1935. Money is transferred from the parent company to the foundation, and thus is accounted for separately from the main business. In the United States a foundation must give away at least 5 percent of its assets every year. The Bill and Melinda Gates Foundation, with an endowment of almost $30 billion and a pledge of another $30 billion from the magnate Warren Buffett, funds thousands of educational programs, and has donated hundreds of millions of dollars to the development and distribution of vaccines for malaria, AIDS, and other diseases.[28] One result of splitting foundational giving from the parent organization is that there is a continuity of giving even in an economic downturn, and so using a foundation represents a persistent commitment to doing good. General Motors maintained the same level of charitable donations in 2005 as the year before, although GM had a bad year with dramatic stock declines and announced that it would reduce its workforce by 25,000.[29]

In short, although some argue that the operation of capitalism has brought great harm to many in the world, it is also evident that corporations have brought about many benefits. Strictly speaking, many of these corporate actions are unnecessary, in that they are over and above what is morally required. The outstanding philosophical issue that we must address is how we judge their actions in light of what are sometimes morally dubious motives.

## Corporate social intervention overseas

We can also use the language of beneficence to assess the actions of companies in their dealings with communities abroad. Corporations have

---

[28] http://www.gatesfoundation.org/AboutUs/, accessed June 3, 2006.
[29] Ian Wilhelm, "Corporate Giving Rebounds," *The Chronicle of Philanthropy* (August 4, 2005), pp. 7–18.

sometimes been instrumental in promoting civic and social programs in their overseas operations, and they have the power to be agents of great good or pernicious wrongs.

It is useful to begin with a look at corporate intervention in a historical light, since many of the issues appear much clearer with the passage of time. During the apartheid era in South Africa (1948–1992), there was official state-sanctioned racial segregation in all walks of life. Non-whites were not allowed in certain areas without a pass, black unions were not recognized, and black education was rudimentary at best. Partly because of poor labor conditions and low wages, owning and operating a plant in South Africa could be highly profitable.

Throughout the period, US businesses were heavily invested in the South African economy, especially in mining and oil. Reaction in the United States was mixed: many investors and campus activists demanded that firms and colleges withdraw their funds from companies dealing with the regime, whereas others felt that the presence of US companies could be a force for improvement, a policy known as *constructive engagement*. In the midst of the controversy, the Reverend Leon Sullivan drew up a set of voluntary – and unenforceable – principles (the Sullivan Principles) that companies working in South Africa could publicly agree to abide by, thus disarming some of the controversy. Of the 284 US companies in South Africa, about a quarter assented to the principles and allowed public review of their operations.[30] Ford Motors, for instance, ran management training centers for black workers and desegregated workplaces, in direct opposition to apartheid policies.

In retrospect, the evil of apartheid is apparent, and the Sullivan Principles espousing non-discrimination and integration are non-controversial. However, as Patricia Werhane has pointed out, there is a moral question with the original sixth principle: "Improve housing and education opportunities for employees outside the workplace."[31] Again, while initially the principle seems innocuous, it actually moves from refraining from harm to active intervention to promote good. Moreover, it advocates doing so by using the

---

[30] John. E. Parsons, "On 'Constructive Engagement' in South Africa," *The Tech* (MIT student newspaper), 105.47 (November 5, 1985), p. 42.

[31] Patricia Werhane, "The Moral Responsibility of Multinational Corporations to be Socially Responsible," in W. Michael Hoffman, Robert Frederick, and Edward Petry, eds., *Emerging Business Ethics* (Westport, CT: Greenwood Publishing, 1990), pp. 136–143.

firm's influence within a sovereign nation. Perhaps companies should be a force for promoting good in this way, but Werhane notes there are significant risks as well. Generally a company is a guest in a host nation, and it is therefore subject to the native laws and customs. The company always has the option to not do business with a regime that acts in a way contrary its beliefs. So, if a country systematically represses women – say, in a way that a US company would not tolerate domestically – it may withdraw rather than try to change national practice.

There are several reasons for Werhane's caution. Following Mill, we might ask if we are interfering for the right reasons and in the right way. In a pluralistic world, what appears to us to be wrong may turn out to be acceptable practice, and we should be wary of being imperialistic, especially when dealing with deeply held religious and social traditions. Additionally, many companies lack the expertise to deal with social issues. This is not to say that a company should not do good in cooperation with a host country when invited to do so: for instance, the pharmaceutical company Merck helping sub-Saharan river blindness victims by supplying free drugs would be unproblematic.

Once more we may have to take a broad perspective about beneficent action and ask whether all things considered it causes more harm than the status quo; if so, the company should cease its activism. In the case of apartheid, the wrong was so grievous that careful corporate intervention could be justified. In contrast, during the 1950s, US concerns, especially the United Fruit Company (UFCO), were directly involved in manipulating development and sometimes regimes in Central America. UFCO provided free schooling for children of employees and built many ports and railroads. At the same time, it discouraged road construction (which would have challenged its monopoly on the railroads) and did everything it could to prevent the government from buying back land from the company. In that case, the overall harm probably did not justify the benefits from corporate intervention.

Many of the social issues that companies encounter overseas are not clear-cut, and it is not always obvious that the host country shares our values. When we beneficently promote the welfare of others, it is incumbent on us as the donors to make sure that the intervention is both welcome and appropriate, or conversely, that pulling out or boycotting a country will be effective and not hurt those we are trying to help. This is why the language of the Caux Principles is unambiguous in demanding collaboration between donors and the groups they are trying to assist.[32]

## Corporate promotion of diversity

The framework of corporate beneficence we have developed also gives us a way to assess corporate action in the face of apparent societal injustice. One element of the Sullivan Principles reads: "Work with governments and communities in which we do business to improve the quality of life in those communities – their educational, cultural, economic, and social well-being – and seek to provide training and opportunities for workers from disadvantaged backgrounds" – an apparent call for business to strive to help some groups within society by providing them with a job and prospects. Notoriously, firms tend to be homogeneous – over 95 percent of corporate chief executives are white males, for example – and women and minority groups are typically underrepresented. The moral question that a firm faces is whether it should act beneficently to advance underrepresented groups and, further, what level of action is appropriate.

Promoting diversity can be very awkward for a workgroup. In the words of Phillip Cox, chairman of Cincinnati Bell: "This is very threatening and difficult for our employee base . . . these are not racist people, but we are all prisoners of the familiar. And that means we don't get up in the morning and say 'I think I'll go out and make myself as uncomfortable as I can by dealing with someone who is very different from me.'"[33] Moreover, there comes a point where the deliberate promotion of members of one group clash with the rights of non-discrimination of another – for instance, deliberately putting an African American woman on an executive fast track may upset the moral maxim of treating everyone equally.

The move toward diversity can be manifested in a number of ways. The emergence of civil rights legislation has outlawed much direct discrimination, and so at its most modest, a firm might follow the law and not

---

[32] "Collaborate with those forces in the community dedicated to raising standards of health, education, workplace and economic well-being": http://www.cauxroundtable.org/principles.html, accessed May 24, 2006.

[33] Jennifer Pellet, "Driving Diversity: CEOs Get It: Diverse Work Forces Make for Better Companies. The Question Is, How Do You Get There?" *Chief Executive*, 198 (May 1, 2004), pp. 48–55.

discriminate against protected groups. Thus in the United States, it is unlawful to selectively refuse to hire people over 40 on the basis of their age.[34] A company would no longer run ads saying "Candidates over 40 need not apply," and would make sure that age is not a topic of discussion during the interview. However, we can see that, all in all, no longer actively discriminating might not be sufficient. The structure and the culture of the firm need not change, and just because discrimination is no longer overt does not mean it will go away – it may persist but in a more subtle form.

In order to stem the perpetuation of harm, it may be necessary to promote the good by engaging in programs that break a cycle of discrimination, known broadly as *affirmative action*. For example, a firm that has traditionally only interviewed candidates from selective universities based on personal recommendations might decide that it is morally appropriate to widen the candidate pool. To that end, it may conduct interviews at colleges that it has never visited before, or actively invite underrepresented group members to apply. We should note at the outset, however, that all forms of affirmative action demand that candidates have the requisite qualifications, so, for example, an engineer needs to be suitably credentialed, and no one without that degree will be considered.

The next major issue to consider is how much diversity is desirable. One kind of affirmative action is as a tiebreaker, where, all things considered, an employer may use diversity to choose between two equally qualified candidates. A stronger version would be where a less (but still appropriately) qualified candidate is chosen. A further consideration might be that candidates from a less privileged background deserve more credit for achieving equal qualifications, given the adversity that they likely experienced along the way.

Sometimes a firm has fixed goals for diversity, known as quotas, but these are less common than they used to be and now companies tend to look for a general ratio without making strict numerical allocations. The change reflects a difference in approach from twenty years ago, when much affirmative action was considered a compensatory mechanism for societal ills such as the horror of slavery. The older view had a number of problems: the beneficiaries were not necessarily those harmed by the practice; it would be difficult to know when enough compensation had been provided; and

---

[34] http://www.eeoc.gov/types/age.html, accessed May 31, 2006.

using the same kind of discrimination against the majority that had been used on the minority was thought to be a case of "two wrongs not making a right." Affirmative action is now more likely to be justified by appealing to a claim that business should reflect the makeup of society in general, both on moral and economic grounds. While this does not entirely address concerns about unequal treatment, it moves from dealing with the past to constructing the future.

As we saw with other applications of beneficence, how extensive it is depends in large part on the motivations involved. Robin Ely of the Harvard Business School has identified three different motivational strands promoting diversity. She calls the first the "integration-and-learning" perspective, which primarily draws on the experiences of the various cultural groups as resources that can be tapped to enable the firm to redefine its markets, products, strategies, and business practices.[35] Research also suggests that increased diversity has been linked to enhanced problem solving and greater organizational creativity.[36]

In contrast, the "access-and-legitimacy" view recognizes that diversity within an organization gives it a strategic advantage and provides entry into previously neglected markets. As one insurance firm CEO recounted,

> The Hispanic market is the largest-growing market for our products in the
> United States, yet none of the people we were having distribute our
> products in those markets were Hispanic . . . Once we started hiring and
> recruiting people from those ethnic markets, we found that our products
> did not relate to these people at all. So we had them put together projects
> to change our products and market efforts so that we can actually access
> the markets.[37]

The third motivation is less strategic. A "discrimination-and-fairness" view takes the position that having a culturally diverse workforce is a moral imperative to ensure justice and fair treatment for all members of society.

[35] R. J. Ely and D. A. Thomas, "Cultural Diversity at Work: The Moderating Effects of Work Group Perspectives on Diversity," *Administrative Science Quarterly*, 46 (June 2001), pp. 229–273.

[36] Jacqueline Gilbert, Bette Ann Stead, and John Ivancevich, "Diversity Management: A New Organizational Paradigm," *Journal of Business Ethics*, 21 (1999), pp. 61–76.

[37] Pellet, "Driving Diversity," p. 54, quoting Michael Roth, chairman and CEO of The MONY Group, a New York-based financial services holding company.

It goes beyond legal minimums and actively counters prejudicial attitudes so that the diversity of the workforce comes to represent just and fair treatment of all employees. Justifications for this diversity need not refer to the bottom line. In the words of the CEO of Albertson's Food chain, "We don't look for any statistics. This has to be in the DNA of a company."[38] Similarly, the head of Kodak, Daniel Carp, described the effort to increase diversity: "Trying to build a commitment to diversity solely on quantifiable dollars and cents diminishes the importance of the endeavor . . . the higher level piece is a top line benefit. This country was built on diverse groups coming together."[39]

As we found in the other manifestations of corporate beneficence, the various reasons to do the right thing are rarely discrete and typically overlap. For example, General Motors, the world's largest automaker, announces on its website:

> GM has long been committed throughout its global operations to hiring people with varied backgrounds. This hiring practice is the right thing to do, but just as important, it creates a competitive advantage for GM. Having a workforce that reflects the marketplace helps GM more effectively reach customers and provide products and services they want.[40]

The case of Denny's restaurant serves as a useful illustration of several issues involved in beneficence and diversity management. On the same day that Denny's restaurant settled a discrimination lawsuit in 1993, six black US Secret Service agents were kept waiting for an hour while white customers were served and then offered second helpings. Other charges against Denny's included that the restaurant apparently demanded that people of color pre-pay for their food without requiring the same of whites. In the 1990s, Denny's had no minority corporate officers, and only one of their 512 franchises was run by an African American; 67 percent of blacks reported that they would not even consider going to a Denny's.

However, the turnaround at Denny's has been dramatic. In 2006, the company appointed its first woman as chair of the board, and by that time over

---

[38] Lawrence R. Johnson, quoted in Brian Grow, Steve Hamm, and Louise Lee, "The Debate over Doing Good," *Business Week* (August 15, 2005).

[39] Pellet, "Driving Diversity," p. 51.

[40] http://www.gm.com/company/gmability/workplace/400_diversity/index.html, accessed May 31, 2006.

half the board and senior management were women or people of color and minority employees accounted for a third of all management. Forty-five percent of the franchisees – 455 restaurants – were from minority groups. Over a million people have attended Denny's diversity training program, which is compulsory for all employees. It has become a major contributor to the Martin Luther King Center in Memphis.[41] In recent years, *Fortune* magazine has consistently ranked Denny's as one of the best workplaces in the United States for minorities and women.

The change was initiated in the face of mounting losses and legal demands. However, Denny's has gone far beyond legal compliance. Under the leadership of Jim Adamson, the company integrated diversity into its performance criteria for managers and has made it a priority in everything they do. Although it is hard to give sole credit to the change for making the company profitable, it seems apparent that Denny's would have floundered if it had done nothing. The head of diversity training promoted active recruitment, searching out executives, franchisees, and suppliers of different racial and ethnic backgrounds. In her words, "Blacks attend black schools. You have to fish where the fish are."[42]

The charge of discrimination still remains, though. A well-qualified white executive could reasonably complain that he was being discriminated against if the position were given to a less-qualified minority candidate. The push for diversity was justified on economic grounds and legally mandated, but that does not answer the moral issue of whether race or gender should ever be taken into account. One argument is that businesses should be color-blind and gender-neutral in hiring and promotion. In response we might consider that the posture of neutrality is not always fair: if an older sibling fights with his little brother, and the parent settles the dispute by sending both to bed early, equal treatment will certainly seem unjust to the younger child.[43] There may be cases where circumstances warrant active intervention, especially if there is a history of unequal power and entrenched attitudes that prevent equal opportunity.

---

[41] http://www.Dennys.com/en/cms/Diversity/36.html, accessed June 1, 2006.

[42] "The Woman Behind Diversity at Denny's," *The Black Perspective* (Spring, 2001), Available at http://www.blackperspective.com/pages/mag_articles/spr01_diversityatdennys.html, accessed June 1, 2006.

[43] The example is derived from Alan Montefiore, ed., *Neutrality and Impartiality* (Cambridge: Cambridge University Press, 1975), p. 7.

Using the language of beneficence, we can see that in the early 1990s Denny's was both causing harm and complacent about what was going on, and hence there was a moral imperative at least to stop the prevalent discriminatory practices. Recall that the affirmative action need not be compensatory and is often designed to reconstitute the structure of a company. The question is not necessarily whether there is discrimination – which, at first glance, selection by gender or race certainly is – but whether it is justified on material grounds that are sufficiently compelling to override other considerations. That is, discrimination is only morally offensive when it is applied on immaterial grounds. It is perfectly acceptable to require that a surgeon have a medical degree or that firefighters can lift heavy objects: the problem arises when choices are made that have no relevance to the case in point.

Here again we have to employ a proportionality test to tell us whether the good achieved through promoting diversity overcomes the potential harm of using race and gender as criteria for hiring and promotion. To help with this calculus, we could widen the issue and look at the notion of merit. Often diversity discussions suggest that merit is traditionally determined by paper qualifications which minority group members may not exhibit to the same extent, with the result that affirmative action in this regard amounts to an unwarranted handout. But if we take a broader view of merit, then we may consider that background experiences and cultural awareness have value just as education and work experience do, thus justifying consideration of minority status, but only in the context of assessing the overall potential of a hire. By the same argument, though, discrimination along these lines would no longer be justified once diversity goals had been met.

Managing diversity has been a success at Denny's. Its bottom-line performance has improved, and employees and customers report greater trust in the brand. At the same time, the Denny's example demonstrates an important lesson about beneficent action. The firm undertook a complete revamping of its approach rather than give only lip-service compliance. In Adamson's words, "I am going to do everything possible to provide better jobs for women and minorities. And I will fire you if you discriminate."[44] It involved re-educating the whole workforce, starting from top management who were described as "all white males – nice people, but all from the

---

[44] Faye Rice, "Denny's Changes its Spots," *Fortune*, 133.9 (May 13, 1996), pp. 134–135.

same geographic area, the same schools, and the same age groups."[45] The entire culture now incorporates mandates of respect for all types of people and the value of diversity. Denny's approach differs from many other companies that have put programs in place that have amounted to wider recruitment and an expectation that new hires will then conform to the traditional culture.[46] Studies show that purported benefits from diversity can only be fully realized if the firm takes a thoroughgoing integrative approach.[47]

## Summary

We have applied the framework of beneficence to these three topics – philanthropy, intervention, and diversity – and have found recurring themes about the delicate balance a firm needs to maintain between economically strategic and ethical issues.

The most persistent disquiet about corporate beneficence in general is that without a great deal of understanding, expertise, and monitoring, it can cause unintended bad results. For example, the socially conscious ice-cream makers Ben and Jerry's started an initiative to buy brazil nuts for a new product called Rainforest Crunch to thwart Amazonian deforestation. The idea was that the forest dwellers would form cooperatives and sell directly to Ben and Jerry's, thus eliminating the middleman and preserving the land.[48] Ben Cohen, one of the founders, announced, "The success of our Rainforest Crunch shows that harvesting brazil nuts is a profitable alternative for Amazon natives who have seen their lands ravaged to create grazing areas or for mining."[49] Unfortunately, the very success of the flavor meant that the cooperative could not produce the quality or quantity of nuts needed, and Ben and Jerry's began to buy from commercial enterprises in the region. The increased demand stimulated large-scale nut

---

[45] "Ray" Hood-Phillips, quoted in "The Woman Behind Diversity at Denny's".

[46] David Thomas and John Gabarro, *Breaking Through: The Making of Minority Executives in Corporate America* (Boston: Harvard Business School Press, 1999).

[47] Nicola Pless and Thomas Maak, "Building an Inclusive Diversity Culture: Principles, Processes and Practice," *Journal of Business Ethics*, 54 (2004), 129–147.

[48] Oma Feldman, "Rain Forest Chic," *The New Republic* (June 25, 1990).

[49] Jon Entine, "Rain Forest Chic," *The Globe and Mail Report on Business Magazine* (Toronto), (October, 1995), available at http://www.jonentine.com/articles/rainforest_chic.htm, accessed June 2, 2006.

farming and prices plummeted. The cooperative could not compete, and eventually native growers sold off their land to big business to recoup their losses, while the government used the increased trade as a reason to cut aid to the region. The case shows that unless a company is extremely sensitive to cultural issues, well-intentioned intervention in a foreign country may result in negative consequences to a traditional way of life and social order.

Beneficent affirmative action may also miscarry. Paradoxically, under the discrimination-and-fairness approach aimed at benefiting minority groups, people of color across work groups described feeling that they were always being judged in terms of their minority status, and management became more reluctant to give them negative feedback and wanted to avoid conflict at all costs, with the effect that they felt membership in their racial group hampered ordinary relations to the point of powerlessness and disenfranchisement.[50]

Beneficence in the form of philanthropy may come with a price to the recipient, too. Schools that accept sponsored educational materials (SEMs) may have children discussing the flourishing wildlife in Valdez, Alaska (courtesy of Exxon), chocolate as part of a healthy diet (provided by Hershey), or the innocuous impact of the greenhouse effect (promoted by the American Coal Foundation), saying that the earth could benefit rather than be harmed from increased carbon dioxide. School administrators may also accept donations from firms that come with corporate logos or have notice boards and newscasts that come with advertising.[51]

These findings reinforce the lesson that beneficence simply imposed from above is at best likely to be ineffective and transient and at worst will transgress the minimal moral requirement of doing no harm. Returning to Wal-Mart, whatever the motives behind their philanthropy, it has been especially effective largely because they have targeted local and specific community projects. It has been adept in leveraging its giving into good public relationships, and this has been a model for other firms. Their tactic has led to a somewhat incongruous dynamic where people may disapprove of big corporations, but are happy with the low prices and social involvement

---

[50] Ely and Thomas, "Cultural Diversity at Work," p. 255.

[51] "Captive Kids: A Report on Commercial Pressures on Kids at School," Consumers Union, Washington, DC (1998), available at http://www.consumersunion.org/other/captivekids/index.htm, accessed June 2, 2006.

of their neighborhood store. We may conclude, then, by recalling an earlier theoretical discussion about impartiality, and how we do feel more responsibility for those we can identify with, contrasted with abstract needs. Whatever form of beneficence a firm engages in, research establishes that it is most successful when the donor and recipients can communicate well, have a shared vision of program goals, and are committed to a long-term relationship.

## General issues for discussion

1. How much do you think we should be concerned about corporate intentionality? That is, if corporate beneficence does good, as opposed to doing bad, or nothing at all, why should we complain?
2. Does it matter what proportion of corporate profits a company gives? For example, in 2002 Wal-Mart gave almost $200 million to charity when its overall profit was about $12 billion.
3. Tax breaks are a significant factor in corporate philanthropy. What effect do you think it would have if companies were no longer allowed to deduct charitable donations?
4. Is affirmative action desirable? What would be a measure of its success?
5. What do you understand by the term "corporate social responsibility"? On a scale from "Do no harm" to "Bring about the good," what level of action should businesses take? What reasons are there to do more or less?

## Case – tobacco philanthropy

Smoking is bad for you. It also fuels a highly profitable industry.

In 1990 the gay, lesbian, bisexual, and transgender (LGBT) community was faced with the HIV/AIDS epidemic against a backdrop of ignorance and discrimination. Jesse Helms, a senator from North Carolina, was a leading opponent of AIDS research funding and civil rights for LGBT people. The activist group ACT-UP (AIDS Coalition to Unleash Power) staged a number of high-profile demonstrations to highlight awareness. One of their targets was Helms, and they proposed a boycott of Philip Morris's products – Marlboro cigarettes and Miller beer – because of the company's longstanding support for the senator.

The boycott did little to hurt sales, but it did create bad public relations. In response to the boycott, Morris launched a traveling exhibit of the US Bill of Rights that purportedly highlighted its concern with civil rights, whether they were for smokers or gays. However, part of the exhibit had a soapbox where visitors were encouraged to exercise their First Amendment right of free speech. LGBT activists used the platform to denounce the company, and the exhibit was soon closed.

LGBT activists and company representatives eventually met, and a Morris vice-president wrote to gay publications emphasizing the company's support for the community. In part it said, "Philip Morris supports legislation to make it illegal for an employer to discriminate against current or prospective employees because of avocational activities."[52] Later the company announced that it would make a donation of over $1 million to AIDS-related causes and continue support "throughout the epidemic's duration," and the boycott was quietly dropped.[53]

The result caused controversy within the LGBT community. Some saw it as a necessary evil justified by an imminent lethal threat, whereas others saw it as blood money from a corporation responsible for millions of early deaths. In the months following, Morris gave money to the Gay and Lesbian Alliance against Defamation (GLAAD) and started to advertise in the gay press. In the years since, it has touted its commitment to diversity, noting its non-discriminatory hiring policy and domestic partner benefits for gay couples, and the Positive Helpings program that feeds people living with AIDS. The company has also sponsored the Atlanta Gay and Lesbian Film Festival and the Miss Gay U-S-A At Large Pageant.[54]

For undetermined reasons, smoking rates within the GLBT community are over 50 percent as compared to about 25 percent in the general adult population.

---

[52] G. Smith, "Philip Morris Speaks Out on Helms/ACT UP Controversy," *Gay Community News* (September 16, 1990). Quoted in N. Offen, E. A. Smith, and R. E. Malone, "From Adversary to Target Market: The ACT-UP Boycott of Philip Morris," *Tobacco Control*, 12 (2003), p. 204.

[53] J. Zeh, "Activists Split on Ending Philip Morris Boycott," *San Francisco Sentinel* (June 6, 1991).

[54] Perry Stevens, Lisa Carlson, and Johanna Hinman, "An Analysis of Tobacco Industry Marketing to Lesbian, Gay, Bisexual and Transgender (LGBT) Populations: Strategies for Mainstream Tobacco Control and Prevention," *Health Promotion Practice*, 5.3 (July, 2004), pp. 129–134.

## Some questions from the case

1. If a corporate donation creates good, does it matter what the company does or why it gave the money?
2. Should Philip Morris be required to announce the source of its wealth and the dangers of its product alongside publicity about its good works?
3. What sort of philanthropy do you think this case represents? Would it make any difference if their donations were anonymous?
4. Would your views change if it turned out that the company gave similar amounts at the same time to lobbyists for both sides of an issue?
5. What distinguishes corporate philanthropy from advertising?
6. One commentator described the donations as "a few tax-deductible crumbs off Philip Morris's very well stacked table." Should we be critical of the source of funds that can be used to promote the good?

# 9   The environment

## Mine tailings

Very little business activity does not create waste and pollution. A fundamental part of capitalist activity is to produce consumer goods – that is, to turn raw materials into finished commodities. In mining, for example, we may have to mine over 200 tons of ore to furnish enough gold for twelve wedding bands. The ore is often washed with a mix of water and cyanide to extract the gold and other minerals such as sulphur and mercury. Ideally, the leftover slurry is treated and kept in holding tanks.

Mines often bring prosperity to the surrounding areas – local people are employed, roads are constructed, and the company may develop local health clinics and other community initiatives – yet they remain controversial.[1] In Turkey, the world's largest gold mining company, Newmont, based in Denver, Colorado, closed its operations on the Aegean coast after residents complained to the European Court of Human Rights about excessive cyanide pollution, despite government support for the development at the local and national level.[2] Newmont also admitted that it released more than 17 tons of mercury into the atmosphere and dumped 16 tons into the sea near Sulawesi Island in Indonesia during a five-year period between 1997 and 2002, but said that the emissions complied with all US and local regulations. By way of comparison, companies in the United States are required to restrict emissions and contain them as much as possible: for instance, the Xcel Energy plant in Pueblo, Colorado, released only

[1] Michael Riley and Greg Griffin, "The High Cost of Gold," *Denver Post* (December 12, 2004).

[2] Registrar, European Court of Human Rights, Chamber judgment in the case of *Ta Kin and others v. Turkey*, application 46117/99 (November 10, 2004), available at http://www.echr.coe.int, accessed May 7, 2006.

16 pounds of mercury vapor in 2003, while their filters captured another 118 pounds.[3]

Newmont has been under scrutiny after a company truck spilled over 300 pounds of liquid mercury when a container fell out of the back of an open truck near the village of Choropampa in Peru. Local children picked up and played with the silvery liquid and later mine officials offered to buy it back, leading to villagers using their bare hands to recover it off the road.[4] Mercury is highly toxic and tends to accumulate in body organs. A liquid at room temperature, it will form easily absorbed microscopic particles if disturbed. Local residents now complain of blindness, neurological damage, memory loss, and muscular pain. Officials from the Newmont mining company say that opportunists have exaggerated claims stemming from mining pollution. They also say that they have responded quickly and thoroughly to any incidents, and they cite illegal miners as a significant source of any contamination.[5]

## The impact of business on the environment

Gold mining is a useful illustration of some of the major issues in the relationship between business and the environment. There is a consistent market for gold, and it offers significant profits to producers. It brings greater prosperity to the mining region by offering employment and tax income locally, and the companies often develop the local infrastructure by creating roads and construction projects for their workers. Regional and national governments often welcome mining companies. On the other hand, mining operations may cause immediate damage and long-term deleterious effects to plants, animals, and people in the area. The landscape is rarely restored to its previous state and may be permanently scarred. The environmental costs are rarely incorporated in the final price to the consumer, are hard to quantify, and are sometimes hidden.

These factors pose problems for business ethics in that most classical theoretical frameworks are primarily concerned with the relations between

---

[3] Jeff Smith, "Mercury Admission: Newmont Concedes it Released 17 Tons of Metal into Air in Less Than Five Years," *Denver Rocky Mountain News* (December 23, 2004).

[4] Peter Hecht, "Peasants in Peru Near Showdown on Mercury Spill," *Miami Herald* (5 March, 2005).

[5] Smith, "Mercury Admission."

people and do not necessarily incorporate our duties to animals and the environment generally. Moreover, there are significant problems in working out the nature and extent of harms involved, since there are both immediate and direct consequences and almost unpredictable future interests. In this chapter we first look at the ways that we can approach environmental issues and then more particularly examine the means to value the environment. We will then consider the move toward sustainability and what implications it has for business practice.

## Approaches to business and the environment

Two of the hallmarks of capitalism are growth and consumption. Countries seek to increase their national product annually. The "rule of 70" is useful here: if we want to find the doubling time of a quantity growing at a given annual percentage, we divide the percentage into 70 to find the number of years. This shows that if an economy grows at the relatively modest pace of 3.5 percent, it will double in twenty years, and some economies like China (10 percent in 2006) or India (7 percent) will double in much less.[6]

While an expanding economy has the promise of greater prosperity, it also increases the burden on the world's resources. The same logic also applies to world populations: in 1900 the world population was about 1.5 billion, and by 2000 it was 6 billion. Each successive billion has been achieved in an ever-shorter time. At current rates, we add at least 85 million people to the planet every year. While estimates of future numbers are largely speculative, it is fair to say that the earth has finite resources. If we continue with present practices, a higher standard of living for the current population will put an additional burden on the environment, as will any increase in population.

Consider many modern personal electrical devices: they operate on integrated circuits, and if they go wrong it is cheaper and easier to replace them than to have them repaired. Similarly, many plastic containers will probably end up in a landfill not long after purchase and last for thousands of years. The plastic products are likely made with energy drawn from burning coal, and production usually creates waste products that we then have to dispose of. These consumption patterns would not be problematic if there were an

---

[6] http://www.cia.gov/cia/publications/factbook/, accessed May 8, 2006.

infinite supply of raw resources. However, at present-day rates we will leave the earth more depleted of its natural wealth for future generations.

Our attitude to the environment is reflected not only in the way we deal with goods, but with services as well. If we go on vacation to Las Vegas, we use fuel that puts hydrocarbons into the upper atmosphere during the flight, and then we will enjoy air conditioning that pours additional heat outside, the city prospers in the desert with imported water and electricity, and we play golf on courses of regularly fertilized and irrigated Kentucky grass.

As an initial step, we should recognize that as producers and consumers we make thousands of small decisions every day that affect our environmental quality, and these decisions are not the choice between having a pristine environment or a polluted one. Instead, we make constant compromises between our convenience and wants and our desire for a clean planet. So, for example, if we decide to drive to work, that has both direct and indirect effects: directly it gets us where we are going earlier and in greater comfort but at the cost of burning finite petrochemicals and producing exhaust. Indirectly, we contribute to a culture of independent drivers that stimulates car production, causes planners to cater to greater traffic demands, and sends signals to the oil industry about consumer preference. Thus we are constantly involved in a trade-off, and in economic terms we will tolerate pollution up to a point where we are indifferent to the greater benefits it brings: perhaps we will be unconcerned about more smog in the air until we have to buy air filters and personal oxygen supplies, and at that point we will have an incentive to change our economic choices.

There are a number of different ways that business can approach environmental questions. First, there are questions of how to value our world. "Deep ecologists" would suggest that the biosphere has intrinsic value and is priceless in the sense that, like love, it cannot be considered a commodity to be exchanged for money. For them, the issue of how to value a forest of old-growth trees would be meaningless, because they do not feel that market terminology can even apply to decisions about the environment. Others feel that there are ways of assigning monetary values and applying cost/benefit analysis, and so the problem to overcome is in refining the methods involved. Additionally, some people believe that the world has abundant natural resources that should be exploited for our benefit, whereas others want to make sure that each generation lives so that the world can be replenished without leaving a legacy of deficit. Another view is that of ecofeminists, who consider the way we deal with the environment as mirroring the domination and exploitation that has historically characterized relations between the sexes, and their view is that we need to regard relationships between each other and the planet in more considerate and cooperative ways.

The classical philosophical approaches that we looked at in earlier chapters hold that ethics is anthropocentric – that is, human welfare is the central concern, and humans are the creators and arbiters of value. However, this assumption has been challenged by those who feel that the environment should be thought of as a total system, where humans have a place but are not at the top of the pyramid. Aldo Leopold (1887–1948), a forestry professor, articulated what he termed "the land ethic" in *A Sand County Almanac*.[7] Leopold used the term *land*, which he considered to be a fountain of energy flowing through a circuit of soils, plants, and animals, with food chains representing upward movement, and death and decay downward. All nature is thus connected, and humans are part of an overall biotic community; from this perspective he believes our role should be as stewards of the environment instead of exploiters:

> Most members of the land community have no economic value. Wildflowers and songbirds are examples . . . Yet these creatures are members of the biotic community and if (as I believe) its stability depends on its integrity, they are entitled to continuance . . . A system of conservation based solely on economic self-interest is hopelessly lopsided. It tends to ignore, and therefore eventually eliminate, many elements in the land community that lack commercial value, but that are essential to its healthy functioning.[8]

The sense of a functioning whole underlies Leopold's approach, leading him to state that "A thing is right when it tends to preserve the integrity, stability, and beauty of the biotic community. It is wrong when it tends otherwise."[9] The impetus for caring for the environment, then, is that it is a system that ultimately serves us, and respect for the internal integrity of the system will result in greater eventual benefits or fewer harms for humans.

---

[7] Aldo Leopold, *A Sand County Almanac* (Oxford: Oxford University Press, 1949).

[8] Leopold, *A Sand County Almanac*, p. 210.      [9] Leopold, *A Sand County Almanac*, p. 225.

A further development along these lines has been the "deep ecology" movement. Associated with the Norwegian Arne Naess, it challenges our current views of personal identity, suggesting that all beings are part of a universal system, and our current concept of individuality is mistaken since different lifeforms are merely different manifestations of an underlying unity.[10] This approach implies that a human ultimately is no more precious than a panda or a tree. Consequently, it would be wrong for humans to interfere with nature beyond fulfilling their most basic needs, and we should adopt practices that will leave the world unspoiled by our actions.

However, notions of intrinsic value are conceptually thorny. If we agree that all living creatures and natural objects have equal intrinsic worth, then there may be little else to say beyond the initial assertion, since it leaves us in a practical stalemate where decisions are either arbitrary or impossible. Thus if we say people and animals have equal intrinsic value and a developer wants to build a subdivision on an area that currently hosts songbirds, then we have no means of deciding whose interests should carry more weight. A more moderate claim suggests that there are degrees of intrinsic value – perhaps humans, birds, and trees all have intrinsic worth, but humans have more than birds, and birds more than trees. This leads to discussions about what features result in more worth and the appropriate justifications for harm, arguments many deep ecologists would resist or discount out of hand. Nevertheless, practically speaking we need some kind of decision procedure: perhaps if the songbirds are in no danger and the tree population is not at risk, then development should be allowed. Still, if we concede, for example, that it is acceptable for human interests to prevail in building an airport while destroying flamingo habitat, does the number of birds affected matter, and should we be concerned if only a few are put at risk, but they are the last flamingos on earth?

Proponents of using intrinsic worth accept that there are major theoretical issues to be worked out, but nevertheless see that framing environmental debates in these terms has tremendous importance in that it completely reverses the moral onus. They say that if the world is seen in purely anthropocentric terms, then we do not need to justify interfering and exploiting it. On the other hand, if we start from the perspective that all

---

[10] John Seed, Joanna Macy, Pat Fleming, and Arne Naess, *Thinking Like a Mountain: Towards a Council of All Beings* (Philadelphia: New Society Publishers, 1988).

of nature is valuable, then we need to justify actions that disturb a natural state. In New Zealand, for example, conservation legislation has taken the view that developers need to justify environmental disturbance, which upends the usual stance of environmental activists having to create arguments for conserving and protecting the environment.[11]

## How to value the environment

Most businesses still draw on traditional philosophical frameworks, and so the question is how best to translate environmental concerns into language that a firm would find persuasive. Thus we now turn to ways of valuing the earth.

The most common form of decision-making about the environment that businesses incorporate uses either a utilitarian or a rights-based model. The utilitarian approach can be articulated using the terminology of cost/benefit analysis based on human welfare. If we buy tuna that puts dolphins at risk, that is a human-centered decision based on the relative value we place on inexpensive food and what dolphins mean to us, and it presumes that we have the authority to dictate the fate of other animals. Thus under an economic analysis, the value of a pet dog is understood as the benefits it brings to its owner, and there are ways we can put a price on it by, for example, looking at the amount the owner spends on the animal and how much she would be prepared to spend in veterinary bills. In a legal forum, if a pet were harmed, then the owner would be compensated. In that sense, humans are the creators and arbiters of value for animals and the environment. Values are usually taken to be instrumental, so that the value of a pristine stream is only what those humans concerned about the stream deem it to be. Similarly, in the political arena, a country may consider development to be in the best interests of its citizens even if it realizes that it may result in environmental degradation.

A practical difficulty in dealing with business and ecology is that the environment is not privately held, and, as we saw in chapter 3, it may be termed a *commons*, derived from an ancient village practice of designating an area where anyone could graze their livestock. In the absence of personal

---

[11] Warwick Fox, "What Does the Recognition of Intrinsic Value Entail?" *Trumpeter*, 10.3 (1993), p. 101.

property rights and external regulation, the grass might become depleted to the point that the area became useless to everyone. Similarly, we share many environmental resources, and there are cases where there is great individual benefit to using the resource while inadequately compensating everyone else involved. For example, if a business releases its industrial waste untreated into the city sewers, it lowers its costs, but passes them on to everyone dependent on the local water treatment. If everyone acted similarly, then we would have a situation in which people do not recognize the mutual enterprise of our existence and only focus on what is in their immediate and local interest, and, what is more, when we realize what others are doing there is a tendency to join in the practice. Along the same lines, it might be responsible, for example, to forgo a helicopter ride through the Grand Canyon because of the pollution that results from such transportation. However, faced with the decision of being able to take a ride before the area becomes so polluted that the canyon cannot be seen, many people will decide to get on the helicopter. Therefore we have to recognize that there is inevitably a tension between our short-term personal gratification and the long-term benefits to everyone who may be affected by our actions.

As well as commons problems, there are other difficulties caused by market failures: environmental effects are often treated as negative externalities, so that the pollution or degradation costs are not considered part of the cost of production. Thus pollution from mining is left untreated, and people buying wedding bands do not pay for the harm caused in bringing the product to market. Most significantly, there are controversies about what cost estimates are most accurate and appropriate.

Another confound for decision-makers is that many effects of business operation are incremental and long-term. For instance, mercury takes a long time to work its way up through the food chain. Similarly, some have denied climate change due to carbon dioxide emissions because the effects are not necessarily dramatic or noticeable from year to year. This leads to what might be termed a *ratchet effect*. A ratchet is a tool that has a locked cog, so that in, say, hauling a heavy object, all the effort can be concentrated on repeated small moves. The parallel is that if the baseline for comparison keeps changing and only reflects small changes, then we are unable to see the overall effect, whereas if we had fixed data, perhaps the state of the world in a given year, then we could use that as a standard rather than looking for minute annual changes. For instance, although we may not perceive much difference from year to year, the emperor penguin population has halved in the last fifty years.[12] Because of the widespread problems in measurement, we will now turn to examine ways of putting a value on the environment.

## Measuring ecological value

The main means of measuring ecological value are revealed preferences, imputed willingness to pay, and expressed willingness to pay. Revealed preferences refers to the standard way of putting a value on market goods, so there is a price on fish or on exotic woods, and furthermore, we can calculate the contribution these goods make toward finished products, say, a table crafted from Philippine teak. We can also put a value on less tangible elements such as a mountain view by the differential that people are willing to pay to live there. In some cases, such as recreation spots, we can look at the amount that people are willing to spend in order to visit. Thus we could do a straightforward cost/benefit analysis to work out whether a forest should be kept as a recreation area or logged for timber: we look at the resources expended by the number of annual visitors over time and compare that to the market value of the lumber.

Economic valuation is made even more complicated by the fact that we are often dealing with so-called passive use or existence value. That is, people may not get any tangible benefit from something they may never use or see – for instance, whales in the deep ocean. However, many people are willing to pay to protect something they may never encounter, merely because they value its existence.

When a company announces the price of its goods, we can get fairly reliable data about how consumers react through their buying behavior; so if the price of gasoline goes up by 15 percent, and people do not change their driving habits, it shows that they are willing to tolerate the price hike, whereas if the price of yellow cars goes up by 10 percent, people would probably shift to buying a ready substitute, for instance, cars of a different color. However, the data in environmental cases tend to be much more hypothetical: we have to ask people how much they would be willing to

---

[12] John Roach, "Penguin Decline in Antarctica Linked with Climate Change," *National Geographic News* (May 9, 2001), available at http://nationalgeographc.com/news/2001/05/0509_penguindecline-html, accessed December 27, 2006.

spend if, say, the giant panda were in danger of extinction. Confounding the data is the fact that people react to dramatic events and news coverage, such as the *Exxon Valdez* oil spill that led to pictures of oil-soaked wild animals; but people care less when the issue is not in the foreground. Evidence shows that we react more to cute or appealing animals, so dolphins or otters stimulate more sympathy than slugs or beetles, for example.

We can also assess willingness to pay by looking at how much people might pay to avoid the consequences of not having a resource. For example, wetlands often act as a flood barrier, and so we can look at what people would have to pay to achieve the same degree of protection. This requires some conjecture on the part of the researchers, especially in light of the fact that people make risk assessments that are not always completely rational – for instance, many people ignore earthquake risks or build in flood plains. Therefore, the value we place is similar to our thinking about insurance: we may not know how much we actually need until something catastrophic occurs.

The most widely used system to fix a dollar amount on the environment is called *contingent valuation*. People are surveyed about what they would be willing to pay for conservation or restoration of an ecological resource. The polling agency has to work out who the relevant population is and what resources are at risk. For example, the question could be posed as a simple choice between logging interests and preserving the habitat of spotted owls in the Pacific Northwest. The way the questions are framed is critical: asking people if they would be willing to pay more for energy to preserve wildlife (a personal loss) may elicit a different response than asking if they want to avoid a price hike (a personal gain) although some animals may be put at risk. Responses may be unreliable because individuals are not asked to make any actual purchasing decisions. Nevertheless, the method does have the potential to provide some data that can be used to develop policy.[13]

A government example comes from regulation of development in order to preserve fish habitat in the Four Corners region in the American West. A survey was created that asked if respondents would be willing to pay into a trust fund that would support the habitat. It specified that all US

[13] See generally the US government website on ecological valuation: http://www. ecosystemvaluation.org, accessed May 3, 2006.

taxpayers would be solicited for the trust fund, and that if a majority supported the fund, the fish would be protected from extinction. Respondents were also told that if most people voted against the proposal, four species of fish would very likely become extinct in the near future. Those voting for the proposal were asked to put down an amount they would contribute. When the survey was sent to a sample of 1,600 households, the average amount pledged was just under $200 each. Extrapolating this amount nationally gives a figure that outweighs the local benefits of development.[14] Still, research suggests that people tend to respond in ways they believe sound good, even though their economic behavior indicates they would act otherwise; so the $200 figure has to be taken with some caution. Additionally, if people had been asked if they would agree to a national $200 tax increase for a very specific preservation project, the answers might be quite different.[15]

## Environmental accounting methods

Traditionally, management decisions about the environment have been made on a market model, and hence it has been important to impute values in order to make a cost/benefit case to preserve the environment. As we have seen, there are a number of ways to do this, and by incorporating the terminology of the market, environmentalists can argue for changing practice. Thus, for example, if consumers are willing to pay a premium for organic food, fair trade coffee, or recycled goods, then they will send an economic signal to producers that stimulate offerings and competition in these areas.

New markets may also alter what companies do. In the 1980s, for example, most car tires were dumped, often causing health hazards as they were a breeding ground for rodents and mosquitoes, and accidental fires sent plumes of toxic smoke into the air. Today, about half of all used tires

[14] R. Barrens, P. Ganderton, and C. Silva, "Valuing the Protection of Minimum Instream Flows in New Mexico," *Journal of Agricultural and Resource Economics* 21.2 (1996), pp. 294–309; D. Brookshire, M. McKee, and G. Watts, "Economic Analysis of Critical Habitat Designation in the Colorado River Basin for the Razorback Sucker, Humpback Chub, Colorado Squawfish and Bonytail," Department of Economics, University of New Mexico, Albuquerque, NM (1994), cited in http://www.ecosystemvaluation.org, accessed June 6, 2006.

[15] See generally the Harvard University Program on Statistical Research, available at http://www.iq.harvard.edu/psr/, accessed May 3, 2006.

are recycled for fuel and crumb rubber, which is used for playgrounds, roads, and hoses. Still, market analyses are highly dependent on public visibility and transparency; if a documentary shows the distress of Peruvian villages affected by mercury, people will respond, but it is economically advantageous for a company with shady environmental practices to keep them secret.

An alternative means by which a business may make ecological decisions is to look at the cost of litigation. If a firm stands to benefit by $1 million by polluting an area, and will only be fined $200,000 if it is discovered and prosecuted, then absent any reputational effects, the company will treat the fine as a license fee. Thus it is important for the courts to be a reasonable gauge of the cost of environmental harms. For instance, after the tanker *Exxon Valdez* negligently discharged oil in Alaska in 1989 – polluting more than 1,000 miles of shoreline and killing hundreds of thousands of birds and marine mammals – the company was fined $287 million in compensatory damages. A cruise line that dumped raw bilge into coastal waters was fined $1 million in restitution. In 2002 a meat processing plant in North Carolina was fined $500,000; it had built a disguised underground pipe system that bypassed its water treatment facility and dumped animal wastes and human sewage directly into the nearby Neuse River. The challenge in all these cases is to make the fines sufficiently accurate to represent the full long-term compensation costs in order to send companies the correct economic signals.[16]

Another way to assess the cost of pollution is for governments to impose regulation that may in turn create a market in tradable pollution permits. For example, in the United States, industries are allocated a number of "pollution credits" that they can then sell to other companies if they fail to use them. The European Union governs the emission of greenhouse gases at some 12,000 industrial sites, and energy-intensive industries and utilities must report their annual emissions in order to get permission to operate the following year. The United Kingdom, for example, has been allocated an annual allowance of 736 million tons of carbon dioxide emissions credits that the government will then distribute to individual firms. If a business has surplus emissions credits, it may trade them

---

[16] FacWorld, *Pollution Litigation Review* (March 2002), http://www.facworld.com/FACworld.nsf/doc/Polllitrev0302, accessed June 27, 2006.

to another company (at present, the value of a ton of $CO_2$ allowance trades for about $10).[17] One potential result of a market for this kind of pollution credit is that the regulating body could reduce the amount of allowed emissions over time and thus could provide economic incentives for cleaner industry. The Kyoto Treaty has a requirement for countries to reduce pollution by set amounts (8 percent under 1990 levels by 2012), and pollution credits are thus a quantifiable way of managing environmental impacts.

Industries have also developed a voluntary standard, ISO 14001, which acts as a benchmark for minimally acceptable environmental management systems (EMS). An independent authority awards the standard when a firm satisfies three criteria: implementation of an environmental management system; having procedures in place to maintain compliance with applicable regulations; and an institutional commitment to both continual improvement and the overall prevention of pollution.[18] There has been a steady growth in environmental awareness in business, and international bodies such as the International Monetary Fund and the World Trade Organization reserve the right to assess the environmental impact of development projects. Furthermore, some governments, such as France, have made it compulsory for publicly quoted companies to incorporate their social and environmental consequences in their annual reports.[19]

## Web of being

Some maintain that there is a "web of being" where all the elements in the biosphere are connected, and harm to one part may result in consequences that we cannot foresee. This does not deny that the value of the environment is relative to human satisfactions, but it reminds us that destruction of remote or seemingly unimportant flora and fauna may be detrimental to our future.

Consider the case of the Pacific yew tree. It became the most valuable tree on the North American continent when it was discovered that it was

---

[17] Laura Cohn, "What Price Pollution? In Europe, the Kyoto Protocol Is Spurring a Brisk Market in Emission Credits," *Business Week* (February 28, 2005).

[18] http://www.iso.org/iso/en/aboutiso/introduction/index.html, accessed May 8, 2006.

[19] Article 116, NRE (Nouvelles Régulations Economiques), http://www.ecologie.gouv.fr/article.php3?id_article=4030, accessed December 21, 2006.

the source of a potentially life-saving drug to combat cancer.[20] It is small and resembles a shrub, and it was often discarded in clear-cut forestry. In the mid-1960s the US National Cancer Institute screened over 35,000 species and discovered that an extract from the yew bark, taxol, could be highly effective in previously incurable cases, especially in ovarian and breast cancers. However, the chemical mechanisms involved puzzled scientists, and it was not until 1977 that scientists understood precisely how taxol interfered with the cancer's growth. By 1991 it was hailed as the most effective cancer medicine discovered in many years.

Over 800,000 pounds of yew bark were being collected annually from forests in Oregon and Washington, since it took the entire bark from six 100-year-old trees to provide sufficient taxol to treat one patient. If alternatives had not been synthesized, the demand for yews would have put the habitat of the spotted owl in jeopardy, and the finite supply of suitable yews would have run out in a few years. Chemists still use the yew in developing the synthetic derivatives, and so they are currently being harvested, but on a lesser scale. Environmentalists point to the yew as a prime example of the continuing need to preserve biological diversity. Because we are unaware of the potential benefits of our surroundings, they claim it is only prudent to conserve as many plants and animals as we can.

## Pascal's wager

We still have to deal with persuading business that environmental issues deserve urgent and direct attention. Because we do not have very clear indicators about the cumulative effect of business practices on the environment, our concerns about pollution and climate change may seem premature and unwarranted, especially given that preventative or remedial measures are likely to make firms less efficient.

R. Edward Freeman has recently suggested that we think of our global future in terms of a two-by-two decision matrix, based on Pascal's wager. Blaise Pascal (1623–1662) argued that it is prudent to believe in God: if God does not exist, then we have lost nothing if we believe, but if God does exist, belief leads to infinite rewards while atheism will result in infinite suffering. Freeman adapts the wager to frame how we should react in

---

[20] http://www.pfc.forestry.ca/ecology/yew/index_e.html, accessed May 1, 2006.

the face of inconclusive evidence about climate change. He says that there is either change or not, and we can take steps or not. This gives us four options. If there is no real change happening, we can do nothing and gain marginal benefits that our present economic decisions offer. If there is no change and we do take steps to reduce emissions and lessen our impact, then it will cost us relatively little. On the other hand, if climate change is real, then if we take steps we may manage to mitigate some of its effects. The worst possible outcome is if it is real and we ignore it. In considering all the possibilities, Freeman argues that in the absence of full evidence, our only reasonable course of action given the enormous downside possibilities is to assume that the changes are real and imminent and act accordingly.[21]

## Sustainablility and the triple bottom line

Many businesses are moving toward sustainability, the belief that we should be able to meet our own needs without leaving a legacy of depleted resources for future generations. Some commentators trace the movement to the 1992 Earth Summit where corporate leaders wanted to explore ways in which they could be more ecologically responsible while at the same time meeting their commitments to increased efficiency. In 1997 the *Harvard Business Review* published a major article that suggested the challenge was to develop a world economy that the planet could sustain indefinitely: that is, business needs to move from expedient solutions to more long-term strategies and competencies that will benefit them in the long run.[22]

Many companies have adopted *triple bottom line accounting*, a term popularized by John Elkington, which is a profound new initiative to promote sustainability.[23] The idea is that to survive in the coming century, businesses need to adopt a wide perspective on what they are doing: they need to be profitable, but they also need stable markets, affluent consumers, and an

---

[21] R. Edward Freeman, Jessica Pierce, and Richard Dodd, "Shades of Green: Business, Ethics and the Environment," in their *Environmentalism and the New Logic of Business: How Firms can be Profitable and Leave our Children a Clean Environment* (Oxford: Oxford University Press, 2000).

[22] Stuart L. Hart, "Beyond Greening: Strategies for a Sustainable World," *Harvard Business Review*, 75.1 (January 1, 1997), pp. 66–76.

[23] John Elkington, *Cannibals with Forks* (Stoney Creek, CT: New Society Publishers, 1998).

environment that will sustain both business and people for the foreseeable future. In that sense, triple bottom line accounting is a prudential instrumental approach that does good for the sake of promoting business, but at the same time is enlightened in that it necessarily furthers human and biotic welfare. The first bottom line is traditional business performance, assessed in terms of profit and loss where the company does well if the bottom line is a positive amount and other factors are secondary. However, given an expanding global market, a forward-thinking company should also consider whether there is a sustainable market for its products and if it is innovative enough to sustain its profitability.

The second bottom line is social, so a company needs to assess its impact on society and the degree of trust and dependability the organization has with its stakeholders. This bottom line considers whether the firm had a net positive or negative impact on the communities it deals with and how that may affect the company's performance. One way of thinking about this is as reputation or good will capital, that is, the amount that a company benefits by having loyal customers or ones willing to pay a premium to deal with an institution they trust. Among other things, this reputation can be undermined by the reaction of socially conscious investors to bad press or by condemnation by non-governmental organizations. Thus if potential customers are discouraged by reports of a firm carelessly killing wildlife or using child labor, then it would be appropriate for investors to receive reports showing the effect of these practices.

The third bottom line is environmental. It considers whether company operations have affected the integrity of essential ecosystems and how it deals with substitutable resources. This is not very different from current practice, in that companies have legal responsibilities in many developed countries to report emissions of various substances and keep within set limits. The change is that the information would be incorporated into a more comprehensive view of the overall impact of the firm. Take as an example the case of coastline fishing in India. Government initiatives in the 1990s opened up waterways to joint ventures with foreign factory fishing ships, and fishing became an efficient industry using modern trawling methods. Fish were also farmed along the coast, and minced fish was often used to foster lucrative shrimp production. The fishing industry has been an economic success if judged solely on the basis of return to investment. However, there is more to the story. Factory fishing drags nets along the sea floor, with subsequent destruction of the marine habitat. It is often so good at catching fish that the stock cannot replenish itself and so diminishes over time. Each pound of shrimp produced has been nourished by 10 pounds of minced fish, and the development of coastal fish farms has been devastating to mangrove swamps and marine forests.

There is also a human cost. Indian traditional fishermen cannot compete with the factory fishers, and the routine use of fish as shrimp feed has led to scarcity. A centuries-old way of life has been threatened by an industry that took most of its catch for export. Many coastal dwellers have been deprived of their means of sustenance. They staged strikes and protests that gained popular support, and eventually the joint ventures were significantly scaled back, and many of the shrimp farms closed.

Triple bottom line accounting requires us to make the different kinds of costs explicit. In this way we can assess the success of a commercial operation not only in traditional economic measures but in clear measures of environmental and social impact as well. Moreover, it illustrates that we cannot easily segment the impact of business: its economic functions are intimately bound up with its impact on communities and the environment.

One of the chief difficulties of triple bottom line accounting is measuring environmental and social impact in a consistent and reliable way, in essence, with a methodology comparable to the Generally Accepted Accounting Principles (GAAP) that standardize corporate profit and loss calculations. The recent Global Reporting Initiative (GRI), which emerged from work done by the United Nations Program for the Environment, and Ceres, the Coalition for Environmentally Responsible Economies, provides some structure for major environmental accountability.[24] In 2002 Ceres was established as an independent body that standardized reporting guidelines, and by 2005 had more than 600 major organizations using the GRI including Ford Motors, McDonald's, Bank of America, Coca-Cola, and Aveda. According to some reports, three-quarters of European companies and half of the major American companies make voluntary triple bottom line reports.[25]

---

[24] The guidelines are available at http://www.globalreporting.org/ReportingFramework/ G3Online/, accessed December 27, 2006. The Ceres website is http://www.ceres.org/.

[25] "New Era of Transparency," *Management Barometer* (September 2002), available at http://www.barometersurveys.com/production/barsurv.nsf/0/ 5642b345fbbcd49085256c3e00658e18?OpenDocument, accessed October 24, 2005.

## Business and heritage

Finally, we can highlight the problems with using purely economic analyses in the case of heritage sites, where there is tension between market demands and something of historic, cultural, or religious value. In the case of Uluru in Australia, competing value systems are difficult to measure and balance.

At daybreak several hundred visitors wait every day for the sun to rise over a spectacular monolith in the northern Australian outback. Uluru, more commonly known as Ayers Rock, rises dramatically from the surrounding desert. Over 1,000 feet high, it turns vividly red and orange in the morning and evening light. Almost half a million visitors come every year to view the rock. There is an upscale resort nearby, and many commercial operators run tours. The area was the subject of lawsuits in the 1980s when it was handed back to the traditional aboriginal tribes known as Anangu, who then leased the area back to the Australian Nature Conservation Agency for ninety-nine years. A condition of the transfer was that visitors would be given access to climb the rock.

The Anangu have lived a nomadic hunting and gathering existence in the desert for thousands of years and believe the world was created by beings whose legacy includes sites where they shaped the landscape and left behind their spirits.[26] Tour operators, who encouraged motel building and other commercial development, had forced them from the area in the 1960s. Ten years later the Anangu established a camp at the base of the rock to reassert their claim to the area, eventually resulting in the deal that established the reserve in 1985. They believe the area to be a sacred site. Under their tribal law, no one but senior Anangu initiates are allowed to follow the trail to the top or to visit special areas, and they believe that the government is allowing their heritage to be desecrated by visitors. They have posted signs banning photography in various sacred sites and worry that overcrowding and damage will rob the area of its unique character, and fear the fragile ecosystem will be hurt by species inadvertently introduced by tourists. They also attach great significance to deaths that occur on Uluru. The climb is moderately difficult, and a chain handhold was installed in 1964 to help people deal with the steep and exposed ascent; nevertheless some thirty people have died in the last twenty years, mainly from heart-related ailments.

[26] www.sacredland.org/world_sites_pages_Uluru.html, accessed April 28, 2006.

Tour promoters offer deals including unescorted climbs, but qualify their advertisements with a statement along the lines of "The traditional owners prefer that people not climb the rock." There are notices nearby stating that the Anangu prefer that people, showing their sensitivity and respect for Anangu law and culture, refrain from climbing. In an attempt to balance the interests of both sides, the Anangu community and the Nature Conservation Agency jointly developed a cultural center dedicated to informing the public about the significance of the site. The proportion of climbers has dropped in the last five years from about half of the visitors to just over a third.[27] Still, many visitors see climbing as a right: in the words of one Australian photographer, "Of course people should be able to climb it . . . Aboriginal people have no more claim on it than any other groups. We as Australians and as tourists are being locked out of this beautiful icon."[28]

In economic terms, the aboriginal people have little to offer; the Anangu could not pay off the tour promoters by compensating them for lost business and thereby protect Uluru from desecration. Moreover, most visitors to the area are there to witness the rock itself, and the fact that it is religiously significant is less important; thus, emphasizing the religious dimension of the site would probably not overcome secular interests. Nor could the Anangu be paid off with any amount, since the significance of the rock is beyond price.

The philosophical response to a purely economic analysis of the case may best be framed in terms of rights, and for our purposes, the rights might append to the site itself or to the aboriginal peoples who regard it as sacred. Nevertheless, if viewed only as an economic resource, the developers will likely prevail. Thus at some point a society might deem environmental, historical, or cultural items to be of special importance and say that they are so significant that they should never be on the market. The United Nations, for example, organized a ban on the sale of ivory that helped protect elephants from extinction, despite the fact that there is a strong market. In a similar vein, the US government resisted development on the historic Gettysburg battleground.

Some philosophers including Mark Sagoff have argued that the only way to deal with these cases is to reject economic analyses and leave ecological, cultural, and historical decisions to the democratic process rather than the

---

[27] Linda Popic, "Should You Climb Uluru?" *The Guardian* (UK) (December 17, 2005).
[28] Ken Duncan, quoted in Popic, "Should You Climb Uluru?".

market.[29] Yet there are still drawbacks. In the Uluru case, the government crafted a compromise that allows visitors to climb a sacred path and enter and photograph places that the aboriginal peoples think ought to be inviolate. Thus any democracy in a pluralistic society inevitably puts the most weight on the concerns of the majority, and rights claims are by no means guaranteed to preserve the environment.

## Summary

Perhaps an answer to many of the problematic environmental issues confronting business can be found by going back to the first principles that anchor notions of property rights, drawn from the work of John Locke (1632–1704).[30] Locke makes a convincing claim that we become entitled to goods through investing our labor in them, and then we may trade them as we see fit. However, he has three important qualifications when talking about ownership. The first is that there have to be sufficient goods to go around; thus we can catch as many fish as we can as long as the stock is not depleted: "at least where there is enough, and as good left in common for others." Second, we may not unjustly infringe the rights of others. Depending how the case is argued, it may turn out that the fundamental religious rights of the Anangu may trump the desire of tourists for a pleasant view.

The third provision is less well known. Locke says we cannot acquire goods if we will not use them; for example, he says there is no right to catch venison if we are only going to allow it to rot.[31] He states that acquiring something that could be useful to others and then wasting it is an offense against the "common Law of Nature" and warrants punishment.

Locke was writing at a time when there were places – such as America – that were both bountiful and underpopulated, to be sure, but his point holds true today when there is little left in common, and appropriation by one party inevitably affects others. It means that we could take from common resources as long as doing so does not harm others' ability to do the same, and that although we can use resources, we may not destroy them

---

[29] Mark Sagoff, "At the Monument to General Meade," *Arizona Law Review*, 42 (2000) pp. 433–462.

[30] I am grateful to Mark Sagoff for this point.

[31] John Locke, *Two Treatises of Government* (London: Dent, 1975), Book II, chapter 5, para. 30, p. 131.

if that leaves scarcity for others – presumably including future generations. Thus, the very idea of property, which is fundamental to capitalism, already implies that we need to sustain the earth's resources. Additionally, these principles of property provide a hierarchy of duties; in short, needs come before wants. Although we may spend at our discretion, if we engage in economic development, we also have specific moral duties: avoid putting people in peril; maintain minimum levels of clean air, water, and soil; and allow people to sustain themselves.

## General issues for discussion

1. How much information about the environmental practices of a business should be available to investors and consumers? What form should it take?
2. One claim is that pollution is often the cost of development: Europe and America experienced times where industrial waste was largely unregulated during times of significant economic expansion. Are there philosophically robust grounds to justify restraint on the part of developing countries today?
3. Is compensation ever due to those harmed by the effects of pollution? Who would pay, and how should it be calculated? What problems do you envisage?
4. Should a business be concerned about wider issues such as the health of the planet or maintaining species diversity? How should it justify expenses put towards those ends?
5. Do we have any environmental responsibility to future generations?
6. If someone wants to routinely drive a quarter mile to work in a large sport utility vehicle and have it idle in his parking space for thirty minutes to warm up before his drive, are there any philosophically valid grounds to criticize his behavior?

## Case – industrial farming

A concentrated animal feeding operation (CAFO), sometimes known as an intensive livestock operation, is a farm that applies industrial techniques to raising animals, typically cows, pigs, or chickens. These farms aim for maximum efficiency by making the most of space, feed, and other resources.

They began in the 1920s when vitamins A and D were synthesized, which meant that animals could grow despite being kept indoors and lacking exercise. However, animals in close confinement tend to spread disease, and this proved a problem until antibiotics became widely available just after the Second World War. Today, half the antibiotics used in the United States are given to farm animals.

The impact of industrialization on farming has been striking. In Ontario, Canada, for example, thirty years ago there were about 19,000 farmers with an average of just over 100 pigs each. In 1996, only a third of the number of farmers raised an average of 418 pigs, and these figures are echoed across farms throughout the developed world. Moreover, some farms are huge: 2 percent of the hog factories in Canada account for a quarter of the annual yield.[32] Three-quarters of the world's poultry are raised in industrial systems, amounting to 6 billion chickens for human consumption. The United States has the largest proportion of CAFOs; for example, 95 percent of the 250 million egg-laying chickens in the United States are in large operations.

Proponents point to the advantages of raising animals in this way. It provides plentiful food at affordable costs; the animals can be managed more easily; it is more likely to be profitable than a small family-run operation; and the product is more consistent, reliable, and safe. Critics point to the dangers of this system. They warn that the large-scale use of antibiotics will lead to resistant bacteria that may put humans at risk; the treatment of the animals is inhumane, as it includes crowding and crude surgery such as debeaking and declawing chickens to stop them from attacking each other in confined spaces; and it produces significant pollution. A single cow, for example, can produce up to 2 tons of manure annually, and according to the Center for Disease Control, the 238,000 feeding operations in the United States create 500 million tons of manure every year.[33] Animal waste is one of

---

[32] Andrew Nikiforuk and Danylo Hawaleshka, "Should We Fear the Factory Farm? Massive Livestock Operations are Raising Troubling Questions about Water Safety," *MacLean's* (Readers Digest Canada) (May 31, 2001).

[33] "Concentrated Animal Feeding Operations," Health Studies Branch, National Center for Environmental Health, Center for Disease Control and Prevention (May 31, 2005), available at http://www.cdc.gov/cafos/about.htm, accessed May 12, 2006.

the chief sources of nitrous oxide, which is fifty times more aggressive than carbon dioxide in its effects on the ozone layer. Typically, animal waste is kept in holding tanks or spread on the land, practices that result in flies and odors. If the soil becomes saturated, waste is likely to seep into the groundwater supply. At the same time, pollution has been loosely regulated. For example, in 2005, the Environmental Protection Agency offered to exempt farms from air pollution laws in exchange for their participation in a study on airborne emissions.[34]

Meat has traditionally been regarded as a luxury in much of the developing world, but demand is expected at least to double in the next twenty years. Countries like the Philippines now have large-scale animal production operations, and China accounts for half the world's pig population. Meat production worldwide has increased five-fold since 1950, and is growing most rapidly in Asia, since industrial processes were routinely part of programs promoted by the United States and international agencies. Local reaction in developing nations has been mixed: residents complain about polluted water and the prevalent odor but are reluctant to offend investors. In the words of one official, "We give these farms leeway as much as possible because they provide so much economically."[35]

In a dramatic shift the World Bank issued a policy document in 2001 that reversed its previous position.[36] It realized that funding large-scale projects put small farmers at risk and threatened the environment, and argued for a strategy "with a people-focused approach, giving high priority to the public goods aspects of poverty reduction, environmental sustainability, food security and safety, and animal welfare."[37] It felt that in the long term, industrial practices would not benefit local farmers and would ultimately lead to destructive pollution.

---

[34] John Nielsen, "EPA Plan Exempts Factory Farms from Pollution Rules," All Things Considered, National Public Radio (USA) (January 26, 2005).

[35] Danielle Nierenberg, "The Commercialization of Farming: Producing Meat for a Hungry World," USA Today Magazine (January 1, 2004).

[36] Cornelis de Haan, Tjaart Schillhorn van Veen, Brian Brandenburg, Jerome Gauthier, François Le Gall, Robin Mearns, and Michel Simeon, Directions in Development: Livestock Development – Implications for Rural Poverty, the Environment, and Global Food Security, Document no. 23241 (Washington, DC: World Bank, November, 2001).

[37] De Haan et al., Directions in Development, p. xiii.

## Some questions from the case

1. Is it immoral for a business to avoid environmental regulation? Suppose you own a farm and the government imposes environmental regulations on farming practices in your area. Are there any philosophical or moral reasons why you shouldn't move your operations to another part of the world that is not regulated?

2. The World Trade Organization has resisted tariffs based on "process and production standards," in effect saying that countries should not be concerned with how products from overseas come to market. This means that although we know the country of origin, we would not know the conditions in which the animal was kept. Would such labeling be desirable, or is it unnecessary?

3. What is the best way to calculate the effects of current industrial farming practices? Are they negative externalities? Should pollution be accounted for in the costs of production, and if so, how?

4. Someone might argue that if farming pollution became an issue for consumers, then they would demand alternatives and this would spur research and innovation. Do you see any difficulties with that line of reasoning?

5. Do you think there are any moral differences between trees and plants, wildlife, and animals produced by humans for consumption? What are the implications of your view?

# Epilogue

## The scandals at Enron and WorldCom

Enron, the seventh largest corporation in the United States, filed bankruptcy on December 2, 2001. At the time it was the world's biggest business failure – Enron had employed over 20,000 people and claimed annual income of over $100 billion. In May 2006, Ken Lay and Jeffrey Skilling, former CEOs of Enron, were found guilty of criminal fraud, conspiracy, and insider trading, among other charges, while many other executives agreed to plead guilty in return for lighter sentences.

Enron started off as a regional power company formed from a merger in 1985. After the merger the new company was saddled with massive debt that it serviced by raiding employee pension funds. In 1988 it faced a scandal when two of its most successful moneymakers, Louis Borget and Thomas Mastroeni, were discovered by auditors to have engaged in insider trading and skimming company money into their personal accounts. The CEO, Lay, took no action, allegedly saying, "I've decided we're not going to discharge the people involved in this, because the company needs those earnings."[1] In the late eighties the United States eased regulations on business, at the same time as a number of so-called "dot com" companies prospered through investor speculation rather than actual production. Enron increasingly moved into diversified areas and became a popular choice of Wall Street analysts because of its consistently high returns. By 2001, Enron stock was regarded as a solid "blue chip" investment, and *Fortune* magazine had named it "most innovative company" for six years in a row, declaring it one of its "ten stocks to last a decade."

[1] J. Barnes, "How a Titan Came Undone," *US News & World Report* (March 18, 2002).

Behind the high earnings there was a complex pattern of duplicity. Some of the innovative schemes were so intricate that analysts and auditors took the company at its word instead of checking them out. Among Enron's tactics was to create offshore independent subsidiaries and then post losses to these companies, giving a false impression of financial health. Other deals were secured by Enron stock, which was posted at its market value and then used as collateral for advances in cash back to the parent company – as if Enron had issued a credit card to itself, created income, but then failed to service the resulting debt. It routinely posted immediate revenue for promised future sales, although the revenue would accrue slowly over time. Meanwhile, the company was ruthless in firing non-performing personnel, but lavished incentives and stock options on those who exceeded their goals. Inside the company aggressive behavior was rewarded and has been described as a "constant test of smarts and status."[2]

Enron was well connected, both socially and politically. It gave substantial amounts to charity, and the baseball stadium in Houston bore its name. It was very generous to local and national politicians. By August 2000, Enron's stock was trading at $90. However, the company faced increasing scrutiny, including investigation by the state of California, which alleged that Enron deliberately congested the power grid to inflate the price of energy. Many executives sold their stock while telling investors the company would bounce back, but others in the market lost confidence, and a year later the stock had lost half its value. The outside auditors, Arthur Andersen, allegedly issued an order to its staff working with Enron to shred all but the most basic working papers. By December 2, Enron sought bankruptcy relief. The government later prosecuted Andersen for its actions, and when it was found guilty it lost its license to do work for the government, essentially dooming that company as well, even though it was acquitted on appeal. Ken Lay died of a heart attack in July 2006, while awaiting sentencing.

Shortly after the markets were rocked by Enron's bankruptcy, WorldCom, a leading telecommunications company, also failed. Its losses amounted to some $9 billion (to give it some perspective, if someone were handed $1,000 every day, it would take almost 3,000 years to accumulate just $1 billion), and 17,000 people were put out of work. Like Enron, WorldCom had been

---

[2] M. Swartz and S. Watkins, *Power Failure: The Inside Story of the Collapse of Enron* (New York: Doubleday, 2003), p. 192.

relatively small until the government deregulated the industry, and then under the leadership of Bernie Ebbers it embarked on a series of takeovers leveraged by its own stock. Ebbers' original company had been created after federal authorities ordered AT&T to break into smaller companies to prevent it monopolizing telecommunications. By 1992, Ebbers had acquired IDB WorldCom and had become the nation's fourth largest long-distance phone carrier. In a series of aggressive buy-outs, WorldCom took over various Internet providers and eventually bought MCI for $34.5 billion.

By the late 1990s, though, the industry faced overcapacity and competition from new technologies, and in order to capture the market, companies engaged in a price war that put several of the major players out of business. While most companies reported lackluster financial returns, WorldCom maintained steady growth and made a bid for Sprint in 1999. However, regulators in both Europe and the United States resisted the merger, causing the company finances to be examined more closely by analysts. Meanwhile, Cynthia Cooper, an internal auditor, realized that there had been some questionable dealings. When her boss stalled after she presented him with the information, Cooper set up a secret unit within the company to revisit the figures accepted by the external auditor, Arthur Andersen. She found several questionable practices: vast sums were moved among accounts in order to cover shortfalls; there were capital expenditures amounting to $500 million but no equipment to show for it; and income had been posted when there was no prospect of actual receipt for years. All in all, she calculated $6 billion in questionable accounting that had turned an operating loss into a solid profit. She took her findings to high-ranking executives, including the chief financial officer, who asked her to delay reporting them to the board. She refused, presented her findings, and the directors then fired most of top management before announcing that the company had inflated profits in the previous year. The company went into bankruptcy shortly afterward, on July 21, 2002.[3]

Ebbers had a distinctly hands-off management style and claimed that he was both unaware of the fraudulent practices and a victim of greedy subordinates. Still, he was charged by the government, and on July 13, 2005, he was found guilty of fraud and conspiracy and sentenced to twenty-five years in prison. In the words of one commentator, "You can't sell yourself

---

[3] T. Padgett, "The Rise and Fall of Bernie Ebbers," *Time* (May 13, 2002).

as a genius to investors but then portray yourself as someone who flunked math to the jury."[4]

Clearly things went badly wrong in both of these cases. Partially the problem was one of confidence. Company stock had funded many of their acquisitions. As long as the market continued to believe there was value in the company based on its statements, the stock held its price. Furthermore, there was a tendency to turn a blind eye to the internal workings of the company as long as everyone was doing well. It is hard to argue with success. In the tale of the "Emperor's New Clothes," people believed that their ruler wore garments that were invisible to fools but visible to those with taste and discrimination, and so they willed themselves to deny the truth, and, of course, every other spectator claimed to witness them too. Eventually the trick was exposed by the voice of a small boy who spoke plainly about what he saw. However, there is a fine line between acknowledging the external reality and claiming the boy was a fool and misled. The truth may be plain to see, but often in business, perception becomes reality. Our perceptions are typically made within a context and modified by what others say.

## Revalidating philosophy

This book is unabashedly philosophical in its appeal to fundamental concepts and their application to business. Part of the design has been to reorient the discussion about ethics. What we often find with big scandals such as Enron, WorldCom, Tyco, Global Crossing, Barings Bank, or Lucent is that they are dramatic and spectacular and frequently point to corrupt individuals with great power abusing the trust of others. These stories frequently read like morality tales, where bad people did bad things, with the resulting lesson that we should not follow their examples. However, they are also important for what they do not tell us, for there had to be a context that allowed these individuals to be influential, as well as a corporate culture that rewarded their behavior. There were many layers of authority within the organization that echoed the tone from above, and few checks and balances that looked beyond the dazzle of the bottom line. Many people were co-opted in the enterprise, and dissenting voices were squelched. But the most interesting feature of these sensational stories is typically missed: these

---

[4] Steve Rosenbush, "The Message in Ebbers' Verdict," *Business Week* (July 14, 2005).

are not just tales of bad apples that need to be sorted from the barrel, but fascinating sagas of how decent people become enmeshed in moral predicaments without an adequate analytical framework to help them sort out the basic principles they should follow.

The regulatory response to these stories is enhanced laws – after all, that is what we should expect from lawmakers. Thus the Sarbanes-Oxley Act of 2002 was quickly created to give greater transparency and accountability, with the aim of restoring market confidence among investors. Yet the law is limited. One consultant said that the first two questions companies usually asked when confronted with the new regulations were (1) what are the minimal requirements? and (2) where are the loopholes? Regulation may force compliance, but it can do little to change the way companies operate.[5]

Our exploration of business has deliberately not been a legal text, except insofar as the law is a reflection of underlying policies built on philosophical principles. Thus it has been most important to establish basic principles at the outset. Moreover, it is instructive that the legal cases against Enron and WorldCom executives were not clear-cut, as the issues were complex, and accomplished legal teams mounted strong defenses. We find that it is much harder to enforce regulation than to put it on the books. For instance, in the case of Richard Scrushy, the CEO of HealthSouth, the prosecution failed to get a guilty verdict despite evidence that he apparently told subordinates to "fix the financials" when the company had overstated its earnings by almost $3 billion.[6] Whatever the legality of a case, though, it is still fruitful to critically assess what has gone on using the tools philosophy has to offer.

Business ethics that confines discussion to dramatic scandals is like closing the barn door after the horse has bolted, and it further implies that corruption is chiefly a question of wrongdoing in big business. The truth of the matter is that we all face moral compromise all the time, every day, and issues that are seemingly petty may have momentous consequences. For example, a worker paid by the number of metal sheets he presses in a day has an incentive to circumvent safety protocols that slow him down; a small town may be devastated when a factory moves its operations overseas; a fast-food restaurant may decide to cook in oil free from dangerous high

---

[5] Personal conversation, 2004.

[6] "Feds Detail Role of Accounting Entries in Scandal at HealthSouth," *Accounting Department Management Report* (March 1, 2004).

cholesterol fats, despite the higher costs; or a mid-level manager may be told that money from a "use it or lose it" account has to be spent by the next day by whatever means necessary. While most of us will not lead a multi-million dollar corporation, we nonetheless face real and immediate dilemmas. Whatever the setting, the first indication that something is amiss usually arises with individuals who have personal misgivings, like World-Com's Cynthia Cooper who had the acumen to realize the moral dimension of what was going on.

It would be relatively straightforward to treat Enron as a case of business gone bad. However, that only provides a temporary and fragmentary view. If we consider Enron in a much broader context, we might view it as an instance where business failed its stakeholders by poor practice and failed on an institutional scale because it became bedazzled by external goods without regard to the wider duties of a company to promote human virtues.

The real benefit from studying business ethics is not that we can draw conclusions from dramatic wrongs, but that we can reflect on the basic principles and concepts that underlie our thinking. That is why we have expanded the conversation from the cases that introduce each chapter to the wider application of general principles that can then be applied to a number of topics. In that sense, business ethics is a primary exercise – it has to be integrated into our lives as employees and consumers as a matter of course, and become a fundamental part of the mission of a corporation. This does not mean that business ethics is a magic wand that will make bad people good or simplify complex issues. On the other hand, it is a far more productive approach than adding ever more regulations. It has sometimes been said that business is amoral – that is, not moral or immoral but an entirely neutral enterprise that reflects consumer demands. This seems entirely wrong. Business penetrates every aspect of our lives and helps construct the narratives that make sense of our existence. Because of that, it necessarily involves the very deepest questions of morality and how we understand justice and fairness, and distinguish right from wrong.

## Virtues in the jungle

The contemporary philosopher Geoff Moore has insightfully adapted virtue ethics to business dealings, and his approach gives philosophical robustness to some popular books on management.[7] For example, a best-selling book has the title *Value Driven Management*,[8] and Stephen Covey's book *Seven Habits of Highly Effective People* has sold over 12 million copies.[9] Both stress that success has to be judged in more than economic terms, that we need to gauge our actions in terms of core human values, and that we need to make sure that whatever we do leads to individual happiness and flourishing.

Moore modifies a virtues framework originally set up by another philosopher, Alasdair MacIntyre, although we should note that MacIntyre himself has been very skeptical that the incentives that drive capitalism could ever be consistent with us living a virtuous life.[10] Essentially, MacIntyre's framework says that we have developed various institutions and what he terms "practices" within them. So, for example, a hospital is an institution, but a doctor practices the profession of medicine within it. To be a good physician there are certain forms of behavior that are encouraged, such as applying specialized knowledge and skills. The rewards within the practice are often internal, and certain character traits are associated with good doctors; these have developed over time and are fostered within professional organizations. On the other hand, there are external rewards, such as pay and status, but these are not unique to the practice – one could acquire them by becoming a lawyer instead, for example. Conversely, someone could be a great doctor without taking the external goods, but it would be impossible to be one without subscribing to the virtues internal to the practice, because seeking internal goods is vital if someone wants to achieve excellence. To put it another way, we could bribe a child to take piano lessons, perhaps, but that will only be effective up to a point. Without internal rewards, she is likely to stop as soon as the external incentives disappear. There is a necessary

---

[7] Geoff Moore, "Humanizing Business: A Modern Business Ethics Approach," *Business Ethics Quarterly*, 15.2 (April, 2005), pp. 237–256; "Hives and Horseshoes, Mintzberg or MacIntyre: What Future for Corporate Social Responsibility?" *Business Ethics: A European Review*, 12.1 (January, 2003), pp. 41–53.

[8] Randolph Pohlman, Gareth Gardiner, and Ellen Heffes, *Value Driven Management: How to Create and Maximize Value over Time for Organizational Success* (New York: American Management Association, 2000).

[9] Stephen Covey, *The Seven Habits of Highly Effective People* (New York: Simon & Schuster, 1990).

[10] Alasdair MacIntyre, *After Virtue: A Study in Moral Theory* (Notre Dame, IN: University of Notre Dame Press, 1984); "Social Structures and their Threats to Moral Agency," *Philosophy*, 74 (1999), pp. 311–329.

tension, MacIntyre claims, because institutions realize the value in promoting internal goods but are themselves largely motivated by external goods. Thus a hospital will seek out funding and prestige, but ironically these can often conflict with the best practice of medicine.[11]

If we apply the distinction of internal and external incentives to business, we can see that corporations inevitably feel the pull toward expansion and avarice, but nevertheless realize there is value in fostering their employees and being responsible community members. Thus someone inside a corporation may be motivated by the internal rewards of the practice – perhaps creating a great product, taking satisfaction in expertly applying skills, or providing great service – although the firm itself is ultimately propelled by competitive forces. Moore describes the nature of someone working for internal rewards as "craftsmanship," where the work itself helps fulfill the worker. This again echoes popular management literature where merely producing goods or services without personal engagement leads to disillusion and lower performance.

In this sense, taking craftsmanship seriously offers a hope that we can resist the temptation to think solely in terms of external rewards as a gauge of personal and professional success. Clearly if we look to pay as a reward, then we will do things that serve to maximize it, and we will move to a culture like Enron's, where very bright people thought that they could outsmart any constraining system to make as much money as possible. The restraint against those forces, it seems, has to be framed in value terms such as justice, honor, courage, and truthfulness – virtues independent of external reward.

This conclusion may initially seem both naive and quaint when contrasted to the harsh realities of the business world, where the law of the jungle appears to dominate. However, most business operates against a background of trust, and multi-million dollar deals are still regularly brokered on handshakes. While Enron and WorldCom were dramatic, they also represent business operating on the ethical margins. The context of business may be tough, but it is still unusual for people to routinely lie, cheat, or steal: the reputational effects alone would mean that no one would deal with them again. Taking our cue from Kipling's *Jungle Book*, the verse describing

---

[11] I have borrowed this example from Tom L. Beauchamp, *Philosophical Ethics: An Introduction to Moral Philosophy*, 2nd edn. (New York: McGraw-Hill, 1991), p. 230.

life in the wild actually recognizes mutual interdependence, not a war of all against all:

> Now this is the Law of the Jungle – as old and as true as the sky;
> And the Wolf that shall keep it may prosper, but the Wolf that shall break
>   it must die.
> As the creeper that girdles the tree-trunk the Law runneth forward and
>   back –
> For the strength of the Pack is the Wolf, and the strength of the Wolf is
>   the Pack.[12]

Still, it would be a mistake to believe that virtuous individuals alone can change the organization from within. Virtuous people will probably fare poorly in an organization with a poor moral climate. Thus the second element is that we should reconceptualize the corporation as a moral agent, like a person, that ought to promote virtuous practices by means of both internal and external goods. A for-profit hospital, then, should aim to provide the best medical care possible and allow the staff to develop the virtues intrinsic to their work. It need not abandon external rewards such as profit (or deny them to its employees), but recognize there are times that internal and external goods will clash, and sometimes the internal goods ought to prevail. For example, it may provide a clinic to the indigent to honor its mission of care, despite the fact that it may be a financial burden and have no significant benefits, even in terms of public relations.

We have seen that corporate culture can have a major effect on employee behavior, and also that it is possible to change it from within – witness the cases of Denny's and Nike, which have both changed their operations to increase the welfare of a wide range of stakeholders. The single-minded corporate goal of return to investors is dated and short-sighted in the age of global trade. Our section on sustainability in chapter 9 demonstrates that a company has to be conscious that it is not only selling goods and products but has a vested interest in developing communities of future employees and consumers. To do that successfully, it has to plan for the long term. The impact a firm has is inevitably intertwined in the social and environmental components of people across the planet, and it ignores them at its peril. We cannot rely on a few saints within companies to change them

---

[12] Rudyard Kipling, *The Second Jungle Book* (Garden City, NY: Doubleday & Co., 1895), p. 23.

from within, though. The evidence is that effective change in culture has to come from the top and be thoroughgoing. The challenge will be to show that the watchword "adding value" often bandied around in business circles actually refers to more than increasing efficiency. Rather, it means that a firm is committed to enhancing the internal goods of their own practice, that is, helping *all* stakeholders to have more fulfilling lives. Many leading firms promote this approach in their mission statements, and we have seen that their commitment of resources shows that these are not just hollow words.

Many writers in the area of business ethics have concentrated on how to make individuals more morally responsible, and some have looked at the character of the corporation. Strangely, though, most have ignored a third element. Time and again we have seen that business reflects the morality of the consumer, a point that cannot be overemphasized. Thus if consumers truly care about the appalling conditions facing low-skilled workers, there are means to rectify these conditions, such as demanding transparency or union-made labels. The rise of the "fair trade" movement shows that consumers have the power to alter the way goods are brought to market. One problem is that these choices are often thought of as a luxury – if the price of coffee or bananas goes too high, then purchasers will resort to cheaper brands rather than compromise their lifestyle. The test is whether relatively affluent consumers would be willing to make meaningful sacrifices to help people they may never encounter. In short, ethical business needs a trinity of virtuous firms, virtuous employees, and virtuous consumers.

## Business and life

Business is a part of human experience. Most of us will be employed, and for many the employment will take up the majority of our waking hours. At its most basic, we all seek to find meaning in our lives and the place of work within it. A crude way of putting it is to ask why we should bother to get up in the morning. In order to make sense of our lives and answer that question, we might reconsider two contrasting approaches that we looked at earlier. The first is a compartmentalized view, where we have private lives, and we adopt a role when we go to work. That segregation allows us to act differently at work and also gives us psychological distance from what we do there. In effect, we wouldn't do things that way if we had a choice, but we abdicate our moral responsibility in our work lives, believing our real lives happen at home with friends and family in our private time. In contrast, we can use the term *integrity* to describe a unified morality that does not meaningfully distinguish moral action we take at work from action at home, or from action in any other part of our lives.

When we try to find meaning in our existence, we each construct a narrative about ourselves and our place in the world that also helps us to connect our narratives with a wider story about the institutions that make up society and its history. Importantly, we cannot describe our lives in terms of a narrative if we adopt the segregated role approach. That is, if we segment our lives into different parts, we cannot see our lives in terms of a grand sweep, connected to others in the society. This insight is closely allied to a notion of personal identity we encountered earlier in chapter 6: if we see ourselves as isolated atoms, then it is much more difficult to consider our lives in a consistent overall way. This is not to say that it is not perfectly valid to think of ourselves as separate or as taking on different roles, but that doing so renders a fragmentary story about who we are and what we are about.

Aristotle used the term *telos* to suggest that our lives are directional, and he regarded each of our lives as an attempt to make as much as possible of our individual potential to attain happiness, which he thought of in terms of fulfillment or human flourishing. If we incorporate a unitary view of our lives, we see that we cannot separate our work lives from our other activities in the sense that they are all part of our personal biographies. It also implies that the way we behave cuts across our various activities: honesty, diligence, trustworthiness, and so forth are exhibited in every aspect of what we do.

If we put these parts together, we find that in order to have fulfilling lives we need to see our activities as part of a whole. This means that we are involved in fostering internal goods at work. These internal goods might be manifested by being a good team player or a helpful colleague, whatever features allow excellence in the operating practice. Capitalism pushes us to segregate our work lives from other parts of our lives, and to pursue external rewards such as pay and status, and companies are currently judged mainly in terms of their economic performance. The very forces that lead to a company succeeding will simultaneously tend to suppress the needs of individuals – for example, employees routinely working diligently for eighty hours a week will have to make compromises in other parts of their lives. Yet if we can break down the opposition and view people as having a single life with different aspects instead of leading several unconnected lives, we might also view things differently. A rewarding job would be one that provides value beyond monetary compensation, and, as seems to be the case, companies would begin to care more about their overall impact on people, communities, and the environment.

The reason for tempering the effect of unchecked capitalism is that ultimately business should serve us, and it does that best when we guide its action in order to promote the common good. In business terms, for example, the urge for profit may tempt us to be less than fully honest or may discourage the company from giving back to the community. If we recognize these forces, though, we can counter them in various ways – by employee activism, ethics hotlines, and ombudsmen offices to allow greater transparency and reporting, as well as consumer awareness. We can also use the vehicles of political action to legislate for our interests and mobilize forces such as non-governmental organizations to pressure and remind businesses to balance their desire to maximize profit with their other chartered duties to stakeholders.

The reason to get out of bed, then, is to make the most of what we could be, and to do so we need to foster institutions and practices that enable rather than hinder the realization of human potential. Work needs to be more than a daily grind described in an English folk song about a decent hardworking couple:

Day and night through thick and thin
They work life out just to keep life in

## Preserving the humanity

If aliens from a distant planet visited us, what would we point to as the highpoint of human civilization? We have great art, wonderful buildings, and spectacular feats of engineering. We have cathedrals rising to great heights built hundreds of years ago by people who knew they would never live to see them completed. The World Wide Web is dramatic evidence of our technology at work, but it might fail to impress beings capable of interstellar travel. We have tamed nature with dams and levees, but we cannot control hurricanes or tsunamis. Our art is largely warehoused and visited by few.

Perhaps we then have to look to the institutions that we have created and the way we deal with one another, and here we can parade the achievements of capitalism. It spurs innovation, creates wealth, and has generated a high standard of living for billions of people. How would our visitor respond?

Consider Alexis de Tocqueville, a Frenchman who visited the democratic experiment of America in the early 1800s. He came from a country with vast disparities of wealth and power and witnessed a new culture with great opportunities open to all, where the engine powering the development of society was business. In his words, "In democracies nothing is more great or more brilliant than commerce: it attracts the attention of the public, and fills the imagination of the multitude; all energetic passions are directed towards it." At the same time, he saw the inherent paradox of business – that if it is not directed to benefit all its stakeholders, it may cause great harm as well as doing great good. He thought if rich and poor saw their interests as competitive rather than cooperative their common ties would break down, and they would have "no connection of habit or duty." He warns:

> I am of the opinion, on the whole, that the manufacturing aristocracy which is growing up under our eyes is one of the harshest that ever existed in the world; but at the same time it is one of the most confined and least dangerous. Nevertheless, the friends of democracy should keep their eyes anxiously fixed in this direction; for if ever a permanent inequality of conditions and aristocracy again penetrates into the world, it may be predicted that this is the gate by which they will enter.[13]

This is probably what our alien visitor would remark, too. Capitalism is a tremendously powerful tool, but if we are going to sustain its benefits world-wide and for future generations, it will be necessary to create safeguards to protect people and the planet. Perhaps our greatest asset is ultimately not a building, an artifact, or even an economic system, but rather our humanity and our feelings of interconnection. In the final analysis that is why we need to constantly remind ourselves to infuse business with ethics.

---

[13] Alexis de Tocqueville, *Democracy in America* (New York: Random House, 1981), book II, chapter 20, p. 454.

# Select bibliography and further reading

### Ethical theory

Aristotle. *Nicomachean Ethics* (Indianapolis: Hackett, 1987).

Beauchamp, T. and Bowie, N., eds. *Ethical Theory and Business* (Englewood Cliffs, NJ: Prentice-Hall, 1997).

Frederick, R., ed. *A Companion to Business Ethics* (Oxford: Blackwell, 1999).

Hobbes, T. *Leviathan* [1651], ed. J. C. A. Gaskin (Oxford: Oxford University Press, 1998).

Kant, I. *Foundations of the Metaphysics of Morals* [1785] (Indianapolis: Bobbs-Merrill, 1959).

Kohlberg, L. and Kramer, R. "Continuities and Discontinuities in Childhood and Adult Moral Development," *Human Development*, 12 (1969), pp. 93–120.

Machiavelli, N. *The Prince* [1512], trans. W. K. Marriott (New York: Alfred A. Knopf, 1992).

MacIntyre, A. *After Virtue: A Study in Moral Theory* (Notre Dame, IN: University of Notre Dame Press, 1984).

Mill, John Stuart. *Utilitarianism* [1861], ed. Samuel Gorovitz (Indianapolis: Bobbs-Merrill, 1971).

Rawls, J. *A Theory of Justice* (Cambridge, MA: Harvard University Press, 1971).

Singer, P., ed. *A Companion to Ethics* (Oxford: Blackwell 1991).

### Capitalism

Friedman, M. *Capitalism and Freedom* (Chicago: University of Chicago Press, 2002).

Moore, G. "Humanizing Business: A Modern Business Ethics Approach," *Business Ethics Quarterly*, 15.2 (2005), pp. 237–256.

Nozick, R. *Anarchy, State and Utopia* (New York: Basic Books, 1977).

Rand, A. *Capitalism: The Unknown Ideal* (New York: Dutton, 1966).

Sen, A. *Development as Freedom* (New York: Anchor, 2000).

Smith, A. *The Wealth of Nations* [1776], ed. Edwin Cannan (London: Methuen, 1904).

Solomon, R. C. *A Better Way to Think about Business: How Personal Integrity Leads to Corporate Success* (New York: Oxford University Press, 1999).


## Feminism

Held, V. *Feminist Morality: Transforming Culture, Society and Politics* (Chicago: University of Chicago Press, 1993).

Noddings, N. *Caring: A Feminine Approach to Ethics and Moral Education* (Berkeley: University of California Press, 1984).

Tronto, J. *Moral Boundaries: A Political Argument for the Ethics of Care* (New York: Routledge, 1993).

Wollstonecraft, M. *A Vindication of the Rights of Women* [1792] (New York: Penguin, 2004).

Young, I. M. *Justice and the Politics of Difference* (Princeton: Princeton University Press, 1990).


## Responsibility

Feinberg, J. *Doing and Deserving* (Princeton: Princeton University Press, 1970).

French, P. *Corporate Morality* (New York: Harcourt Brace, 1996).

Hart, H. L. A. "Varieties of Responsibility," *Law Quarterly Review*, 83 (1967), pp. 346–364.

Velasquez, M. "Why Corporations Are Not Morally Responsible for Anything They Do," *Business and Professional Ethics Journal*, 2 (1983), pp. 1–18.


## Rights

Donaldson, T. *The Ethics of International Business* (New York: Oxford University Press, 1989).

Etzioni, A. *The Spirit of Community: Rights, Responsibilities and the Communitarian Agenda* (New York: Crown, 1993).

Koller, John M. *Asian Philosophies* (Englewood Cliffs, NJ: Prentice-Hall, 2006).

Paine, T. *The Rights of Man* [1791] (New York: Penguin, 1984).

Stone, C. "Should Trees Have Standing? Toward Legal Rights for Natural Objects," *Southern California Law Review*, 45 (1972), pp. 450–501.

Sunstein, C. A. and Nussbaum, Martha C., eds. *Animal Rights: Current Debates and New Directions* (Oxford: Oxford University Press, 2004).

United Nations. *The Global Compact*, available from http://www.unglobalcompact. org/AboutTheGC/TheTenPrinciples/humanRights.html.

Waldron, J., ed. *Theories of Rights* (Oxford: Oxford University Press, 1984).


### Autonomy

Cialdini, R. *Influence: The Psychology of Persuasion* (New York: Collins, 1998).

Equal Opportunities Commission (USA). *Federal Laws Prohibiting Job Discrimination: Questions and Answers* (Washington, DC: Government Printing Office, 2002), available from http://www.eeoc.gov/facts/qanda.html.

*Age Discrimination*, available from http://www.eeoc.gov/types/age.html.

Faden, R., Beauchamp, T., and King, N. *A History and Theory of Informed Consent* (Oxford: Oxford University Press, 1986).

Milgram, S. *Obedience to Authority: An Experimental View* (New York: Harper & Row, 1975).

Mill, John Stuart. *On Liberty* [1859], ed. Gertrude Himmelfarb (New York: Penguin, 1982).

Social Accountability International. *About Social Accountability*, available from http://www.sa-intl.org/index.cfm?fuseaction=Page.viewPage&pageId= 472&stopRedirect=1.


### Beneficence

Carnegie, A. *The Gospel of Wealth and Other Timely Essays*, ed. Edward C. Kirkland (Cambridge, MA: Harvard University Press, 1962).

Elkington, J. *Cannibals with Forks: The Triple Bottom Line of 21st Century Business* (Chichester: Capstone Publishing, 1997).

Snider, J., Hill, R. P., and Martin, D. "Corporate Social Responsibility in the 21st Century: A View from the World's Most Successful Firms," *Journal of Business Ethics*, 48.2 (2003), 175–187.

Thewlis, M., Miller, L., and Neathey, F. *Advancing Women in the Workplace* (London: Equal Opportunities Commission, 2004).

Wulfson, M. "The Ethics of Corporate Social Responsibility and Philanthropic Ventures," *Journal of Business Ethics*, 29.1–2 (2001), 135–145.


### Environment

FacWorld. *Pollution Litigation Review*, available from http://www.facworld.com/ FACworld.nsf/doc/Polllitrev0302.

Freeman, R. E., Pierce, J., and Dodd, R. *Environmentalism and the New Logic of Business: How Firms can be Profitable and Leave Our Children a Clean Environment* (Oxford: Oxford University Press, 2000).

Jameson, Dale. *Ethics and the Environment: An Introduction* (Cambridge: Cambridge University Press, 2007).

Leopold, A. *A Sand County Almanac, and Sketches Here and There* (New York: Oxford University Press, 1949).

Sagoff, M. *The Economy of the Earth* (Cambridge: Cambridge University Press, 1988).

Seed, J., Macy, J., Fleming, P., and Naess, A. *Thinking Like a Mountain: Towards a Council of All Beings* (Philadelphia: New Society Publishers, 1988).

# Index

£16-99

# Ethics and Business

In this lively and accessible book, Kevin Gibson explores the relationship between ethics and the world of business, and how we can serve the interests of both. He builds a philosophical groundwork that can be applied to a wide range of issues in ethics and business, and shows readers how to assess dilemmas critically and work to resolve them on a principled basis. Using case studies drawn from around the world, he examines topics including stakeholder responsibilities, sustainability, corporate social responsibility, and women and business. Because business can no longer be isolated from its effects on communities and the environment, these concerns are brought to the forefront. The book also captures the dynamic nature of business ethics in the era of globalization where jobs can be outsourced, products are made of components from scores of countries, and sweatshops often provide the cheap goods the public demands.

KEVIN GIBSON is Associate Professor, Departments of Philosophy and Management, and Director of the Center for Ethics Studies at Marquette University.